Aspiring to Excel

Leadership Initiatives for Music Educators

G-5789

Aspiring to Excel

Leadership Initiatives for Music Educators

Kenneth R. Raessler

Foreword by **Jeffrey Kimpton**

GIA Publications, Inc.
Chicago • www.giamusic.com

PEANUTS reprinted by permission of United Feature Syndicate Inc. (page 94)

TOLES © 2001 The Buffalo News. Reprinted iwth permission of
UNIVERSAL PRESS SYNDICATE. All rights reserved (page 279)

G-5789
© 2003 GIA Publications, Inc.
7404 S. Mason Ave., Chicago, IL 60638
www.giamusic.com

ISBN: 1-57999-216-1

Printed in U.S.A

To my grandchildren:

Julia Elaine Denison
Madaliene Elizabeth Denison
Eric Alexander Denison

—may each of you always *Aspire to Excel*.

Table of Contents

Foreword
Aspiring to Excel

When my longtime friend and colleague Ken Raessler first told me about his book *Aspiring to Excel,* he spoke passionately about wanting to provide future generations with an understanding of the processes of excellence that must become a part of the successful career of music educators. As I started to draft my own thoughts for this foreword, a personal experience came to mind that immediately put into context the commitment and excellence that is the foundation for Ken's career and book.

Over the past two years, I have been hospitalized three different times at the University of Minnesota Medical Center, a major teaching and research hospital. At 6:00 a.m. each morning, the eight residents of internal medicine would troop into my room with my charts and quiz me about the previous day's activities and the night I had spent. Throughout the day, various residents would return to discuss my condition. At the end of the day, the residents would again return and ask more questions. After they left, I could hear them in the hall, quietly reviewing all the details and information. About 10:30 each evening, one lonely resident would return— always the same one during each visit—and review the day's events and findings. As a teacher, I was fascinated with this process of inquiry, and one evening I asked the final resident, Eric, about this continual process of examination, questioning, and analysis. His response was quite telling. "We have to make this right. What we learn today will be critical to what we might do tomorrow for you, or next week with another patient. It is all cumulative knowledge and layers of experiences. Without these different interviews and the comparison of data and experiences, we won't be able to figure out how to make you better. And we won't be able to succeed as doctors. This is all part of the learning process."

I was struck by this statement, and I still am to this day. What is different between those who *aspire to excel* in medicine and those who *aspire to excel* in music? Music educators combine the analysis of data and experience with the understanding of emotion and feeling. Music educators must have keen understandings of the psychology of our students, the physiology of the body in the production of music, an understanding of the social and aesthetic import of our art and our teaching. Music educators must be willing—and patient enough—to chart the incremental advancement of our students through data that leads to the eventual health of our patients (read students and program). The clinical use of the cumulative data, practices, and experiences we employ as teachers is how we become masters of the *processes of excellence* that are key to success in any field. The intensity of the process of inquiry is the essence of how anyone in *any* profession must *aspire to excel*—throughout his or her career.

Some may find this analogy inappropriate for the music education profession. After all, society may not judge what we do as important as saving lives or curing sick patients. Doctors make more money than music educators. But perhaps we should think differently. It is the desire to *excel* that is required in any profession, regardless of how much we make, who we serve, or how much we are needed in society. Perhaps what we do is, in many ways, a way of saving lives, or curing patients, by creating antidotes of creativity, emotional expression, aesthetic enjoyment, and personal expressiveness. If that is the case (and I do believe it is), then the processes that are used in finding the *answers* and *solutions* to the challenges of teaching and leading in music should be the same as those used by the doctor. The zeal to find these solutions to physical or aesthetic wellness should be the same. It is that zeal that is the spirit behind Ken Raessler's remarkable career and the bedrock foundation that supports his book, *Aspiring to Excel*.

What does *Aspiring to Excel* provide to the profession? This book underscores the fact that long-term rewards come from patient effort, tremendous amounts of planning in curriculum and program design, shrewd strategies that build strong relationships with colleagues and community, tremendous political acumen, and a whole lot of just plain hard work. This book is not a "how to" for instant success. Those who read it in hopes of knowing the "ten steps" to a successful music program will be sorely disappointed. Professionals don't rely on slogans and a bumper sticker. If there is one key lesson that readers must take with them from *Aspiring to Excel*, it is that those music educators who aspire to excel are as concerned with the *processes* of teaching and administration as they are with the *outcomes*. Processes take time, commitment, reflection, and persistence, and are applied differently in each situation. Yet each situation, each experience, each day, and each job yields a new layer of knowledge that creates a framework on which to develop personal and programmatic goals. The deeper the layers of experience and success, the more leadership can be encouraged to grow—for all the right reasons. Leadership is the sum of many processes working together. One doesn't acquire leadership; it is not automatic. Leadership is earned.

Ken Raessler has established himself as a leader the hard way: he earned it. Ken began his career forty-five years ago as many of us did—fresh out of college, full of zeal, idealistic, eager to create a program. What is remarkable about Ken is that he is concluding his career in precisely the same manner. Four decades of commitment— in small and large districts, higher education, consulting, and state, regional, and national leadership—have left Ken with a buoyant optimism that is remarkable. Some will read these chapters and rationalize that Ken's career took advantage of easier times in public education. I disagree. Teaching and leading in this profession has *always* been hard work, regardless of the environment of public education or its historical period. If we can attach to our work only *half* of the buoyant optimism that Ken has after four decades of work, this profession will be far stronger than we could ever have imagined.

As you read this book, you will quickly find out that Ken has developed a tremendous series of lists of the things that he felt were useful and worked—or didn't work—in the last forty-five years. He has kept these lists religiously, and in fact, the lists became sort of a running joke during our work together in editing this book. I kept my own list about Ken that I think the reader needs to remember.

- Ken never stopped learning. He constantly sought the acquisition of knowledge—through coursework, mentors, master classes, workshops, clinics, teacher observations, community forums—about music education, program development, and excellence. He is as eager to seek new experiences today at age seventy as he was at twenty-two—which tells us something about commitment to this profession.

- Ken was never afraid to cultivate people from whom he could learn, whether respected teachers and leaders from whom he could seek advice and counsel, or people he watched in the process of teaching and administrating. Ken loves people, and he cultivated, learned from, and continues to learn from the people of this profession—at all levels of responsibility and leadership.

- Ken always had a ready willingness to ask questions as a means of looking for new solutions. He used questioning to deepen his understanding, challenge old beliefs, and formulate new ideas. He has never stopped asking questions.

- Ken was never afraid to take a stand, admit a problem, seek new methods or organizational structures—in short, demonstrate leadership—regardless of the circumstances or the consequences. But he knew when to take action because he had carefully acquired the data and the experiences to know what to do next.

Let me close by returning to my experience with the medical profession. Word quickly spread throughout my doctors and nurses that the director of the school of music was in the hospital. Everyone was eager to share his or her musical experiences with me. I was amazed at the number of interns, residents, and doctors, nearly 90 percent by my count, who had—or continued to have—extensive experience with music. On the evening that I quizzed Eric about the design of the residency, I asked him what he was going to do at 11:00 p.m. after an eighteen-hour day, since he had to be back at 5:30 a.m. for preparation for morning rounds. His answer was something I shall never forget. "Professor Kimpton, I played piano for sixteen years. I have about thirty minutes of paperwork, and then I am going to the meditation room where there is a wonderful grand piano. I will play Bach or Beethoven, Chopin or Debussy for about fifteen minutes, maybe more. It is the only way I can keep my life in balance right now. I look forward to this part of the day all day long. It is what helps me keep myself—and my patients—alive."

Why do we *aspire to excel?* Like Eric, who worked eighteen-hour days so he could make fifteen minutes of music each evening, the answer lies in how much we want ourselves to succeed in the long, hard struggle of our professional careers so that we—and others—

can continue to be alive with music. *Aspiring to Excel* is a strange combination of intensity, hard work, music, faith, love, optimism, perseverance, skill, and commitment. If Ken Raessler helps us understand that much in this book, then he has made a remarkable and lasting contribution to this profession. I would have expected no less.

Jeffrey Kimpton
Director, School of Music
University of Minnesota
Minneapolis, Minnesota
October 2002

Preface

As a three-year-old, my parents took me to my first parade in Middletown, Pennsylvania. I was a shy little boy, but when the first band marched by, I knew I belonged. I simply went out on the street and marched with the band. Ever since, I've been hooked for life.

In the fall of 1954, I began teaching music in Belvidere, New Jersey. I was fresh out of undergraduate school at West Chester State Teachers College (PA), eager to teach but still very young in experience and knowledge, as any first-year teacher is at that stage. But I knew that I wanted to be the best music teacher I could be, and I set my sights—at each stage of my 45-year career—on clear aspirations for growth, achievement and, above all, sustained excellence. I *aspired to excel.*

Aspiring to Excel will address the importance of leadership and excellence in the education of students through music. As a K–12 music teacher in Belvidere, junior/senior high school choral music educator in East Stroudsburg, (PA), graduate assistant in music education at Michigan State University, senior high school choral music educator in Hatboro-Horsham High School (PA), college music professor and director of music education at Gettysburg College (PA), supervisor of music education in the Williamsport (PA) public schools, director of the School of Music at Texas Christian University in Ft. Worth, clinician, author, NASM national accreditor, speaker, presenter, and consultant, I have set forth goals and aspirations on which I have worked deliberately every day of my life. I specifically list these positions because it is important for the reader of this book to know the many ways in which I have known and experienced music education, and *aspired to excel*. It has been a life's work, it has been hard work, but it has been a life of enjoyment and reward.

This book is not a "cure all" but may possibly be an "Aha." The book will not solve all of the problems of this complex profession, but the ideas established herein could be a new beginning, indeed, something for future leaders in music education to build upon. The suggestions expressed in this book may well be something whose "time has come."

Perhaps the ultimate purpose of this book is to stress the need for both leadership skills as well as the quest for excellence in the music education profession. Leadership without the sincere quest for excellence simply falls short. If you don't have both, it will be difficult for you to excel! On the other hand, my experience has demonstrated that *real* achievement simply does not happen without quality leadership and a true devotion to excellence.

Of course, my career has witnessed many changes in music education, and I do not doubt for a moment that future music educators will face some similar challenges as those I experienced. The diversity of the music education profession appears to have created a fragmentation to the point where there is limited communication or understanding between, for example, the elementary music teacher and the university musicologist. The unique quest of providing music instruction to students from early childhood through higher education has consistently created debate within the profession about the value of each component part of this profession. The title "music educator" has generally been attributed to the public school music teacher. However, it is my thesis that *everyone who teaches music* is a music educator, whether a music theorist, musicologist, composer, music educator, conductor, or director of a performing group. Everyone teaches music. The sum of the parts equals the whole.

One of the joys of my professional experience has been the

opportunity to actually teach students from the kindergarten level through the doctorate about the substance of music and music teaching. What a unique and joyful experience! Thus, this book is dedicated to all "music educators" regardless of the level or designation of that which they teach. The important issue is that they *aspire to excel* at the teaching of music.

I have observed that the true leader will constantly—and almost instinctively—*aspire to excel*. In that quest, the leader will be quick to recognize and celebrate excellence in others, embrace their success, and share in their joy. Indeed, success and excellence can be contagious. It is not unusual to encounter those colleagues who do not share this quest. Thus, they appear humbled, uninspired, and inadequate, or they find fault, affix blame, rationalize, or become defensive. Whatever the response, true leaders will be so busy with their own quest for excellence that they will share it openly and freely without condition. When *Aspiring to Excel* becomes the norm, there can be no instance where it could pass by unnoticed or unappreciated. A continuing commitment to quality will allow music educators to begin focusing on what is right rather than what is wrong, with us and with others.

During the past fifteen years, I have presented seminars in both leadership and excellence to music educators throughout the United States. Those experiences, and my own years of work in so many facets of this profession, have served as the genesis for this book. It is my hope that those who read the book will come to sense the same exuberance and excitement that the students in my graduate seminars exhibited. What a great and unique journey excellence and leadership can make when joined together. Please join me in this quest as you read this book—and *aspire to excel*.

Kenneth R. Raessler, Ph.D.
Professor and Director Emeritus
School of Music, Texas Christian University, Ft. Worth, Texas

Acknowledgments

This book has been in my thoughts for many, many years in one form or another. It has made many transitions, leaps, and turns during these years, and finally it has come to fruition. I am deeply indebted to my good friend and colleague for many years, Jeffrey Kimpton, Director of the School of Music at the University of Minnesota, who not only wrote the Foreword to this book but also provided me with another set of eyes as we traveled through the content editing phase of the book. It is difficult to adequately express appreciation for his many hours of editing other than to boldly state that his wisdom was irreplaceable.

I have been blessed with an incredible family who have lived through this hectic and wonderful life with me. To my wife, Joyce, of forty-three years and counting, I owe much of who and what I am. Her love has known no bounds and is unending. To my children, Laurie and Todd, I owe a great deal of gratitude for their constant support, interest, and concern, and for their willingness to share their father with so many wonderful people. They both *Aspired to Excel,* and indeed, they did excel—Todd as a hotel GM and Laurie as a mother.

Numerous persons have touched my life, influenced my thoughts, and shared my professional dreams. To acknowledge each and every one would be impossible; there are simply too many, yet there are those who must be acknowledged.

In a lifetime, if one is fortunate enough to find one soul mate, then that person has been blessed. I have been fortunate enough to have located four. In addition to Jeffrey Kimpton, there is Dr. Peggy Bennett of Oberlin College, Dr. Russell Robinson of the University of Florida, and Dr. Tim Lautzenheiser, professional mentor to the entire music education profession. These persons will never know the impact they have had on my life, but let it be said that it was powerful.

I have been fortunate to have worked with three outstanding bosses in my career. Dr. Oscar Knade, then Superintendent of Schools, and Dr. Eleanor Patton, then Associate Superintendent of Schools in the Williamsport Area School District, and Dr. Robert Garwell, then Dean of the College of Fine Arts and Communications at Texas Christian University. They exemplified the leadership qualities espoused in this book. Without Oscar and Eleanor, there would be no Wiliamsport story to tell, and without the trust, understanding, and encouragement of Bob, the TCU experience would not have been nearly so successful. My friendship with Dr. Knade dates back to undergraduate school, when he came to my dormitory room every Monday evening to listen to and "conduct" Paul Lavelle and his "Band of America" as it played on my small, tan, plastic radio.

My three golf partners, Larry Eason, John Widnor, and Warren Boling must be acknowledged, for they have been so very patient while I *aspired to excel* on the golf course. I never really accomplished the aspiration, but I keep trying. They have lived through the writing of this book, and even showed interest at times. They each, in their own professional lives, have exemplified the leadership qualities articulated in this book.

Thank you to Alec Harris for his trust, patience, and encouragement, to Linda Vickers, who was extremely effective in proofing the manuscript, to Robert Sacha for his meticulous graphic design and designing of the Tables, to Yolanda Durán for her aesthetically appealing artwork, and to Liz Branch who carefully typed the original manuscript

And yes, there are more. There are those colleagues where the interaction was less frequent but nevertheless significant and influential on my professional thought. I will always be indebted to them for their friendship and collegiality.

Colleagues around the nation who have influenced my thinking throughout the years include:

- Chris Azzara – Eastman School of Music
- Don Beckie – University of Redlands
- Willa Dunleavy – Fort Worth Independent School District
- John Dunphy – Villanova University
- John Feierabend – Hartt School of Music
- Robert Floyd – Executive Director,
  Texas Music Educators Association
- Edwin Gordon – University of South Carolina
- Richard Grunow – Eastman School of Music
- Janet Herrick Stucznski – Williamsport Area School District,
  Lakeland College
- James Jordan – Westminster Choir College
- David Jorlett – Artistic Director,
  Northern Pines Music Foundation
- Michael Kumer – Duquesne University
- James Lee – Coastal Bend College
- Clifford Madsen – Florida State University
- Don Muro – Freelance musician, author, and clinician
- Natalie Ozeas – Carnegie Mellon University
- Diane Persellin – Trinity University
- Darhyl Ramsey – University of North Texas
- Bennett Reimer – Professor Emeritus,
  Northwestern University, clinician, and author
- Tom Rudolph – Haverford Township School District,
  clinician, and author

- Scott Schuler – Supervisor of Music, State of Connecticut
- Sue Snyder – Entrepreneur, author, and clinician
- Marguerite Wilder – GIA Publications, author, and clinician

Colleagues from the public schools and universities where I taught and with whom I shared dreams, goals, and aspirations include:

- Adam Baggs – Texas Christian University
- Richard Coulter – Williamsport Area School District
- José Feghali – Texas Christian University, Gold Medal Winner, 1985 Van Cliburn Piano Competition
- Tom Gallup – Williamsport Area School District
- Douglas Gordon – Williamsport Area School District
- German Gutierrez – Texas Christian Univeresity
- Paul Kellerman – Williamsport Area School District
- David Knauss – Williamsport Area School District, Mansfield University
- Mary Lippert-Coleman – Williamsport Area School District, Past President, Pennsylvania Music Educators Association
- Garland Markham – Williamsport Area School District, Cobb County (Georgia) Public Schools
- Albert Nacinovich – Williamsport Area School District
- John Owings – Texas Christian University, Gold Medal Winner, 1975 Casadesus Piano Competition
- Judy Shellenberger – Williamsport Area School District
- Judy Solomon – Texas Christian University
- Walter Straiton – Williamsport Area School District
- Ruth Whitlock – Texas Christian University
- Clement Wiedenmyer – East Stroudsburg Area School District
- Curt Wilson – Texas Christian University

- Robert Zellner – East Stroudsburg Area School District, Gettysburg College

And finally, but nevertheless of great importance, I must honor all my music colleagues, particularly at Gettysburg College, the Williamsport Area School District, and Texas Christian University. Thank you for making this thing called a *career* so engaging.

Chapter 1

The Look of a Leader

Over the past fifteen years, I have taught many seminars in leadership in music education. I always start my seminars with the same two questions. First, "Why did you choose music as a profession?" The strong majority of the hundreds of music educators I have taught speak of their passion for performing and the valuable personal experiences they have had with music. They often talk about the powerful mentors they have had and the role they have played in their professional development. Those mentors have primarily been music educators.

Then I ask the second question. "Why did you choose music education as a career?" This time the answers are quite different, but in many cases, they sound like this. "I just wanted to be a music educator after I found I could not make a living through music performance."

Have you ever heard or experienced this thought? Many have. And each time I hear this response in my seminars, it makes me sad. When the raison d'être for becoming a music teacher is only to acquire the financial means for making a living, music teaching becomes the alternative to music performance. I call it the "if I can't make it in performance, I can always teach" syndrome. Granted, many of these performers turned teachers make excellent music educators, and we should be thankful they chose the profession, regardless of the negative way in which it was expressed. But even more precious are those who first and foremost want to be music teachers and yet continue to perform to enhance their teaching.

Once the conviction to music teaching has been established, the leadership and commitment to excellence must become prominent. It is not an automatic response. This is a learned response—one that comes from hard work, inquisitiveness, commitment, many experiences, and a layering of skill and relationships.

Let us consider a little scenario. Possibly you have been there. It goes something like this:

Music Teacher:
But I just wanted to be a music teacher after I found I could not make it in performance. Now I find I need to be a music educator, musician, director of extra curricular activities, and a public relations expert! C'mon, enough is enough.

Music Leader (Mentor):
But...music has always been fun; however, no one ever said it was easy. Music teaching may be different from music performance; however, one is not easier than the other. It is just that financially it is generally easier to earn a living with music teaching than music performance. Unfortunately, many times people associate music with a hobby and, thus, expect music performers to play for "fun" (i.e., free; without pay) unless they have established a professional career and have a manager to protect and market them. On the other hand, musicians may enter the education arena through many different

	doors, with little or no true understanding of the demands of a music education career. It is, indeed, an exhaustive and exacting career choice.
Music Teacher:	But there are only twenty-four hours in a day. This is not a job; it is a way of life.
Music Leader (Mentor):	Yes, it is a profession, and a profession signifies a way of life rather than an hourly employ. Please understand that your decision to become a music teacher is not necessarily the easy way out. To become a music educator at any level of the educational spectrum is quite challenging. Thus, you must realize that anything worth having is worth working for. The music teacher (the leader) must also be a problem solver and learn to persevere.
Music Teacher:	Sometimes it just seems like no one really cares whether music lives or dies in this place. I am convinced they only want me to function before or after school. The "basics" are the only prime-time activities, and music may occur whenever...or never. I am non-mandated, and at times it seems like a disease similar to leprosy. Many colleagues in other schools say the same thing.

Stephen Sondheim, in the song *Putting It Together*, from *Sunday in the Park with George*, succinctly describes the process of leadership in the arts with the following lyrics:

Be a nice guy.
> You have to pay the price, guy.

They like to give advice, guy.
> Don't think about it twice, guy.

It's time to get to work.

Art isn't easy.
> Even when you're hot.

Advancing art is easy,
> Financing it is not.

A vision is just a vision if it's only in
> your head.

If no one gets to hear it, it's as good as
> dead.

It has to come to life!

Perhaps Sondheim wrote this song about music educators! Yes, the leader has to pay the price regardless of how he or she entered the profession. The credential range of music teachers is quite vast, from the private music teacher who needs no credentials other than a shingle stating the intent to the public school music teacher who must be certified in multiple areas (unless there is a severe shortage of music teachers). Of course, higher education counts degrees as entry certification, with the Ph.D. or DMA as the preference. Thus, the entry points into the music education profession are vast, with requirements ranging from a shingle to a Ph.D. or DMA.

The amount of leadership a music educator might display is not in proportion to the number of degrees the music educator holds. I have worked with some wonderful, adept, sensitive, strong, visionary leaders who only possessed a bachelor's degree and countless hours of other courses and workshops. They were magnificent. Leadership is about the relationship between experience and vision, and the ability to communicate the result of that experience and vision to the great variety of constituents in music education, education, and society.

Former President George H.W. Bush often talked about "that vision thing" and was mercilessly parodied by comedians. Yet "that vision thing" *is* the essential ingredient that is so important to quality leadership. The teacher who *aspires to excel* is almost by default a visionary and, thus, a leader. Why is this? Because without vision there is no goal, without a goal there is no progress, and without progress the program becomes stagnant or atrophies. I have served as a consultant for many K–12 music programs in which there is great fragmentation, in staff continuity and communication, in organizational structure, in curricular sequence and design, and in instruction quality. In higher education, I have seen the same thing far too many times, where there is no integrated sequence of instruction from the freshman year to the senior year, between and even among disciplines. The unfortunate result is almost always the same: without sequence and articulation, there is no vision. And without vision, it is often difficult to shape the sequence or the articulation. One does not precede the other; they are concurrent processes.

While this may sound very utopian to the reader, we are all aware that a number of challenges are put before us that make the talk of structure, sequence, organization, and vision a daunting task in our daily lives. Issues such as site-based management, block scheduling, departmental autonomy (band, choir, orchestra, general music, music theory, music composition, musicology, applied music, etc.), and a fragmented music program and curriculum present challenges in the continuity of learning that are formidable. And yet I firmly believe that without continuity there is no sequence and, thus again, there is no vision. This is as true in individual music programs (your own building) as it is in district-wide programs in which there is dedicated administrative leadership.

Perhaps this takes us to the point of my book. It is doubtful that we are going to return to the days in which there were dedicated music supervisors who controlled district-wide music programs. The issue of leadership has changed in contemporary education. It is not so much about anointed leadership—administrators who carry this title and authority. It is very much now about individuals who have leadership skills, a broader and deeper kind of individual leadership. Instead of a music program having a leader (singular), by virtue of where public education is today, we must have many leaders (plural) in our music programs. Consequently, what can the leader in music education do to encourage programmatic organization, a sequence of instruction, and a quest for quality and excellence? The answer is obvious—and yet complex. We must *become, act,* and *be* leaders by example. We must establish the *look of a leader*, developing those qualities an individual must possess to deal with, understand, and influence other people. By adapting and practicing the following leadership characteristics, true leaders will not be content with the status quo but will be compelled to take an active role in effecting change.

General Qualities of Leadership

Let us begin with the basic leadership qualities an individual committed to leadership must possess. The following exhaustive list is not meant to inhibit potential leaders. Rather, it is meant to encourage leadership, entrepreneurial behavior, true accountability, and an understanding of how students learn. Initially, a leader needs to possess those generic qualities with which many can identify—traits, in no particular order, such as:

- Sense of humor
- High energy level
- Tolerance for change

- Ability to listen
- Vision
- Enthusiasm
- Self-confidence
- Appreciation of the efforts of others
- Appreciation for the success of others
- Sensitivity to the needs of others
- Willingness to take risks
- Optimism
- Respect for others
- Unselfish love
- Credibility
- Trustworthiness
- Honesty
- Risk taker

Qualities of Leadership for the Music Educator

The above qualities frequently come to mind when one thinks of leadership, whether it is a music educator or any other professional. But there are more of these attributes that are unique to the music education profession. The following traits relate directly to the music educator who demonstrates good leadership qualities in order to build program excellence and cohesiveness, and to effect change. A leader in music education will need to (in no particular order):

- Possess a vision for the goals of the music department.
- Develop a professional and political presence and attitude.
- Develop a community-minded public relations and service image.
- Possess a deep aesthetic and creative soul that will command artistic respect from students, colleagues, and

superiors.

- Possess the ability to establish an exemplary model of musicianship in both teaching and performance.
- Possess a true understanding of the program of music education, early childhood through grade twelve, or the totality of higher education programs in music, depending on the area of employment.
- Possess the ability to tackle the intricate and monumental problems that will occur within the department as well as from the outside, especially when they could affect the program negatively.
- Possess the ability to sort out the smaller, incidental problems before they become major problems.
- Command the respect of musician colleagues and celebrate their artistry.
- Understand the delicate balance between aesthetic freedom and censorship.
- Possess the desire to bring all together for the good of the whole.
- Have the personality and compassion to be trustworthy, thus gaining colleague confidence concerning personal matters that may affect either their professional life or the professional lives of others.
- Possess the strength to speak frankly to those faculty colleagues who go out on their own, attempting to create their own musical empire.
- Possess the ability to find good in colleagues when they have an "unpolished moment" and to lend them support.
- Develop the ability to spot raw talent in colleagues as well as prospective colleagues going through the interview process. This is, of course, assuming that music faculty involvement is a part of the interview process.

- Possess the courage to request involvement in the interview process of prospective colleagues.
- Possess a sense of futurism, which allows the individual to envision the upcoming needs of the music unit.
- Demonstrate organizational strength, which gains the respect of both colleagues and superiors.
- Be impeccable with your word and speak with integrity.
- In the pursuit of musical excellence, steer clear of a perfectionist mentality, which offends colleagues and causes irritability when minor things go awry.
- Be careful not to take issues personally. Nothing others do to you or say to you is because of you; it is because of them. This is a difficult quality to embrace, but it is so very important. Think about it.
- Be careful not to make assumptions. Be bold enough to ask questions when something is not clear and then communicate precisely your response to the issue.
- Always do your best. When you have done all in your power to complete something well, the feeling is exhilarating.

In summary, the leader in music education will advise, anticipate, defend, discuss, expedite, identify, honor, initiate, justify, listen, pacify, question, understand, wait, yield, and envision. A tough challenge? Yes! An important challenge? Absolutely! An impossible challenge? Never! Without leaders in this noble profession, the profession will falter.

Basic Understandings of Leadership

Perhaps you are saying, "This isn't me. My situation is great. Things are going really well. I have support, budget, great parents, terrific administration." Certainly, "if it ain't broke, don't fix it." But schools today can change in a heartbeat. A supportive board of education can be voted out. Superintendents last about five years. A strong principal advocate can retire. A budget can be voted down, or the state economy can take a turn for the worse. There is no such thing today as constancy in education. The political realities of education require a nimbleness to adapt to changing circumstances. The ability to negotiate change is a key attribute of leadership.

With this in mind, let us approach the understandings one needs to be successful as a leader in music education. What are some of the attributes individual leaders must know and be able to do within the profession of music education? How do those attributes help us survive in the professional environment—K–12 and higher education—in which music education exists? A leader must realize the following:

- Change is an inevitable certainty.
- As soon as one goal is realized, another has been established. Goal setting, like excellence, has no conclusion.
- Great teachers are not necessarily the ones who are the most knowledgeable. They are the individuals who can best communicate their knowledge to others.
- Individuals respond and behave according to how they feel, not what they know.
- An angry exchange of words changes few minds because neither person is really listening to the other. This is demonstrated clearly in television discussions where it appears everyone is talking at once, and even the viewer has difficulty understanding what is being said.
- One must become analytical about the behavior of others. What could be the justification for the behavior that another exhibits?
- No one can make you angry; you make yourself angry. You

are the only one who can learn to be in control of your emotions.

- The longer you remain calm and in control of your emotions, the more likely you are to remain in control of the situation.
- One must learn to be an observer in his or her own life. It is important to view what happens to you objectively, evaluate your response, and determine your own best course of action.
- Respond to people rather than reacting to them. Reactions are many times offensive.
- It is many times necessary to distance oneself from the person who has a tendency to irritate and upset you…and seems to do it repeatedly.
- When a person earns your rejection, give it, but give it in a gentle and caring way. Again, respond rather than react.
- Do not communicate in writing more than you have to, especially with controversial or emotional matters or reprimands. Many things may be taken out of context and, thus, not really express the true intent of the written message.
- Leaders will experiment and take risks. They are open to ideas and are willing to listen; they attempt untested approaches and accept the risks that accompany those approaches. They break free of self-imposed limitations.
- Leaders balance the paradox of routines. Routines can smother challenge and creativity, yet they are needed for orderly functioning. The trick must be to not allow the routines to overwhelm all of the time and energy.

Some of these understandings will be repeated in more detail throughout this book, specifically in Chapter 13: Avoiding Burnout.

Suffice to say, this list affirms one essential fact of leadership: true leaders must be deeply engaged in what they are doing. They must personally believe in the value of music education and the value of leadership *in* music education. They must communicate this value to others with clarity, passion, and pragmatism. They must celebrate this art and be committed to meaningful activities and actions that bring satisfaction to all who participate and teach this art. Only then will the *look of a leader* contribute to the *life of a leader* in a meaningful and fulfilling way. Yes, the true leader is a unique entity. The true leader is indispensable to the future of music education in this country.

Warren Bennis, Professor of Business at the University of Southern California, possibly said it best:

> The manager administers, the leader innovates.
> The manager maintains, the leader develops.
> The manager relies on systems, the leader relies on people.
> The manager counts on control, the leader counts on trust.
> The manager does things right, the leader does the right thing.

Leaders, of course, are those people we would follow into battle. Managers are the people we would follow into budget meetings.

BE A LEADER!

Chapter 2

The Life of a Leader

The life of a leader is not always an easy one. It requires tremendous tenacity and perseverance, constant thought and care, compassion, and courage. There have been many instances in my career where I made decisions that were not necessarily popular at the time they were made. But good leadership is about the unequivocal possession of knowledge that supports the decision—popular or not. Leaders must possess the information, facts, analysis, foresight, political sensitivity, pragmatism, and short- and long-term vision to know why, when—and, more importantly, how—to make the right decision. The *effective* leader is also the effective *teacher* who shares information with those affected as the decision is being shaped.

In almost every instance, there were happy endings to the controversial decisions I made. In the final analysis, when I look back on years of experience, it is the ability to stay the course, to keep teaching (yes, even in administration) what the purpose, structure, sequence, organization, value, and vision of the music education program is supposed to become. This is as true today to those who teach in music classrooms as it is to those who hold the title supervisor, director, superintendent, or dean.

The study of great leaders throughout history will support my beliefs. Bottom line, a leader must command the respect of others. This is as true with those who have district-wide administrative clout or authority as it is for those who are singular leaders in their buildings or departments. How does one command that respect? Certainly some of the necessary qualities come to the individual innately. However, many more of these traits are acquired through learning, experience, and maturity. The purpose of this chapter, then, is to examine these life aspirations and, in essence, create the profile of a true leader.

Initially, the life of a leader must be exemplary. "Exemplary of what?" one might ask. The answer, though not a simple one, must center on commanding respect. Others must respect the quality of life and the lifestyle of the individual who is a leader. If the leader does not command respect, then the basic and fundamental reason of why people follow leaders is lost. Leaders have an organizational style that is predictable, sound, and ethical. Leaders must lead from a record of success in the management of the process of their personal and professional lives, be it as concrete as finances or as indistinct as aesthetic taste. Certainly in the field of music education, musicianship and musical accomplishments will strongly influence the opinion of people about their leaders. The countenance and the confidence of these individuals must exhibit some sort of success, and their success breeds—and is a predictor of—future success. Thus, the *perception* of success is an important element in the *reality* of success.

Integrity is also an important aspect of effective leadership—integrity in dealing with colleagues as well as superiors, but most of all integrity with oneself. Integrity is not learned; it is earned. And the person possessing integrity will not go by unnoticed. The person who has integrity is the person who has the look of a leader. Leaders must be true to themselves and celebrate their existence. To assume a profile of someone else in an effort to establish personal integrity is unnatural—and deceptive. To become what some other group thinks a leader should be is synthetic and false. A leader who has *true*

14

integrity is on a personal, never-ending quest to find and eventually love his or her own personal uniqueness. This is not an easy quest, nor is it an issue of self-centeredness, but it is a quest of paramount importance if the leader is to employ the individual talents he or she has been given wisely and without apology. The result of this internal quest many times will produce a true entrepreneurial spirit, a valuable element in the *look* and the *life of a leader*.

I have found it important, as one internalizes one's being, to learn to seize the day, solemnize what it has to offer, and concentrate on the present, for looking back often causes frustration ("If I had only...."), and concentrating too much on the future can create worry ("What if...."). While you can learn from the past and apply that learning wisely in the present, you secure the future by seizing the immediate opportunities at hand. You must celebrate the day and *be here now!*

Styles of Leadership

I have observed many models of leadership that I thought were effective (and some that were not, but we learn from these, too!) and have read about the great leaders of history. The words and ideas I offer here are the result of experience, observation, and history. I have learned that there is nothing quite so basic to leadership as the difference between authority and power. Authority and power are very different, and the life force of the authoritarian is quite different from the life force of the powerful. The teacher who has authority but no power may well be the study hall teacher who has the authority to control behavior but somehow appears powerless to control the students and their learning behaviors. This is the person who is in charge but not in control. The authority without the power simply does not produce positive results.

I have lived through eleven presidents of the United States during my lifetime, and in most cases, history has already established their leadership styles. With no political bias, it is clear that a president who had the major *look of a leader* was John F. Kennedy. He received the authority when he was elected President, but it was his persona that gave him the power. During the short years of his presidency, the country was totally enamored with "Camelot," and this image remains today. Even though there were questions about his personal integrity, he was still able to project political integrity as President. There was an elegance, a refinement, and a polish that people cherished. John Kennedy had developed the ability to command respect and to inspire confidence. To a lesser but nevertheless effective degree, Bill Clinton possessed these same qualities.

Conversely, Harry S. Truman commanded the opposite *look of a leader*. He enjoyed his reputation as a "give 'em hell" President. Today, he probably would have been labeled a "micro manager." In a very different way, he also inspired confidence. What was it in the character of these two totally different leaders that commanded the same sort of allegiance and respect? It was *power*. Authority is given or delegated. Power is earned or taken.

The differences between authority and power need to be investigated. In K–12 education, there is always a leader or authority who controls public school music teachers, whether a supervisor, principal, or superintendent. If that leader has also gained the respect of music teachers, then the music teachers award that leader with power. There is not a great deal of consensus in most K–12 districts, although those authorities who are true leaders are working to institute more consensus-building relationships. But in K–12, even if the leaders do not have respect, power is taken because authority is very clearly defined in a hierarchical ranking.

The same structure between authority and power can be found in higher education, but the role of the faculty and how they award power to a leader is different. On most university campuses today, there is a continuing tension between faculty and administration over the "right" of the faculty to make decisions—or at least participate in the decision-making process. In the university setting, the traditional relationship of faculty to authority lies in a governance system that is based on the old concept of "shared" power or shared governance, often through consensus when and if that is possible. In higher education, power is both earned and taken by a process of dialogue with faculty—after sometimes lengthy or convoluted debate. In higher education, the process of sharing that unequivocal knowledge discussed earlier is critical to leading faculty towards consensus.

In K–12, authorities and leaders move ahead after they make decisions with or without consensus or debate. Accountability lies with a higher authority: the school board or state. In higher education, it is different. Sometimes shared governance doesn't work. Some faculty want both the authority *and* the power, and they continually press, naively, because they don't understand the difference between the two—or the necessity for two separate processes. Many faculty (see Chapter 12: Music in Higher Education) are too wrapped up in their own disciplines to see the larger or collective vision, no matter how clearly it has been shared.

I clearly recall informing a university music faculty of a decision I had made on my own, although I had discussed the problem with many faculty individually. I knew I had the support of 90 percent of the faculty. Even though I had shared my concerns, one faculty member questioned why I had not consulted with the entire faculty before making that decision (the question of dialogue and debate bringing consensus). My response was that I knew what their reaction would be, knew how much support there was and, thus, wished to avoid going directly against the wishes of a few in a confrontative situation. This decision created much tension at the time, and probably some never forgave me for making it. I needed to do this, however, to follow my own vision (see Chapter 1: The Look of a Leader). In this instance, I used my authority but took the power. Clever leaders at the university level grant to the faculty that which looks like a lot of authority, but most are much less inclined to delegate real "power," especially when the faculty numbers more than fifteen to twenty—influence, yes, but power, no.

So how does this all relate to leadership in music education, and more specifically, to individual teachers who may operate as separate entities? As a music educator, you are awarded authority over your students, but you usually have little or no administrative authority except in your classroom. Based on the administrative authority you have, it becomes essential for you to develop strategies to influence decisions and gain more authority over your day-to-day professional existence. You must assess how much authority you have to do your own job. How much influence do you have with your colleagues or with your superiors to be persuasive in decision-making? Do you have input into the development of curriculum, or are you told what to teach and when to teach it? How much input do you really want in decision-making, or is it just easier to sit back, let things happen, and then complain about the results? (That is *not* the *look of a leader*.)

You may have more authority than you think. For instance, you may have significant authority to determine the design, structure, and sequence of your curriculum. You probably have the authority for repertoire selection, for discipline and classroom management, for the planning and implementation of instructional activities, or for the use of technology. How you use that authority is a critical component of your individual leadership. How well you lead in using that authority in music education is the way you earn power. Just as there is a relationship between administration and faculty over the processes of authority and power so, too, is there a relationship between authority and power in the classroom in which the music educator is the authority. How you exercise your authority, in curricular design, teaching competence, through motivation, inspiration, and your own aspirations for excellence, will determine how you are given power by your students. Students will give you power through their commitment, expression of emotion, achievement, increased self-confidence, and their own desire for excellence. It is a shared process, perhaps more natural in design and authentic in purpose (and certainly less political) than the balance of power and authority between central administration and faculty.

Thus, you must establish at some point in your career whether you would rather just function in your own domain or truly develop the ability to have input into your professional existence. *This is leadership*. The true leader could not allow someone else to have total control over his or her professional life. It simply is not professional. Leadership is taking control over that which you *can* control and working to improve that situation while *aspiring to excel* in the domain in which you are the leader. By doing so, you are demonstrating leadership that will be noticed by others. Your success creates the *look of a leader*, a look that is grounded in achievement, success, and vision.

Whether or not you have developed this ability to influence, it is important for you to ascertain the style of leadership you feel comfortable with and that provides you with the most success. Every leader has developed a style of some sort. Even the leader with a bland leadership style is exhibiting a style of leadership, although probably not very effective. Since leadership is not something we *do* but rather something we *are*, it is important to develop a style that is effective and matches your own personal qualities. It is important to know who you are (self-confidence) and where you want to go (vision).

Some people find success in a democratic style of leadership that invites colleagues to work together and participate in decision-making. Such a person encourages cooperation and supports the creative thinking of groups of individuals. George W. Bush appears to be exhibiting this leadership style. He has earned the reputation of delegating power to others and then giving them the authority to execute their judgments. Other styles fall at the opposite end of the continuum by leading in an autocratic manner. Certainly the well-known Pied Piper of Hamlin had an autocratic style of leadership. He made one kind of music, and the rats just followed him to the end. There was no consensus or discussion about the process—it was *his* way. I know music educators today who are clearly Pied Pipers, and let there be no mistake—it is *their* way or the highway. In a more controversial analogy that will probably raise some eyebrows, I believe Jesus Christ was a very autocratic leader. He had a singular philosophy based on love and kindness, and he was able to exhibit that great love and kindness as he led others.

Leadership styles can also be exhibited in your teaching style, which is an often-overlooked kind of leadership. Some prefer a quiet kind of leadership in the classroom, while others prefer a highly structured and systematic approach. Still other teachers like to delegate tasks or challenges to groups of students and are comfortable with a team approach, which can sometimes be chaotic.

Successful teaching and quality leadership are based on fairness, trust and, yes, love and kindness. Setting high expectations for faculty or students can be the ultimate form of caring. The love and kindness issue has two very important aspects: the ability to give love as well as the ability to receive love. People frequently have more difficulty receiving love than giving it, even though the desire to receive love is a common trait. We must learn to allow love to enter the equation of good leadership. All too frequently we feel as though we are not deserving of love and, therefore, if we truly let it happen, we will appear as unworthy, soft, or weak.

Now, back to the autocratic style of leadership. As stated earlier, Harry S. Truman was well known for his autocratic "the buck stops here" style of leadership, and history has shown that it was an effective style for him, possibly even without the love and kindness. The only love I can recall him exhibiting was when he verbally criticized—to the press and, thus, the nation—the critics who gave his daughter poor reviews after her Carnegie Hall debut. He did exhibit love for his daughter. I wonder how well she received it. By the way, Harry Truman also played the piano, but the only thing the public ever heard him play was *Missouri Waltz* (he was from Missouri!).

On the surface, one might conclude that a democratic method of leadership might be the preferable style. It certainly is American. In my opinion, however, the right style or the best style will vary from individual to individual and from situation to situation, and will be shaped as much by the experiences one has in life and teaching as it is by individual personality. I have never known a *successful* leader who was completely democratic or absolutely autocratic. I have, however, been acquainted with some unsuccessful leaders who attempted to be totally one or the other. I have also experienced people who thought they were leaders but never led; this produces anarchy, and anarchy in education is chaos. The type of leadership style that is most effective is the one that is wisely chosen on the continuum from autocratic to democratic.

Again, though, the most important thing is that you establish a leadership style that is effective for you. The music education profession desperately needs leaders who are at the front of their profession developing a plan for the success of their music programs. In the application of love and caring, the good leader must learn when to step forward and when to step back, how to shift from being democratic to autocratic. The best leaders are those who can sense when to make that shift innately and do so in a way that challenges and inspires others to accept their leadership, whether faculty, colleagues, or students. When leaders lose support from colleagues or students, those who are true leaders will go back and analyze their approach and adjust the degree of democratic or autocratic style they have used. Successful leaders will do this intuitively and constantly; unsuccessful leaders will never do this, continue using the same approach, and fail.

The Quest for Excellence

The life of a leader is a constant quest for excellence. Those who don't care about excellence or growth are not going to be leaders. It is that simple. An effective leader is a person who always shows respect for others and their opinions and, consequently, gains their respect. That is very hard because sometimes leaders must show respect for those who have disagreed or worked against them in the past, or whose opinions they do not really value. My good friend Jeff Kimpton (who wrote the Foreword for this book) and I have often talked about how our wives are often not able to understand how we can go back to work and deal with a faculty member in an even and fair manner after the person has tried to undermine our leadership. This is a very important part of the job of leadership. In fact, learning to carry on when others oppose you is a trait of loving and caring that leaders must have for their colleagues—as well as their institution or program if it is to be successful. If leaders carry major grudges that prevent their ability to always look at things fairly and objectively, we both agree that leadership would be severely impaired, if not destroyed.

Leaders who *aspire to excel* are flexible, open to change, and dedicated to the mission of music education: educating individuals through music. They must be free from the need for ongoing approval from others (although a little bit of approval does make one have a better day from time to time) because they understand that leadership does not always foster popularity and certainly does not guarantee it! You can please some people all the time, and you can please all people some of the time, but it is virtually impossible to please all people all of the time. Leaders are non-judgmental, good listeners, and have very keen abilities to analyze and interpret the behavior of others—constantly. They understand that insecure persons exhibit the qualities of competitiveness, fear, anxiety, and paranoia, and frequently want to "get even" or "get revenge" when they feel they have been wronged. They often want to blame others for their own failures or inadequacies. Secure individuals are cooperative, accepting, loyal, honorable, and supportive. They always seek to understand. Unfortunately, they are sometimes taken for granted because they never intentionally create problems or draw attention to themselves.

Creative individuals exhibit the qualities of enlightenment, risk-taking, generation of ideas, and suggestion of new strategies. And they certainly "march to their own drummer." These individuals will demand time and attention from a leader, but they will be productive in the long run.

Where does your persona fit in these profiles? Don't worry, the human condition always contains—indeed welcomes— imperfection. In fact, good leaders know this and accept this because they are always trying to make something better.

Effective leaders, by nature, are dedicated to the enhancement of progress because inherent in their leadership is a strong sense of vision that is supported by steady progress. Common phrases used by leaders are, "How could we...?" "Do you suppose...?" "I wonder...." "Wouldn't it be interesting to try to...?" "Why don't we consider...?" and "Some research on this matter might just show...." Leaders would not be inclined to say, "Yes, but...," "We never did it that way before... ," "We tried that one time and...," or "That would never work...." There are always some folks who deter progress—I often call them the "yes-buts"—but real leaders will quickly realize that these negative statements, at best, promote the status quo, interfere with progress, and enhance retrogression. No real leaders will tolerate that for very long.

Effective leaders will invite participation by all but never depend on it. They will be accessible to others, show interest in their thoughts or concerns, be courteous, exhibit good judgment, and motivate others to act. Good leaders are generally creative individuals and are, therefore, willing to take risks. This in itself requires the careful judgment of drawing a line between risk and caution. One thing is certain: effective leadership always requires at least some degree of risk-taking because "nothing ventured is nothing gained." And why do good leaders take risks? It goes back to the issue of having *unequivocal knowledge*. They have analyzed, researched, looked ahead, scouted the territory, and know the territory. They have a vision as well as the knowledge and information to take risks to advance that vision. This is a key difference between leaders and managers.

Over the years, thousands have been asked by way of questionnaire and survey what characteristics they admire in leaders. The ones described below have emerged consistently at the top of the list.[1]

- Leaders animate the vision and make manifest the purpose so others can see it, hear it, taste it, touch it, feel it.
- Leaders demonstrate personal conviction. They believe in the message and effectively repeat it many times.
- Leaders foster collaboration by making certain all parties understand each other's interests and how each can gain from collaboration.
- Leaders build trusting relationships, are able to consider alternative viewpoints, and make use of other people's expertise and abilities.
- Leaders are able to give voice to other's feelings.

- Leaders make themselves vulnerable to others.
- Leaders listen.
- Leaders make other people feel strong.
- Leaders serve and support others.
- Leaders recognize and acknowledge the contributions of others.
- Leaders stay in touch with the outside world.

How Others View the Music Education Profession vs. How the Profession Views Itself

Music educators must consider how other education professionals view the profession of music education. We all know that we are "different"; others know we are "different," and many administrators at both the public school level and in higher education sometimes show frustration over that difference. It is that difference that creates the tension between music educators and the education establishment in this country. Others view music educators as expensive, temperamental, self-serving, an entity unto themselves, and the lowest faculty-to-student ratio in the academy. As music educators, we think we are dedicated, hardworking, creative, underpaid, and misunderstood when doing the most for our students and institution. Our colleagues in the school of education at the university level view us, at times, as unyielding, self-sufficient, self-important, and inflexible. We feel others do not understand the special and unique experiences music educators are supposed to have. We say, "Why do music education majors need to take those courses in the School of Education? Those courses are just a waste of time and we need those credits to offer better music courses to our students." We say, "Our courses provide the students with all they need to know to go out and be a music teacher." They say, "Your students need our courses to understand the large context of the public school."

On the other hand, as music educators we see ourselves as more committed, more dedicated, more effective, more "put upon," more necessary, and more vulnerable than our counterparts in other disciplines. We say, "How many other educators need to recruit people to have a balanced and sizeable ensemble?" "How many other educators have to maintain an inventory of instruments and keep them in playing condition?" "How many other educators need to be concerned about acoustics, practice rooms, and concert halls?" "How many other educators need to sell hoagies, magazines, and candy to raise funds for the various facets of their program?" And finally, the big push, "How many other educators put on public performances of their work?" We equate public performance with accountability and testing. Other academics do not view public performance as accountability at all because it does not test individual achievement or knowledge, but rather group performance.

I would have hoped that over all these years the "we vs. they" syndrome would have faded into the past as the education establishment came to understand the role and value of music education. Alas, this is not the case. Thus, the continuing dichotomy between these two perceptions has served to constantly make music educators a profession in crisis. These sharp differences in the way others view music educators as opposed to the way we view ourselves are the root causes for the perceptions that cause conflict, jealousy, envy, and misunderstanding. We live in a world of perception, one in which stereotypes are easily formed, supported through media and our very own profession—perceptions that are oftentimes interpreted as fact. The old adage that "everyone is innocent until proven guilty" has now become "everyone is guilty until proven innocent."

While you might not think the media plays a role in the shaping of the perception of music education, it does. Do you remember the McDonald's ads of the early 1990s, when the band descends on a restaurant playing very badly and dances around with fries and a burger and then sounds wonderful? There is a perception that school music is quaint, sounds bad, and is a joke at times. Therefore, the *life of a leader* has much to do with the development of a positive perception. The perception of excellence is far more difficult to attain and maintain than the perception of ineffectiveness or inefficiency. Of course, one perception is tied to leadership and good teaching; the other is tied to failure. (The issue of perception will return frequently in later chapters of this book.)

Sometimes we can be our own worst enemies in contributing mistaken public perceptions about the profession of music and music education. The fragmentation we experience between K–12 and university; or between band, choir, and orchestra; or between classroom vs. performance; or between theory and musicology doesn't help our cause. If we aren't united in purpose internally, how can we ever expect others to understand the *what* and *why* of what we do. Although there is a great deal of communication between high school and college performing group directors for recruiting purposes, generally there is little interest, respect, or cohesion between any of the other factions of the profession. It seems that we are so busy concentrating on our own area that little thought is given any other area of the profession. True leaders will explore and attempt to understand every aspect of their profession.

When tension arises within the profession, it saps energy that could be much better spent working toward common goals. Energy is the lifeblood of music teaching and performance. One of the challenges in leadership in music is that we deal with people who are highly creative, emotional, and have very strong individual musical skills and talents that take years to perfect. Because music is both an individual art and a collective practice, the balance between individual and organization, musician and group, teacher and teachers is a delicate one. People in the arts have not historically been known for cohesiveness due to the individual nature of each musical art form. Good leadership understands and makes the effort to bring cohesion to this diversity. Effective leaders walk in the shoes of other members of their profession. They constantly are thinking about how others view the challenges and opportunities that lie before them. They are always working to create and share appreciation of the valuable part each colleague plays in the totality of the profession.

I find that the lack of sensitivity about the whole is especially true in higher education among performing group conductors who compete for the same students and for the same funds. They compete with applied faculty for power over their students, battle over philosophical differences concerning vocal technique or orchestral repertoire, and try to manipulate student involvement in opera or marching band. The leaders in our profession must recognize and celebrate these differences, and also do all in their power to bring these differences together into a unified whole. We need each other desperately, and while it is healthy to discuss, debate, and work toward individual goals, it is equally unhealthy to have internal tensions between individuals or areas in the profession that ignore the common bond that is so necessary to our existence.

I am constantly amazed when I speak to music educators who cannot tell me how many music faculty members there are in a building, a K–12 department, or a school of music. Some have stated that they have not even met other music faculty members in their department, school district, or school of music, and I am not referring to only large music education units. Do we need leaders in this complex profession? We certainly do, and honest, non-judgmental self-evaluation must become a way of life. If we do not believe that the sum of our parts is essential to the whole of our profession, then we are going to be in big trouble.

To the average American, the desirability of a profession is frequently based on potential earnings and the perceived social status of the profession. Parents, guidance counselors, admissions counselors, and friends constantly remind us of this. Even when we advise students (and sometimes our own children) concerning the choice of a career, we advise them to choose music or music education "only if you have to." As music educators, we are viewed as having a limited earning potential and limited social status. College professors, at times, earn less money but have a higher social status than those in K–12 public education. This is particularly true for males. If female, the husband in another profession may provide the social status because music teaching rises in social acceptability as a second income.

I recall, when playing golf at a local country club where I lived at the time, overhearing in the locker room a club member say, "When did they begin admitting teachers into the club?" This is a sad commentary for all educators, regardless of discipline, because education is so important to the heartbeat of a nation and is, in fact, the foundation upon which this American democracy rests. How do others view us? Obviously as a frill when one has enough money and when all other matters of life are in order. And if they are not? Well, this is where leadership comes in!

A Profession or a Job?

It remains imperative that we view ourselves as professionals in the field of music education. When you ask yourself the question, "Am I involved in a profession or a job?," the answer simply stated is that the job is only part of your profession. Until you understand this, your professional life will never be totally fulfilled. The word "profession" is defined in *Webster's Dictionary* as "a calling requiring specialized knowledge and often long and intensive academic preparation," whereas a job is "a regular or hourly remunerative position." It must be noted that the word "professional" dictates who you are and prescribes a certain way of life that is ongoing. Like leadership, a profession is a way of life; a job entails only hourly commitments. A profession is concerned with the long term; a job is only concerned with that day and those hours worked. True professionals make their life their art. True leaders are professionals.

This chapter would not be complete without acknowledging that you cannot be all things to all people, nor can you be all things to yourself. That simply is not human. Real leadership can be exhausting and frustrating because you often spend the greatest amount of time working with the smallest percentage of the people who are the least secure, competent, happy, prepared, and professional. But real leaders know that if there is to be real success, helping those people to improve—or move along to other jobs—is as critical to the long-term success of the program as is developing long-range strategies and vision. It is difficult to assess what to do today and what to work on tomorrow without constantly taking your work home with you mentally every night. This theorem is particularly poignant to me. Leaders must learn to find quality time in their own lives, whether through exercise, family, hobbies and, yes, enjoying and listening to music. Balance is important. I must confess that I was never totally able to separate thinking about my profession from my personal life, but then this is another aspect of love and caring for the profession that can be a good sign, too.

Finally, I must stress that leadership is frequently not the easy choice or the easy path to take. The individual—*you*—must want to make a difference. Certainly outstanding leaders must be role models; they will, however, experience frustration and disappointment from time to time. Dr. Frederick Miller, Dean Emeritus of DePaul University in Chicago, stated in a speech to the Texas Association of

Music Schools that:

> Disappointment and frustration often become the fuel for
> burnout…. Frustration and disappointment are not the same
> thing, but they have something in common….
> Disappointment occurs when outcomes do not match up
> with hopes. Frustration occurs when outcomes do not match
> up with expectations.

Yes, the life of a leader is a complex one, but it must be an exemplary one with vision and passion leading the way. The old adage with which leaders have historically identified seems appropriate here:

Many can talk the talk,
but only the true leader will walk the walk.

Amen.

---

1 Kouzes, James M., and Posner, Barry Z. *The Leadership Challenge: How To Keep Getting Extraordinary Things Done in Organizations.* San Francisco: Jossey-Bass, 1995.

Chapter 3

Historial Perspectives of Music Education

As I have taught seminars, workshops, and courses across the country, I continue to be amazed at the lack of historical knowledge that my students have about the 150+-year history of music education. Perhaps I shouldn't be surprised since youth often do not know, and as the old Texas expression goes, "Who brung ya to the dance." Or to put it in another way, you won't know where you're going until you understand where you have come from. I write this chapter not so much as a history lesson, because I do not presume that the entire history of music education could be contained in just one chapter. I do think, however, that there are lessons from history from which we can learn and that this history *is* the reason why we are where we are today in this profession. If we believe in the old adage that history repeats itself, then we need to know what historical events have had the greatest impact on the profession so we don't repeat past mistakes and waste precious time. Good leaders need to know this history so their vision for the future is even clearer.

Leadership has been evident from the beginning of American music education. Lowell Mason, in 1837 or 1838 (depending on which historical treatise is consulted), persuaded the Boston School Committee to include music in the curriculum of public schools as a regular subject. This marked the first time the teaching of music was supported by public taxes to the same degree as other subjects. Mason was probably an autocratic leader whose true intentions were the placement of vocal music in schools in order to teach children to read music so singing would improve in the churches and choral societies of Boston.[1] But he, too, had his problems with school authority. He was removed in 1845 because he would only hire members of the Congregational Church to teach music, except for one Unitarian who was later dismissed for an unknown reason. In 1884, it was stated by H. W. Day, publisher of the *American Journal of Music and Musical Visitors*, "There are certainly Methodist and Baptist teachers, and those as make no particular religious professions, who are truly able and competent to teach, but they are not employed."[2] This might well have been the first instance of the issue of separation of church and state with regard to music education!

History reminds us that leaders were responsible every step of the way in creating a vision for music education, in every discipline of our profession. The school orchestra movement actually started in London in the late 1890s and early 1900s by the Murdock Company, a string instrument manufacturer that created school orchestras as ways of advancing interest in string music and, obviously, string instrument purchases. Americans Albert Mitchell, Paul Stoeving, and Charles Farnsworth witnessed this phenomenon in England and came back to America wanting to do the same thing here. They were leaders with a vision; they started the string orchestra movement in Boston in 1913—a movement that quickly found other advocates across the country as this country's professional orchestra movement was beginning to grow. By 1917, there were three times more orchestras in American schools than bands![3] (For a more detailed look at the genesis of the school orchestra movement, please see Chapter 10: Instrumental Music Education.)

This was to change, though, when American military band members came back from Europe at the end of World War I. The rise of collegiate band programs had exploded at the turn of the century and really accelerated after World War I. Some universities had formed bands to support football as early as the 1890s, specifically Minnesota in 1892 and Illinois in 1896. Bands first marched on the field in 1910, and as college band programs expanded in the early 1920s after the war, virtually all were marching by the end of that decade.

The band movement in public schools began to grow at the same time. Military band members, flushed with excitement over the musical experiences they had had during the war and seeing the rapid spread of school orchestras, began to organize bands in junior high and high schools. These veterans found ready partners in American band instrument companies that had experienced great growth in making instruments for military bands and needed new markets now that the war was over. Leaders who had a passion and a vision for what bands could bring to American youth included people like H. E. Nutt in the Chicago public schools, Charles Jenkins in the famed Joliet, Illinois schools, William D. Revelli in Hobart, Indiana, and Mark Hindsley in Shaker Heights, Ohio. The band movement—and the music industry—initiated the national band contests in 1923, held annually in Washington, DC. School bands from all over the country would come to compete for the national championship.

It was only natural that high school bands would want to emulate the college model, particularly as a new crop of instrumental music educators trained in college programs moved into positions of leadership around the country starting in the early 1930s. Marching bands, of course, became even more prevalent in most colleges and universities after World War II, and so did marching bands in high schools.

This progression of events probably changed the manner in which the public viewed music education more than any other event in the history of the profession. The public became more and more aware of music in schools—but as an exhibition, not as an educational experience. In the minds of many, music coupled with competitive athletics established a stereotype and a perception that music education is an extracurricular subject and an entertainment medium—a dilemma that plagues our profession to this day. *This* is why history is important.

In higher education, this concern has not been as apparent. The study of music, per se, has retained academic merit. This is especially true in the study of music as an academic class (music history, theory, and "appreciation"). The performance of music, however, is awarded less credit and less academic prestige. It is interesting to note, however, that there are more scholarship monies available for performing group participation than academic music encounters. This is especially true with marching band!

General music, too, has an interesting history of strong leadership. The practice of singing in school began to take hold in earnest in the 1870s and was, in large part, supported by the textbook companies and publishers with their singing books. Music institutes, organized by book companies such as the American Book Company and the Ginn Company, became popular and were often held at the normal schools preparing teachers. The book company institutes actually preceded and motivated the creation of specific music pedagogy experiences at colleges and universities around the United States. These institutes helped classroom teachers learn how to bring singing skills and music reading into the classroom. If the classroom teacher could not sing adequately, a record was provided. The results achieved in this manner were modest, at best.[4]

As time progressed, classroom teachers needed assistance, and trained music teachers were first hired to help classroom teachers better teach music. These first music teachers were called "music supervisors" because they supervised music instruction in an entire school building. I can personally recall using the *American Singer* during my elementary school years and actually teaching from the series during my early years in the profession. MENC was actually called the Music *Supervisors* National Conference when it was formed in 1907.

In school districts around the country, music teachers with an almost evangelistic zeal advocated for elementary music for every child becoming a foundation for a K–12 system of music education. Harriett Clarke, who trained at the Potsdam/Crane School of Music, came to Wichita, Kansas, and started the elementary music program in 1888. Many other advocates in other towns and cities around the country shared those ideas. Listening became a part of the elementary school curriculum as the Victrola Company created the national listening contests in the 1920s, again to sell more victrolas and create a new market for listening materials as part of a comprehensive education in music. The growth of elementary music continued most rapidly after World War II, particularly as schools were seeking greater specialization from all teachers and as elementary teachers began receiving planning and preparation periods as the teachers union movement grew—provided, of course, by elementary music specialists.

While there is a similar history in the development of the American choral music education program, I am for purposes of brevity not including it here because a detailed discussion can be found in Chapter 11: Choral Music Education.

Music programs exploded in size, quality, and curricular inclusion during the 1950s and 1960s. Instrumental programs expanded into the elementary school, and junior high programs became training grounds and mirror images of high school performance programs. The music industry exploded with materials, from elementary textbook series with recordings, posters, and motivational materials to a flood of string and wind instrumental music series that created a dynamic school publishing empire—Rubank, Belwin, Carl Fischer, Kjos, Southern, Theodore Presser, and many more. Any school that was "worth its salt" had a music program, and competitions—solo, ensemble, band, orchestra, choir—all exploded as a way to prove the worth and merit of a music program. This laid the groundwork for the conflict between music education as an academic subject and performance as a means of justifying that subject that we live with today.

That tension between education and performance in music has been around since the earliest beginnings, and no one should forget that. Samuel Cole in 1903 came closest to the present philosophy surrounding general music, when he wrote:

> The real purpose of teaching music in public schools is not to make expert sight singers nor individual soloists. I speak from experience. I have done all these things and I can do them again, but I have learned that, if they become a means to an end and not a means, they hinder rather than help because they represent only the abilities of the few. A much nobler, grander, more inspiring privilege is yours and mine; to get the great mass to singing and to make them love it[5]

We should also not forget that the treatment of music as an expendable part of the curriculum has deep historical roots that predate our current national problems. No one should forget the frenzy this country experienced in education when the Soviet Union launched Sputnik I in 1957 and overtook the United States in the race for space. Math and science education exploded in importance, and I can remember with great clarity the lump in my throat when the school board of East Stroudsburg, Pennsylvania, talked about reducing the music program so more time could be spent in math and science education—in 1958! (Fortunately, our music program wasn't cut, but it did prevent an orchestra program from being started.) This is the earliest time I can remember having to become an advocate for my program and to defend its existence. Little did I know that it would become an almost full-time job for so many in our profession.

As music began to develop a rationale for the inclusion of music as a regular course of study, we passionately—but probably naively—used arguments that were tenuous at best. We used the affective rather than the cognitive to justify our programs. The argument that "a boy who blows a trumpet will never blow a safe" played to the notion of music as a positive *moral* force rather than a positive *academic* force. We sold music as a means that would underscore democratic principles, the values of working together, good mental health, profitable leisure time, and positive human relations, and in doing so sidetracked our arguments that music was of paramount educational, creative, and curricular importance. Frankly, when I look back at this time, we appeared shallow and laid a foundation that ultimately did more to assign music to the curricular sidelines than it did to make it more fundamental. We must know this history so we do not repeat it; I fear, however, that we do tend to continue to repeat this history.

At the same time, research in the study of music as a cognitive discipline—an academic, creative, and expressive force—was exploding. It seems odd that we were laying the groundwork for an advocacy movement to justify music in the curriculum at the same time major leaders and researchers were developing a pedagogical and philosophical foundation about the importance of music learning. The research and teachings of Jaques-Dalcroze, Carl Orff, Zoltan Kodaly, Shinichi Suzuki, Edwin Gordon, Bennett Reimer, the Manhattanville Music Curriculum Program, and Comprehensive Musicianship, to name just a few, were all hallmark events in our profession. They contributed to a vast resource of philosophies, pedagogies, and curricular materials that real classroom leaders in music education can and do use to substantiate the seriousness of music study. But too often I fear they are negated by our non-musical justifications, and the true leader in this profession knows the difference.

How leaders learn those differences, and the value of those philosophies and pedagogies is, of course, part of the history of music teacher education. Teacher education in music has had a tentative history. The system of higher education in this country was originally established around the English system, and most universities and colleges established during the first years of this country's history staunchly subscribed to the rich grounding and experience of the liberal arts, which they felt was essential for the educated person. During the evolution of the music education profession, this liberal arts tradition viewed specific training in teaching pedagogy as being of questionable academic merit. The Boston Academy began classes for teachers to improve church music in 1830. This led to the establishment of teacher's conventions for pedagogical purposes, but the increasing demand for public education in this country required a greater number of teachers, and these conventions were soon followed by the normal school movement in about 1865.

Normal schools were the first effort to establish a process for the training of teachers. In 1865, there were approximately fifteen normal schools in five states. Admission requirements were low to non-existent. One only needed to have an eighth grade education to be admitted. The primary goal of these schools was to prepare teachers for classrooms in rural areas. The curriculum of the first normal schools was one year in length and gradually expanded to two, three, and finally four years of instruction by the early twentieth century. In large cities, urban teachers received their teacher training in special high school programs that maintained classes specifically for students to be trained as teachers. While Harvard, Yale, Brown, and Princeton avoided teacher education programs at the undergraduate level, the normal schools actually began to *add* components of a liberal arts education to the preparation of teachers; they eventually became comprehensive state universities offering many degrees well beyond teaching. However, the condescension between the classic liberal arts and music teaching pedagogy still exists today, and I believe it is the historical precedent for the often-low status of music education in the musical academy of this country.

In the late 1800s, specific college instruction began for music teachers even though the curriculum was still basically designed for general classroom teachers. At this time, it was rare for music teachers to have a position teaching only music; they were usually certified to teach many subjects. As I previously stated, the music institutes of the book companies were the genesis for a specific program in music teacher preparation. In 1871, the Pennsylvania State Normal School at Mansfield became one of the first normal schools in the country to create a separate department for music education. Oberlin followed in 1876. The growth of music teacher education was slow among the nation's colleges and universities. In fact, in 1916, very few had programs for the specific training of music "supervisors," as those who were certified to teach music were called. The reason for the "supervisor" designation was because their role was to supervise the elementary general classroom teachers as they taught music to their students. I can personally recall that as late as the early 1950s, music majors at West Chester State Teachers College in Pennsylvania (another former normal school) were labeled "music sup's," and music majors around the campus commonly referred to one another with pride as such. Thus, the label "supervisor" did not disappear quickly, and all music majors through the 1950s were awarded the degree of Bachelor of Science and were certified to "Teach and Supervise Music, K–12."

In 1884, the Crane Normal Institute in Potsdam, New York, achieved national recognition by emphasizing the commonality between the preparation of a music teacher and a musician. Here, another leader, Julia Crane, founded a rigorous program that linked pedagogy, performance, and some aspects of the liberal arts tradition. The liberal arts in the late nineteenth century still subscribed to the philosophy that the Bachelor of Arts degree represented a pre-professional degree leading to such professions as law, medicine, dentistry, and the ministry. Crane broke the mold and created the specific curriculum that led to a professional undergraduate degree in music education. As professional music schools gradually began to form in higher education across the country, the model of an inclusive professional degree in music and music education took hold.

The early twentieth century brought the first sustained efforts to broaden the training of music teachers into the academic mainstream, in part because music instruction was becoming more routine in American public schools. Schools of music were created at many of the largest comprehensive and land grant universities in the early 1900s, which linked music teacher education with music performance. In normal schools turned state teachers colleges, one could often only go there for music education, as performance degrees weren't offered. In conservatories, one went for performance because music education wasn't offered. Ultimately, out of the national demand for both teachers *and* performers, nearly all schools offered both areas, and this spread to the liberal arts colleges and universities that had so long excluded both performance *and* music education from their curriculums.

Isn't this an interesting history bringing us to where we are today? Most colleges and universities today, with the exception of those in the Ivy League and a scattering of other universities throughout the country, offer degrees in both music and music education at the undergraduate level.

I wish this were not true, but music teacher training today continues to struggle to find its home. State teachers colleges are now state universities, all working to become research institutions and greatly influenced by the broadly based liberal arts curriculum that confounded music education study one hundred years ago. It often takes music majors five years to attain a bachelor's degree because they must meet so many requirements—liberal education, music performance, music history and theory, music pedagogy, the "education" requirements, observation and practicum requirements, and state certification requirements, not to mention the mandatory standardized test before only temporary certification is granted—all of this increasing at a time when there is a national shortage of teachers, and entry-level salaries still rank with those of police officers and sanitation workers. It seems amazing to me that the "typical" music education student still does not usually possess the breadth of "general education" courses to qualify for Phi Beta Kappa. An additional sixth year would be required to achieve this honor.

Through many years of consulting in higher education, I have observed that some colleges and universities have embraced a music education program, but with less than the serious intent this commitment demands. In far too many cases, the *real* reason for offering the degree in music education is an economic one: these programs attract students. Music education students play in performing groups. The true dedication to the training of music teachers and the actual concern for program quality appear secondary to the concern over the quality of applied and performing programs. I have seen this lack of commitment demonstrated again and again when a school of music requires that student teachers leave their cooperating schools to return to campus to attend a rehearsal by a performing group. I have even seen schools of music where the loss of scholarship is threatened should a student not comply. If we cannot solve these issues, we will forever face the national dilemma of insufficient numbers of music educators.

I close this chapter knowing that it is wholly insufficient to stand alone as a history of music education. What I hope I have accomplished, however, is to help the reader understand that where we are today is based on a foundation extending back nearly one and a half centuries. Possibly this proud past combined with the exciting hope for the future will indeed command the respect and support of all people. It will always be important for the future leaders in this profession to know its historical base and from whence it came. This is essential in order to put the dreams and aspirations for the future in the proper perspective.

1 Birge, William Bailey. *History of Public School Music in the United States*. Washington, DC: Music Educators National Conference, 1966, p. 25.
2 Keene, James A. *A History of Music Education in the United States*. Hanover, NH: University Press of New England, 1987, pp. 115, 116.
3 Ibid., p. 271.
4 Birge. *History of Public School Music in the United States*. p. 353.
5 Ibid., pp. 161, 162.

Chapter 4

Building The Necessary Support

Where I was is gone–done–over–
    But I will not look back
Where I am is now–I must be here now–
    I must concentrate on it with all that I have.
    But…
Where I shall be is now being built, and my vision
    and advocacy will build that!

I want to make a confession. I have *never* in my 45-year career as a music educator started a new position with great support of any kind. I never took a position that was ready-made and already established. I seemed to be like a friend of mine who likes to buy old houses and fix them up. I am a builder, not a maintainer. And so I have always had to work to build the support system for music education from the ground up because I knew no one else would be a support system for me. It was exciting, rewarding, stimulating, and difficult. But it was enduring, and it is why I can look back on my many positions and see them continuing to excel—even ten, twenty, forty years later. They continue to achieve because many members of the community—parent, faculty, student, business, civic, and cultural—aspired to want the music program to excel. An effective leader helps create *many* leaders throughout the community who can claim ownership to program success.

Building the necessary support requires tremendous patience and a clear knowledge of the various constituencies served by music education. There is a system of support within your school and your district; the leader who *aspires to excel* must find and cultivate that support system. There are the vital networks of parents and students who can quickly tell each other the kind of job you are doing and share their enthusiasm about the program. There are connections with business and civic organizations, from the chamber of commerce, Rotary, or other service organizations to senior citizen associations or neighborhood associations in larger urban centers. There are the collections of cultural organizations that might exist in your community—theater groups, symphonies, choral associations, or community bands. Each of these has a vested interest in the health and vitality of the community and of an engaged and successful youth, and in having a positive demonstration of excellence by their local school district.

I continue to be surprised that my students in seminars and workshops are not very aware of the networks of support systems in their communities, nor are they aware of how much they need them. I could never have built the programs I did without these people. It seems as though younger music educators today don't think these people make a difference or have influence over them. They do—and they can. Even if you are the only music teacher in a small school, there is a support system. In urban schools where students are bussed in from all over the city and the network of organizations might lie within a small neighborhood—or many neighborhoods—there are support systems you must know and build upon.

I might suggest making an inventory of support systems and organizations within your school, district, or community. After you have a listing of all of them, and their different potentials for support, you will need to figure out how to make a personal contact with the various organizations and individuals, and develop a sphere of influence in each. You will also need to figure out, in advance, what you will say about your program and how you will connect these people *with* your program. Don't develop this network only when your program is in trouble. Develop it when your program is strong.

What *will* you tell them about your music program? Remembering the previous chapter on history, will you tell them about the affective attributes of music, the cognitive benefits, or both? Do you know why you should do this? How will your students demonstrate their achievements? How will you describe the curriculum and purpose of your program? What will those who come into contact with your program come away knowing and believing? How will you help them see a value in what you do, and what your students do? How will you structure frequent interactions for this network to return to experience what you do?

Too often, music educators look to external advocacy materials to substantiate their programs rather than connecting the intrinsic value and merit of the program to their own school and community. Recent writings in the MENC "Music Makes You Smarter" campaign stated that a new study by Dr. Francis Rauscher (University of Wisconsin, Oshkosh) and Dr. Gordon Shaw (University of California, Irvine) demonstrated that laboratory rats exposed to the music of Mozart appeared to be smarter than those exposed to minimalist music. They also indicated that there had been moderate test gains in groupings of students who played the piano in some California classrooms. Our profession quickly seized on that information, much of which is thin on its merits as substantiating research, and went crazy. This was supposed to be the big "aha" moment, a time when research clearly substantiated the study of music. Zell Miller, Governor of Georgia, proposed as part of his state budget to make classical music tapes available to all newborn children in the state so it would make Georgia children smarter. Of course, at the same time, he removed from the state budget the funding requested to increase the number of music teachers in the state.

I am not sure public perceptions of music education are really any different today than they were after the MENC campaign or the neonatal tapes of Mozart for Georgia children. People simply won't change their perceptions or place greater value on something with which they have no personal connection. That's why it is crucial for there to be an authentic and consistent opportunity for you and your students to build those connections, based on the validity of your program and its curriculum—not on specious research findings that most people either simply don't believe or think is marketing and media hype to begin with.

Throughout this book, I will avoid using the term "advocacy." Webster defines "advocacy" as "pleading and defending." We must be careful when we use quick slogans and clever campaigns that we do not adopt a pleading and defending tone in a way that is not becoming of the music profession. If you have a good network of community support, others can more eloquently speak to the benefits of music and a quality program of music learning than you. I have found it appropriate and successful to establish a demeanor that invites other persons to speak and respond rather than a demeanor that gives the appearance of knowing all the answers. Music educators could better spend their time teaching well. I am convinced communities will change their attitude about music if they hear the values of music from their peers and friends rather than from you.

So what does this all have to do with building community support? What does it have to do with the overused word "advocacy"? Where will this all end? Should we expose all children to Mozart in order to research their intellectual growth and spatial reasoning? Mozart is just one of many composers. What happens if we play Mahler, or Sousa, or Randall Thompson? Why do school districts continue to eliminate music teachers in spite of the "Music Makes You Smarter" and many other "campaigns"? Is there a chance that at times more claims are being made on behalf of music education than can be delivered?

Perhaps it might be wise to go back to the true purposes of why we have music in the schools and remind our network of supporters of the premise that music is a valid educational offering in its own right—one of many elements that enhance the quality of life. Certainly this is a goal of education. We know music contributes to attitudes toward life, as well as the motivation and discipline needed to learn and excel. These things matter and are basic to our art form, yet they are all but ignored because they are affective behaviors, difficult to prove statistically. To use the arts primarily to teach that which is not truly distinctive about music seems to undermine the real reason for music in our schools. While I understand the need to show the interrelationships between music and other educational processes, I have a concern that we lower the importance of music in its own right and create the perception that music is just a contributor to the "more important subjects," such as mathematics and reading.

I have additional concerns about promising more than we can deliver in the total educational process. We really aren't sure that Mozart per se makes you smarter, no more so than we know that Wheaties makes you a champion. One thing we do know for certain because there is statistical proof: students who choose to participate in music courses and ensembles are generally better students and do well in standardized tests. However, it has not been proven that music is the cause of their intellectual success. Possibly it is just that more intellectually capable students are involved in music study. Or possibly it is that the process of music study *is* a critical factor in intellectual development, which is the premise of Howard Gardner (see Chapter 6: Developing a Comprehensive Curriculum in Music). But just because some students choose to take music and do well doesn't mean all students must take music. Some come from homes where music study is encouraged; others come from socio-economic classes that can afford instruments and lessons. Some come from homes that value the largely Western European art music that is the primary focus of our music education programs.

Claims that music study leads to higher grades and higher achievement and test scores may lead to disappointment and lack of credibility because the evidence is indeed thin across all students, socio-economic classes, and cultural and racial backgrounds. Sometimes it may be better not to give our public what they want but rather to help them understand what they ought to want, and why. Should this not be a part of our educational mission? Is this not what building support for music education is all about? It is important to build support for music education for all the *right* reasons, and there are many. So what are the right reasons?

Many music educators I have come to know across this country think that building support for music education is a financial issue and is most important during times of budget cuts and belt-tightening. These periods of time always seem to bring about reductions in funding for the arts at national, state, and local levels in both the private and public sectors. These tough financial times, when tough decisions face school boards, also exacerbate the tension between the "peripheral" role of music versus the "academic" subjects that must be preserved. When the chips are down and the budgets are lean, this is *not* the time to start building community support. Community support must be constant, ongoing, deep, wide, and part of a belief system in the value of music for students and the community that will weather any economic storm or organizational restructuring.

There must be community support for student achievement in all areas, for education as a foundation for the community and for a quality of life in which music contributes to the human condition. Could this just possibly be at the very root of our national problem in education, for logically, the better the "human condition" of the learner, the more successful the learning? It would seem that the human condition nurtured by the arts should be the root and the basis of education.

The true measure of the quality of a profession cannot be measured by how well it does during the "good years," but how well one manages to survive or even progress in times of austerity. We see again and again that in times of national crisis, tragedy, and austerity, the country turns to music to express the deepest emotions or as a tool to influence public thought. True, music will always be a necessary part of the national psyche. But what about music in education?

Let's think about getting out of the cocoon and speaking to the community. This should not be limited to any one group of people, for there are many who need to carry the torch. The individuals important in building community support include 1) yourself; 2) your students; 3) your peers in your own discipline and in other disciplines; 4) administrators; 5) boards, clubs, and foundations with whom you deal, especially the school board; and 6) the community.

You

You are the least effective advocate for your own profession. I'm sorry to tell you that, but it is true. The public would expect you to be an advocate; it is best if you let others create a climate of support for music education in your community. You can certainly *influence* the advocates and provide important and powerful material. The foundation of support must be simple: the development of quality programs that are properly funded…the creation of opportunities for musical learning both within and outside of the school or university. Social, business, and civic groups must have a positive image of the music program and know what it contributes to the community, school district, or university. Your primary goal must be to assist in the development of an outstanding music program in your school district or your university, for this will speak for itself. Yes, you are a conduit for information about issues and challenges to supporters of the program. Your work behind the scenes, however, will pay far greater dividends than if you are personally leading the charge.

Students

The ability to communicate with music students is crucial to building community support. Those teachers who are able to relate to their students do so by conveying an excitement and passion for music. Members of a community can discern an ambiance that surrounds a successful teacher, and they know when students respect that teacher. The difference between popular and unpopular teachers is the level of excitement and passion they have for their students and for the subject they teach. Students know the difference between a teacher who lives to teach and a teacher who only teaches for a living. It is interesting that music educators are the only teachers who call themselves "directors" and view themselves differently. Music *directors*, however, must also remember that they are first and foremost music *teachers*.

Many students carry music with them throughout their life because a teacher aroused a passion in them and helped them understand the educational purpose behind their school musical experiences and how they can carry them into life. Successful music teachers must communicate the passion and the programmatic objectives of music to parents, promoting the idea of amateur music involvement for a lifetime and expressing pride in their participation and support. Quality music ensembles are only one part of the demonstration of musical involvement; individual achievement, a strong curricular framework, and a stimulating classroom music program are all part of the mix. As the entire program improves, students get excited and involved, and become the program's best communicators. Student success breeds program success.

All students will seek out those teachers they admire. The passion students demonstrate for music is the result of a passionate teacher and high teaching competence. We have all seen and heard music programs with passionate children and enthusiastic teachers that aren't very good. Passion and enthusiasm on the part of students is an affective reaction, but a high level of student achievement is a cognitive reaction related to a fine teacher. Good music programs have both. The fact that music students "hang out" at the music room speaks both to their love of music and their devotion to their music teacher. The wise teacher will understand that it is more readily possible to captivate a student's heart than the student's brain, and thus, the teacher who brings a passion for music to the students must be captured with both the students and the art form. The very best support for music education will come from motivated students who have had a positive experience. It must be music for a lifetime.

Peers

Music Peers:

Good music programs develop from a logical sequence of learning, but the cohesiveness of the music faculty contributes greatly to this end. Music educators must take ownership of the entire music program, whether K–12 or university. The music faculty has to work as a team and agree on the importance of the program, its goals, and a sequential curriculum. If there is not a relationship between the many music teachers in the district or department—if they are only a series of discrete programs that lack any kind of curricular or faculty continuity—the purpose of music in education is weakened, badly.

When I was an administrator, I wrote monthly letters to my faculty, both in K–12 and in university positions, in which I shared my hopes, discussed challenges, and brought new ideas or philosophies forward for them to consider. I did this to build a sense of community, to help focus faculty attention on curricular and programmatic issues, and to keep them up to date on contemporary issues. In addition to regular meetings, this memo helped set the tone for the program. Certainly I had an advantage being a full-time music administrator. Even in those districts in which there is no regular music administrator (and those are the majority these days), music teachers *must* find a way to establish a regular system of communication.

Non-Music Peers:

The music teacher/professor relationship with peers in *other* academic disciplines is an ongoing challenge, particularly at the public school level. In higher education, the peer relationships fall into a more cohesive format because these sort of professional relationships are academically and physically non-threatening. Collegiality among non-music peers in higher education comes much more readily at the university level because there is less competition between faculty for funds, students, or administrative support, and personal matters such as salaries and grievances are kept very private.

The opposite exists at the public school level, where all faculty are treated as one in terms of salaries, rank, and privilege. Teachers unions fight for this, thus inhibiting entrepreneurial behavior on the part of the individual teachers. When an individual teacher emerges from the status quo grouping, antagonism and jealousy develop. As music educators attempt to build support with their non-music peers, old stereotypes and misperceptions can cause them to appear "different," "special," or even at times "bothersome." Some of our non-music peers are jealous of our community visibility. Others find us aggressive and excessively passionate about our programs. Many music educators tell me that non-music teachers in their buildings wish they could only work with high ability and motivated students. There are other stereotypes and misperceptions that are hard to get out of the minds of non-music peers. They do exist, such as the following:

- Music is extracurricular, not curricular.
- Music is entertainment.
- Music classes at the elementary level afford the classroom teacher a free period.
- Music is just like athletics.
- The music teacher places unrealistic demands on student time to the detriment of "academic" study.
- Music pulls students out of class and real "academic" study.

How do we deal with these perceptions held by our peers? How did these stereotypes develop in the first place? Perhaps music teachers have been so dedicated to their students and programs that they have isolated themselves from the school or district structure that is a support system. As music teachers, we must do the following:

- Become a part of the whole school or district.
- Discuss in a friendly manner a perception we notice a colleague holds, for this stimulates the important element of communication.

- Communicate the values and curricular beliefs of the program with our peers.
- Take an active interest in the work of our colleagues and praise them and the good work they do.

One thing is certain: we will continue to have difficulty justifying our existence as long as these perceptions exist. We must work to eradicate them diligently, intelligently, and consistently because they are crucial to building support in our schools. We now have the National Standards for Arts Education that will not change our cultural landscape overnight, but they do represent a critical curricular rallying point for change. We have to watch the balance of our programs, for we run the risk of being even more excluded from the mainstream of education if our profession continues to "genuflect in humble adoration before the kinetic plumage of the marching band."[1] We simply must continue to convince our non-music peers—and/or "academic" colleagues—that we, too, are "academic" and supply a segment of education that no one else can provide.

Administration

Justifying and defending music programs to public or private school and university administrators continues to be a challenge for even the most experienced music educators. We have spent 160 years trying to learn how to effectively convince those in decision-making positions that music is essential education. Those administrators who make decisions about music programs often base those decisions on a personal system of values that possibly is reflective of a non-musical background or a negative personal experience with school music.

Yet research in the 1990s in the state of Ohio dispels that notion. Dr. Barbara Payne, Associate Professor of Music at the University of Hawaii, Manoa, investigated how school administrators felt about many of the statements that are frequently included in justification documents. The study requested information about each administrator's musical background and included the extent to which each had participated in school music ensembles. It is interesting to note that the study showed no difference in how the justification statements were perceived based on previous participation in school music. Apparently the participation in school music, or the absence thereof, had no real effect on the values they placed on their school music programs.

Other results obtained from the 250 subjects who provided information showed that:

- They perceived the strongest values of music education to be, in rank order:
  - Improving self-esteem
  - Providing an opportunity for success for students who have problems in other areas
  - Providing a means for students to increase the aesthetic quality of their lives
  - Providing a more well-rounded education
  - Training students to use a form of communication
  - Providing knowledge and appreciation about man's cultural or historical artifacts
  - Developing potential and talent
  - Providing a means for students to enrich their lives through self-expression
  - Developing self-confidence
  - Public relations

- Providing a means of increased satisfaction
- Developing creativity
- Improving motor coordination
- Self-discipline
- Developing critical and analytical skills
- Developing citizenship
- Teaching a unique symbol system
- Needs no justification
- Providing a means for using leisure time
- Assisting in learning other subjects
- Exposing students to our cultural heritage
- Helping students who have difficulty in other areas
- Increasing perception
- Providing a means to participate in rites and rituals
- Allowing students relief from more structured classes
- Helping students find the "good life"

- Over half of the values were non-educational, with over three-fourths of the values being non-musical.
- Only nine of the twenty-six values listed were musical values, while fifteen of the values were educational.
- Male administrators were more likely to assign a positive value to statements associated with social development or miscellaneous benefits (leisure time, rites and rituals, good motor coordination, using leisure time, etc.).
- Female administrators were more positive than males concerning the musical and intellectual values of music.
- Administrators over the age of forty were more likely to see music as a form of leisure time activity than those under forty.

- Administrators from small towns and rural areas were more positive about music education's ability to improve self-confidence than subjects from large cities or metropolitan areas.
- Administrators from rural areas were more positive about the effect of music on the development of creativity and imagination than those from more populous areas.

Even though this study was completed almost ten years ago, I see little difference today.

At one point during my tenure as a public school music supervisor, the administration was very supportive of a competitive marching band until they learned that the marching contests were held the same night as the school football games. The high school principal became very upset when I suggested that the band would no longer be able to attend football games on competition nights. He suggested strongly that I had my priorities confused. My response was that I was doing what was best for the band program and would have the ninth grade band at the games, including a half-time show. He objected to what he called the "band scrubs" doing the game. My response was that I was doing what I was hired to do, and if the presence of the band was that important, they might consider moving the football games from Saturday to Friday evenings. As one might suppose, that suggestion was not well received; however, the upper administration and school board did support my proposal. The ninth grade band did play at the football games on competition nights. Many times the competition band would get back to the football game in time to present its competitive show at the end of the game, and surprisingly the bulk of the fans remained to see the show. Before long, the large following the band had for its competitions began to significantly affect the attendance at the football games, and thus, it became not only a school spirit issue but also an economic one. Money talks! Thus, football games were changed from Saturday night to Friday night, and remain so today.

I maintained this approach at the university level as well. When the new football coach convinced the university to replace the artificial turf with grass on the game field, the athletic director gave notice that the band could no longer practice on the field because the marching would harm the grass. After some negotiation, we procured a practice field that lacked a high vantage point from which the director could see the formations. When we requested a cherry picker, the university turned us down. After much negotiating and many strong suggestions that no cherry picker would mean no band at the football games, the administration succumbed, and a cherry picker was purchased.

It is important to show appreciation to administrators for their support, to make certain their names are on the programs and they are properly introduced at the concerts and performances they attend. Keep administrators aware of the music curriculum, the importance of curriculum sequence, and the positive results of a well-constructed curriculum. Stress the importance of classroom music—not just performing music—and communicate both the positives and the needs of the music program. Opening the lines of communication and keeping administrators informed about important issues, both positive and negative, regarding the music program is essential. Involve administrators at all times, in sharing credit for program excellence and in finding solutions to continuing challenges. Remember, administrative involvement leads to ownership, which in turn kindles pride and consequently leads to support. Administrative support is the end result all music educators seek and must have.

School Boards, Clubs, Foundations, Civic and Cultural Organizations:

As music educators, we must play the politics of inclusion and get out of the little cocoon in which we sometimes live. There is a larger community that surrounds us that we must embrace. We cannot become an elite and separate entity in our communities. We must avoid a programmatic isolation that is often a byproduct of wanting to be independent, for this results in a breakdown of communication with the larger cultural and civic community. The arts generate a strong statement about the quality of life in a community, and it would follow that a strong arts program in the schools is a keystone in further building that quality of life.

Building a broad base of community support must be handled in a sensitive manner. Direct contact with school boards, foundations, and civic and cultural organizations can be threatening to school or university administration. The most successful way to do this is to work together with people in your district and administration so you are viewed as a team player, a community entrepreneur, and an advocate for the institution you represent. Once again, building the necessary support is often better accomplished through someone else other than the music educator.

School Boards:

These elected officials have great control over education in this country. How we help them know what we do is a delicate but important task. Deciding to bring two hundred parents to a board meeting on the night the board is voting on a budget cut is not the way to work with a school board—it is too late! That work should be consistent, ongoing, and involve three ways in which school boards can be engaged in the music program: information, engagement, and communication.

Each year in Williamsport, a report entitled "Music in Williamsport: An Annual Report to the School Board and Taxpayers in the Williamsport Area School District, Williamsport, Pennsylvania" was published. The report, which was sent to all local media, included information about music department finances and budgets; per-pupil costs; community support; news from elementary, middle, and high school programs; guest performers; faculty achievements; and photographs. Not only was this an effective public relations venture, but it also eliminated speculation and rumor about various aspects of the program, especially per-pupil cost and the ratio of students to faculty.

Board members can also be involved in other tangible ways, through invitations to special rehearsals and concerts, by asking board members to speak on the value of music education at public events, or by bringing groups to perform in the lobby prior to a board meeting. Sometimes it helps to have distinguished citizens, students, and parents address the board. Willa Dunleavy, Director of Choral and Classroom Music in the Fort Worth Independent School District in Texas, used Music In Our Schools Month to bring voices to the Fort Worth Independent School District Board. Willa introduced teachers and students who had excelled musically. She put together a group of speakers who spoke on behalf of music education in Fort Worth schools, including a community member who spoke about the history of music education in the school district; the president of the Texas Music Educators Association; the director of the School of Music at TCU; the CEO of Rhythm Band, Inc., a music company in Fort Worth; and Van Cliburn, internationally known pianist and resident of Fort Worth, who concluded the presentation by eloquently speaking on the importance of music to the soul of a human being. After the presentation, the school board president stated that he "had never heard such eloquent speeches in this room [the board room] in all his years on the school board." Willa effectively used others to present her message.

During a critical budget time in another school district, the music parents organized a letter writing campaign where students involved in the music program wrote letters to school board members. You must be careful in using this approach, but if the writers know how to share personal insights and passions, it can be very powerful. One of the most moving letters was written by a young woman whose parents paid tuition for her to attend the school district because of the quality of the music program. This letter, in part, read:

> ...Since we were not pleased with the music program in the town where I live, my parents and I researched the music program of five school districts in the area. I chose [this school district] for its high academic standards and its outstanding music program. This means that I need to commute twenty miles one way, everyday, so that I can experience the many wonderful music opportunities. I feel really dedicated and committed to this program...if you were to remove music from my academic program and my schedule, you would be removing a part of me, a part of my soul. Music isn't merely something you do; it's a ritualistic sharing of your very being. Those who partake of music have a desire, moreover a need, to express their sensitivity, thoughts, and emotions to an audience. The raw feelings of the soul expressed through music, and the electric heat of a natural high received before and during a performance, are things that should never be repressed or seized, especially on the basis of monetary funds or lack thereof. Once we stop expressing ourselves with song...we risk becoming a cloned, brain-dead society of dull, boring, and partially educated

people. Please vote in favor of music. It is something extremely relevant to us. WE DO CARE![2]

Incidentally, the board voted in favor of music! Here's another example of how others can speak on behalf of music rather than the music educator.

Clubs, Civic and Community Organizations:

When I ask music educators in my seminars around the country to name the service or civic organizations in their community, I often get blank stares. Yet these networks of civic, service, and social organizations are an important part of the fabric of a community. Consider how the school music department can help and be helped by the local Rotary Club, Lions Club, or Kiwanis Club. Each club has a different agenda with which music educators can identify and on which they can capitalize. Should a music program play for a Lions Club supper? If they do, has a bond been established that might help support a future music project? Or perhaps on a higher level, will that contact with you and your students create a sense of value that could have an impact in a future school budget vote?

I have discovered that every time a group reaches out to the community, the community responds many times over. The groups are myriad in most communities: Junior League, AAUW (America Association of University Woman), women's clubs, arts organizations, neighborhood organizations, chambers of commerce. Do not hesitate to call upon them. They may not necessarily give you outright financial support, but that's not the reason why you are doing this. You build relationships with these organizations to build support for the cause of music in the schools. An example of this might be the Young Person's Concert of the local symphony, where they might research the background of the program, go into the schools to prepare the children (students), provide busing and chaperones for the concert, and arrange seating at the concert. The bottom line is that all of these clubs and leagues are dedicated to the support and betterment of the community. Use them!

Foundations:

It is important for leaders to become aware of the various philanthropic foundations in the community and to keep them aware of the music education program. Their prior knowledge of the program and its impact on the community will make it easier to convince a foundation to provide grant money for projects that will enhance the program and the community. Foundations are more willing to invest in organizations in which they have confidence their money is going to be used wisely and for good purposes. Purely and simply, it is political. The funds for musical and educational projects are difficult to acquire without participation in the political climate of a community. In public schools, foundations often support programs in schools that are of deeper importance to the community and its cultural life. Try to review websites of foundations and look at previous patterns of grant making. Many foundations list the types of grants they have funded in past years.

At the university level, I have worked closely with the advancement (development) office to acquire funds for various projects and new facilities. Success was realized, but unlike the public schools, I had help. I did not need to do it myself. However, if the school of music were not viewed as a quality asset to the university and the community, it would not have been possible to raise the $16 million for an addition to the main building of the school of music. The quality of the program is in direct proportion to the ability of foundations to support the program.

I would suggest that before approaching an individual or organization, you investigate the proper application procedure. Remember to remain an entrepreneur, but do not be obnoxious or overly aggressive. In fact, when possible, it is again good to use a third party who is uninvolved but carries some respect in the community or with the board. Never have a family member involved in any way, and be certain to attempt to show the need beyond that which the school district should supply through local taxes and through their normal budget processes. Above all, prepare a logical, organized, and targeted proposal that is well written, documented, and has clear benefits.

Community

In an era when programs are scrutinized and sometimes curtailed, community support is probably the most essential element in building public support. There are many supportive activities that can accomplish the goal of keeping the community aware and indeed even excited about the program.

An all-district concert is an effective public relations tool because it displays the sequence of instruction from the elementary level through the high school. It is important that this all-district event run vertically from a curricular aspect, rather than horizontally. An all-district elementary or middle school event by itself simply does not display to the public the total curriculum and skill development sequence. When an audience observes the continuum of experience from elementary to high school, both parents and students see firsthand how far they have come and where they can go. In urban areas, one can replicate this concept by using schools in a geographic area or regional district. These are big events that take time and effort; I would suggest rotating choir, band, and orchestra on separate evenings and in a yearly rotation.

Sometimes it is good to hold a rehearsal in front of the audience to demonstrate firsthand what is involved in preparing a performing group for concert. Parents and the community are impressed when they experience the behind-the-scenes process of education rather than always the end result. This has often been referred to as an "informance" rather than a "performance."

It is most important to constantly keep the community informed about concerts, activities, and achievements through the local newspapers, radio, and television. Although reporters may appear to be uncooperative, a creative music educator with leadership attributes will be able to find some aspects of an event that will interest the media. Rather than submitting anything typical or traditional, find new angles and creative venues. The media loves human-interest stories or unique angles to a concert. I was successful in getting publicity when I had triplets performing in a concert, sent out a picture for a feature with a long row of tubas, and yet another with a long row of string basses. A press release with a listing of the repertoire just doesn't do it anymore. The media loves photos of students engaged in actively performing. The media will often respond to unusual promotional presentations and ideas that help to support your message to the community.

Even though some of these ideas are not brand new, we must use them to support our programs and emphasize that music learning is crucial for students and education. We must build support groups so school music is not an entity bearing little relevance to the musical life outside the school setting. If our public constituents do not see a basic connection between school music and the deeper experience of the arts, music education will remain, at best, a peripheral subject.

I am thrilled with the number of city music organizations (symphonies, opera companies, arts foundations, etc.), particularly in urban areas, that receive grants for educational programs in the schools under the rationale that school outreach is important because of the reduction in the number of music teachers in the school districts. While I am most supportive of these musical thrusts into the educational arena by local arts groups and foundations, it is important that their work augment the music in the schools taught by music specialists rather than replace it. It would be self-defeating to have the local arts groups replace the music teachers as a visitation rather than ongoing instruction. School districts must not be able to claim that a wonderful presentation by a local arts organization could possibly be a substitute for a much-needed music teacher. We must all work together on this matter!

John F. Kennedy stated during his presidency that, "The life of the arts, far from being an interruption, a distraction in the life of a nation, is very close to the center of a nation's purpose and is a test of the quality of a nation's civilization." I close this chapter by paraphrasing that statement:

The life of a program in music education, far from being an interruption, a distraction in the life of a community, is very close to the center of its purpose and is a test of the quality of its future in the arts.

1 Down, A. Graham. *TMEC Connection*. Fort Worth, TX: Texas Music Educators Conference, Fall 1990.
2 Excerpts from the letter of Erin Gay to Jan Harrison, School Board member, Williamsport, Pennsylvania, Summer 1988.

Chapter 5

Relationships

This may become the most valuable chapter in the book for many because healthy relationships and effective leadership together are essential for success. We must develop those relationships that nurture our energy, create positive environments, and support our personal and professional goals. I am not naïve enough to propose that all relationships are positive, and while I have suggested that it is best to distance yourself from those who have earned your rejection, you must develop relationships even with those who oppose you, being careful not to let that relationship damage your essential self or sap your energy as a leader and a human being. Above all, relationships are the lifeblood of programmatic and professional support. We must be genuine, honest, and candid in our relationships, and know when a relationship has changed or does not work, and for what reason.

My years in music education were evenly divided between public school and university settings in many diverse positions. These eclectic experiences were full of rich, varied, and worthwhile relationships that really defined how I was able to achieve excellence in such diverse settings. Each position has been vital to the development of my being as a teacher and an administrator, and important to the product I produced in this profession. It was through these relationships that I gained the valuable insights into the many facets of music teaching and leadership that are required to be a successful music educator. In short, you *learn* from relationships.

One colleague might refer to me as stubborn, but another might think of me as determined. The way those colleagues view me is based on the quality of our relationship. I prefer to work more closely with the person who looks upon me as determined, because a determined person accomplishes goals. Our ability to nurture or sustain relationships has to do with how we handle good relationships and bad. If people seem unreasonable or self-centered, love them anyway, but from a distance. If you do well and people respond with envy, do well anyway. If you are successful, you may win false friends and make true enemies, but try to know why they feel the way they do, and don't let those differences in attitude prevent you from succeeding anyway. The good you do today may well be forgotten tomorrow, but that should not change your relationships or your ability to achieve.

We all know that it is human nature to favor the underdog, yet human beings love following a winner. Relationships must be built in order to be a winner. When you have given the world the best that you have and still feel unappreciated, then you probably have not helped those with whom you have relationships understand the efforts you have made. When what you have worked to build is destroyed overnight, you must continue to build and develop relationships. Give the world the best you have anyway, for when love and skill work together, you can expect a masterpiece. But it is doubtful that a masterpiece in music education, which involves teaching and people and music, can be done without quality relationships.

There are times when music teachers are lonely people. I think this is sometimes self- inflicted. We teach a different language. We are in isolated parts of the building because we "make noise." We may have an itinerant assignment in which we are only in the building for a short period of time. As stated in the previous chapter, sometimes we don't want to have relationships with those who are not supportive of our programs or us. Music education will never take its place in the school, university, or community if we are not constantly working to develop new personal relationships with our fellow music teachers, students, peers, administrators, communities, and learners of all ages. This will be the source of strength for music education in the future.

Let's begin by focusing on you, the leader, in this exercise of building relationships. There are some essentials necessary for sustained leadership.

- Be flexible in your teaching and your attitude about teaching. Understand that music is just one of many subjects taught. Music is an important part of learning and the life experience—but not the only part.

- Celebrate the energy inside of you that constitutes who you are. You have time. You have talent. You have unique resources. You have energy. The greatest of these is energy! We need to nurture that energy by connecting it to those who share and appreciate your energy levels. We sing about the body electric so, therefore, we must also celebrate the body electric.

- Make every effort to function as a pioneer. A pioneer is bold enough to know the difference between complying, growing, and experimenting with change. We frequently experiment with students, but how much do we experiment with ourselves?

- Attempt to define your strengths. Conversely, what are your shortcomings? Do you enjoy building and creating excellence, or are you more content to be a maintainer once excellence is established? Knowing who you are and the strengths you have help you develop relationships that accentuate those strengths and the different personalities with whom you work. For instance, I learned early in my career that I was a "builder" and always needed just one more mountain to climb. Without that "mountain," I seemed to lose the thrill of accomplishment. I had to learn to recognize that not everyone with whom I had a relationship was a builder. Relationships come when you can understand your own strengths and use the different traits of others effectively.

- Understand that there are many things that cannot be changed—history, how other people act, the values of others, or the inevitable over which you have no control. It seems worthless to become overly concerned about those things over which you have little or no control. Rather, pursue those things that you can truly impact.

- Establish your own vision, mission, values, and high priority goals. Begin with the end in mind and work from there. The vision must remain constant and be based on your own value system.

- Think about silence as a worth that brings no risk.

- Remember the value of praise, not only to others but also to yourself. Make sure you occasionally give yourself a pat on the back, for the best way to gain the respect of others is to first respect yourself.

Relationships with Students

Many times, as both a music teacher and music administrator, I felt powerless and small, overwhelmed and inadequate, engulfed in the feeling that perhaps my efforts were insignificant and that my life's pursuit of bringing the joy of music to others was futile. Have you ever felt that way? It is a natural thing to feel. I think it is a normal thing for teachers to question whether or not they are making a difference. In my case, when I reflected upon the students, the relationships I had with them, and the influence I had and could have on their lives, it brought me back to reality. As I watched their enthusiasm and enjoyment as they achieved in music, I realized the amazing power I actually did have. That is real power!

Relationships with students are built through motivation; inspiration; steady, consistent, and fair discipline; caring; carefully sequenced instruction (and the ability to recognize when students don't "get it"); and the ability to laugh and enjoy those unique personalities. Teachers have the power to uplift and create and, when red hot, the intensity to inspire. This is a powerful part of teaching, one that must be respected and nurtured because it is at the very heart of quality student relationships. With just one look, you can let a student know that everything is well with the world and that he or she has a perfect right to aim for the top of the hill! You can use your hands and body and facial expressions in class or rehearsal to create tremendous musical moments. As students experience music at greater levels of sophistication and understanding, it deepens the relationship you have with them.

The power you have in your student relationships makes you a considerable force in the school, district, and community. In the eyes of your students, you are the system. You have the power to lead them to places they never knew existed, to build them up when society turns them down, to catapult them further than you will ever reach, and to push them gently but ever so assuredly into the unknown with information for a future none of us will ever see. Empowering them is of the essence, for if their teachers at times feel powerless and small, could you understand how insignificant they must sometimes feel?

The adults who make the greatest difference in a student's life are not the ones with the most credentials, the most money, or the most awards. Rather, they are the ones who care the most. It takes just one person to make a difference in a student's life, and there is no reason in the world that the person cannot and should not be you! This requires a level of competence, caring, and honesty that allows you to stand apart from non-music colleagues. When a positive relationship with you and music is allowed to enter the arena of learning, we ensure that music will enter the lives of students and that all learning will indeed become significant, vital, and exciting.

Relationships with Peers

Peer relationships[1] among music faculty and non-music faculty are tremendously important in the educational process. We must work to develop quality relationships with other music colleagues so everyone will willingly work with one another and stand up as advocates for *music*—not just one aspect of the program (band, choir, orchestra, etc.) or one segment of the profession. Harmony, blend, and balance are musical goals we all strive for, but are these same qualities not equally as important outside of the classroom or rehearsal hall as you deal with your teaching colleagues? We all know there are individuals who thrive on petty faculty intrigue and vindictive backbiting. We have all experienced abuse of student relationships when students are encouraged to take sides in faculty disputes. This is the antithesis of the quality relationships among peers needed to ensure music program success. Because it is so prevalent, it has as much to do with the fragmentation and factionalism of our discipline as anything. This simply must not occur—whether in the university or in K–12 music programs. The responsibility for creating positive faculty interaction lies with strong faculty and administrative leadership.

By training and temperament, music educators are emotional and impassioned about the art they pursue and teach. This often extends into their professional peer relationships. Could it be that at times we bring the wrong tools to build relationships and solve problems with our colleagues? What stands us in good stead in college/university study—the ability to dissect an issue, argue its merits, compete with others, quantify, and criticize–simply does not work in interpersonal situations that require compromise, harmony, and participation in the total process of human interaction. Just because music (and arts) education has been behind the eight ball of school change, curricular reform, or university funding does not mean that we should extend that defensiveness into our own peer relationships.

The emotional and creative passion we bring to music sometimes makes us appear hypersensitive, intellectually arrogant, or incredibly selfish in an attempt to protect just *our* part of the music program. If you do not understand the actions or attitudes of another individual, simply ask why rather than speculate behind the person's back. Speculation encourages an antagonism that is totally unnecessary and accomplishes nothing. Given the fragile state of our profession in the educational mainstream, we simply must not foster any sort of curricular fratricide. When these kinds of actions occur, we must remember that our students are put in no-win situations, and consequently, more losers than winners are created.

I remember trying to get this idea across to teachers in a district where I was supervisor, with teachers who were having a hard time learning to play together in the same sandbox! I used a quote from the best selling autobiography *Iacocca*,[2] *the* controversial former head of Ford and Chrysler Corporations. In this book, Iacocca remembers a conversation with Vince Lombardi, the legendary football coach, about his formula for success in producing a winning team.

[The coach] has to start by setting up the fundamentals. A player has got to know the basics of the game and how to play his position. Next, you've got to keep him in line. That's discipline. The men have to play as a team, not as a bunch of individuals. *There's no room for prima donnas*. But there have been a lot of coaches with good ball clubs who do not win the game. Then you come to the third ingredient if you are going to play together as a team: *you've got to care for one another*. Each player has got to be thinking about the next guy and saying to himself: if I don't block that man, one of my fellow players is going to get his legs broken. I have to do my job well in order that he can do his. The difference between mediocrity and greatness is the feeling those guys have for each other. Most people call it team spirit. When the players are imbued with that special feeling, you know you got a winning team.

I tried very hard to keep peer relationships on a positive, focused, professional, and civil level in all of my positions, and it is a tough, ongoing, and difficult job. If we as musicians and music educators cannot behave with benevolence and civility toward one another, how can we expect our students—or anyone else—to view us any more kindly? If we cannot reach agreement with one another, how can we expect others to reach agreement with us? To become mature in our relationships is part of being educated rather than merely knowledgeable in a particular area of expertise.

Each of us is only as good as all of us, and it is the "all of us" that must come first. The acquisition of tenure or programmatic fame in the course of developing a program does not eliminate one's responsibility to be a part of a team of peers. If you allow problems to become opportunities for positive change, your professional life and that of the music education profession might just take a major step forward.

Relationships with Administrators

The root and body of the word "administer" is "to serve." Good leaders and good administrators must juggle the delicate balance between serving and leading to be certain leadership, in the long run, becomes the dominant trait. To craft a relationship with administrators, we must realize that they are the pilots of a complex ship and they need to make many navigational decisions during the year. They, like we, need to constantly adjust to currents and winds of change, new techniques, and new technology, for no day is the same. Much of what was written in Chapter 4 on building administrative support for music education also applies in this chapter with regard to developing relationships with administrators.

Relationships with administrators are not one-way streets. An administrator has as much responsibility for positive interaction with a teacher/professor as the teacher/professor has with the administrator. Administrators need to talk to teachers, not at them, and teachers/professors need to talk with administrators, not at them. They need to work with teachers, not against them or in spite of them. On the other hand, when a teacher/professor is given responsibility by the administration, that empowerment does not mean entitlement. Above all, an authentic relationship with an administrator must be based on the fact that administrators are human and must play the cards as they are dealt. No administrator can be all things to all people, and an administrator cannot be viewed as inadequate if he or she is unable to solve your particular, personal problem.

Keeping these things in mind, how does one build a relationship with an administrator? Just as teachers need the same kind of encouragement as their students, so too do administrators need to feel trusted and worthy of mutual respect. Open dialogue and discussion and the ready sharing of information between teachers and administrators help all parties develop relationships that are professional and ongoing. The most important matter in developing a quality teacher/administrator relationship is that both parties *want* and *work* towards that relationship. They must appreciate the other, respect the other, communicate with the other, and treat the other as a knowledgeable professional. Each needs to value the accomplishments of the program and celebrate it as a source of pride to both the educational community and the local community.

Relationships with the Public

While many of us think we can only *communicate* with the public, building relationships with the public is an important element contributing to the success of music education programs. How we as teachers feel about the music education program is secondary if the public does not value and support this program in its schools and community. Relationships with the public can take on many delineations; however, these relationships need to be used for more than merely giving out information or manipulating public opinion or reaction. Communication helps establish the values of the program, build an image, bring people together for program improvement, and communicate success. While relationships with the public are less defined because of the large number of people that must be influenced, there are ways that positive and intimate communication can be used to create positive relationships. The difference between relationships and communication is an interaction between the person and the program—students, directors, faculty, and parents.

Dr. Joseph D. Brown, Professor of Marketing at Ball State University, came to Williamsport, Pennsylvania, for two days in December 1987 to interview key figures in the vital music education program of the Williamsport Area School District. In Case Study

No. 1, *The Williamsport Image*,[3] produced in May 1988 by Gemeinhardt, the conclusion was reached that the music education program must be "a program not merely on paper, but a vital program which extends into the community and affects its cultural base; a program in which no one area upstages the other, for excellence that becomes the norm must be experienced by every part of the department."

Certainly the issue of relationships with community could be a book in itself. I would suggest that relationships need to be as personal as possible, with frequent interaction between teachers and students, parents, community leaders, the general public and, above all, music. Press releases and advertisements are minor representations. To be effective in creating support for music education programs, relationships with the public must be rich in their human and musical interaction.

Each individual school and program must also have important relationships with parents and, in particular, parent booster groups. These are important resources that can help create additional networks in the school and community that should be explored but not exploited. Parent booster groups can be great for raising money and awareness, providing volunteer support, chaperoning, and working with civic and service organizations in the community. The music educator, however, must remain in control of the program, including musical decisions, repertoire, organization, and structure. The music educator must also be able to determine the balance between support, advocacy, and aggressiveness. While the parent's organization can be a tremendous help to music programs, it must also be monitored closely. The booster organization can never become an autonomous arm, and clear guidelines concerning the responsibilities and limitations of the parent's group must be established.

The mystique of professional relationships seems complex and complicated in the sheer volume of effort that is demanded. Yet these relationships are a core of music education program success and professional recognition, and are an essential component of the activities of leaders who *aspire to excel*. Done well, the development of these multiple relationships will cause morale to soar, music departments to work together more cohesively, and program goals and values to be carefully defined so idealism can flourish. Idealism fosters vision. This philosophy of relationships, brought to life by a profession wanting to cultivate these relationships, might just be the necessary thrust that will make music programs healthier in schools, districts, universities, and communities. There is really nothing revolutionary in this chapter—just plain common sense. But if these relationships were actually employed, the result for music education would indeed *be* revolutionary.

Relationships are life–ah, so fragile–here today–
 gone tomorrow
Life–death–hope–despair–
 give it all you've got, and it will be all right!
Everyone is not created equal—make the best of what you have
 and you'll make it—and everything will be all right!
Human dignity—hold your head high—
 you know you have it!
Interrupt the monotony, break the routine, capture the
 imagination,
 nurture the hopes.
Communication is so difficult—don't just talk, listen—because
 you need to know—silence is work without risk—
 and it will be all right!
But I must not know so much that I care so little.

Sensibility, love, hope, happiness, but
How?
Why?
When?
Where?
Everywhere!
And in the end, it will be all right!

— K. Raessler —

---

1 Portions of this chapter are edited from an article by Dr. Kenneth Raessler in *Yamaha New Ways* titled "Each of Us Is Only As Good As All of Us!" Fall 1993, Vol. 8, No. 7.
2 Iacocca, Lee. *Iacocca*. New York: Bantam Books, 1984.
3 Brown, Joseph D. Gemeinhardt Case Study No. 1, *The Williamsport Image*. 1989.

Chapter 6

Developing a Comprehensive Curriculum in Music

A sequenced curriculum is both basic and essential to an effective comprehensive music program. If any music educator or any music education program is to truly excel, then ongoing curriculum development is a key ingredient to program excellence and success. It is the *sequence* and *interrelationship* of the curriculum that is essential to the program—a sequence that must begin with clear goals for early childhood and extend through the elementary, middle, and senior high school years, with a culminating experience for pre-baccalaureate learning in performance and classroom music experiences. This music curriculum must be balanced between conceptual learning, experiences, and performance opportunities. The curriculum should be comprehensive in experience and sequential in concept. Perhaps most important, the curriculum should be coordinated by a designated curricular leader who is selected or elected from the music faculty at large. And the music faculty must work together to ensure that the integrity of the curriculum is an essential core of the music program.

Too often we face a music curriculum that is a collection of unfocused activities and experiences, primarily oriented towards quick outcomes rather than a sequential series of carefully planned learning experiences leading toward well-defined goals. Disparate and disconnected experiences at various levels can never be connected and made a curricular whole. *The School Music Program: A New Vision*[1] gives music educators a flexible blueprint for a music curriculum that allows for individual teacher creativity while emphasizing a standards-driven curricula. I stress the word *blueprint*, for while a teacher may not necessarily support all of the aspects of the prescribed *National Standards for Arts Education*,[2] they can still subscribe to the sequential aspect found in these documents. The *Opportunity to Learn Standards*,[3] another document published by MENC, clearly articulates the curriculum, scheduling, staffing, materials, equipment, and facilities needs in order to make the sequential curriculum work. The *Opportunity to Learn Standards*, as does this book, addresses the "what to do" as opposed to the "how to do it" for the music educator. The three books mentioned here are essential and basic to the library of every music educator, especially to those who *aspire to excel* in curriculum development and implementation.

A comprehensive music curriculum is a valuable asset for any music program, and it will develop its own support system as it prepares students to become music consumers as adults. Of course, this assumes that music educators will demonstrate a clear and ongoing concern about both future consumers and performers as they prepare students for adulthood. Frequently, the greatest emphasis is placed upon the performance factor of music programs, with little more than lip service given to the balanced and comprehensive education of the future consumer of music. Music is something to be experienced and enjoyed for a lifetime, even when it is not pursued as a potential profession. I am not aware of any statistics that substantiate that those whose only experience is in performing music also pursue a life of musical enjoyment as a consumer. If effective, a comprehensive music program will produce students who will enjoy music for the rest of their lives, playing in community bands and orchestras, singing in church and community choirs, or filling up the seats of a performance hall. After all, if we do not have audiences in the future, there will be no need for the performers, composers, conductors, teachers, or scholars of music. Those who *aspire to excel* will recognize that it is essential to demonstrate curricular concern for both performer and consumer.

Too often, in our haste to put our students frequently in front of the public eye as a means of substantiating music in our schools, we over-emphasize the extracurricular aspects of the program. That is not to say that this entertainment is not important to our program visibility and public perception. A music program that only attempts to entertain does a disservice to its students, yet a program that ignores the entertainment component has few supporters outside the school building (and sometimes inside the building as well). Music educators must distinguish between the curricular and extra-curricular aspects of the program and keep them in balance. When either aspect of the program gets out of balance, then we risk developing a program that cannot stand on its own merits.

What can the comprehensive music curriculum do? First and foremost, we must remember that music is an art, and as such shares concepts, expressive potential, and learning processes with all other areas of the academic curriculum. This is rarely explored to its maximum potential, and too often we isolate music from the total educational experience of the school. A second consideration involves music as a discipline, which allows students an opportunity to combine music learning with experience to develop unique ways in which they can display their greatest talent. Third, it is important that students come out of schools—and the school music experience—with some sense of worth and confidence. For some, this can come from mathematics, history, theater, or athletics. For others, it can come from experiences provided by music.

So it seems to make little sense to remove the privileges of participation in music because a child is weak in another subject area. It merely allows students to be weak in two subjects and serves to deprive them of valuable creative and academic potential, self-worth, and confidence. The Texas "no pass, no play" law, also adopted elsewhere, takes dead aim at music (and, of course, athletics.) I am very sure we will soon recognize that punitive rules such as these could have been avoided had our music programs been more carefully integrated into the curriculum and total academic programs of our schools.

The process of what actually should be the content of any subject area has always caused debate among colleagues. This, of course, is a healthy exercise as long as it does not create excessive conflict. For some, factual knowledge is the critical element. For others, cognitive skills become the quest. For still others, the conceptual understanding of the subject matter is the essential goal. It would seem that the understanding of concepts is more basic to learning than the accumulation of factual knowledge or the mastery of skills, although all of the above must occur at times in the educational process.

The "new curriculum" advocated in *The School Music Program: A New Vision* cites seven categories that will lead to a more inclusive curricular structure.[4] They are:

1. "Skills and knowledge as objectives" – The music curriculum, as stated earlier, must be broad enough to stimulate both future performers and future consumers of music. It must also be sequentially constructed.

2. "Diverse styles of music" – Does the music curriculum reflect the multicultural mix of the students and parents it serves? Does it reflect the multicultural mix of the United States...and the world? Does it include music outside of the art music tradition?

3. "Creative skills" – The traditionally performance-driven music curriculum of the past must be expanded to also include the creative activities inherent in improvisation and composition.

4. "Problem-solving and higher order-thinking skills" – The curriculum must go beyond the acquisition of factual knowledge, with the focus on education rather than entertainment.

5. "Interdisciplinary relationships" – The discrete art of music must maintain its own integrity in the curriculum, but serious attempts should also be made to embrace relationships between music and other academic disciplines.

6. "Technology" – The arts and technology greatly affect one another. Not only is art shaped by the technology with which it is created, but the process of producing the art also shapes the technology. Technology belongs in the music education domain. Thus, the music educator must use it and not oppose it. The new age of communication is more than merely the age of the computer. It is an era of innovative new technology, innovative new sounds, and wonderful new opportunities to express ourselves with creative new musical ideas. When technology is introduced into the music curriculum, the result will probably encourage more male participation in the process; in fact, males usually outnumber females in these classes.

Technology, however, should not be used for its own sake but rather to achieve the overall objectives of the music curriculum.

7. "Assessment" – Assessment is here to stay, and so it should be. The music education profession must respond by identifying the important kinds of intellectual and aesthetic behaviors necessary for establishing what students really need to know and be able to do in the music classroom, as well as how authentically their achievements can be assessed. There is an acute need for the entire process to speak to the educational importance of aesthetics, to express aesthetic qualities, to encourage aesthetic values, to reflect human motivations, and to fulfill the affective functions of the real world. The affective is dying, and leaders must work diligently to prevent its death.

As I have developed curricula with countless numbers of music teachers in the past, we have initiated the philosophical considerations of curriculum development by listing basic assumptions we knew we had to either embrace, question, or discard before getting into the specifics of the curriculum development process. Some of these include:

- Concentrate on motivating the students' desire to learn.
- Eliminate the "teach the best and shoot the rest" mentality. Remember that music is for all children, and your curriculum must really support that philosophy.
- Work to dispel the feeling that the arts are only for the privileged. I recall attending the grand opening of the Meyerson Symphony Hall in Dallas—one of the magnificent concert halls in this country. A wonderful grand opening—black ties, caviar, champagne, lights,

limousines, valet parking, TV reporters, celebrities, etc What a glorious occasion! Except…there were a group of citizens walking about outside the concert hall with placards stating, "The arts are for the wealthy," "Our taxes paid for this hall," and "We cannot afford to attend our own concert hall." This concern has since been successfully addressed, but at the time, it was a poignant moment and a powerful statement.

- Work to stop the perception that music education is only entertainment. We know it is more than that, but how many others share this knowledge? The public must be educated about what this profession really represents. We are educators, and we teach music; we are also musicians, but the teaching of music is our primary profession. Indeed, this profession teaches that the journey is just as important as the destination, and the process is essential for the product.

- Be aware of the distinction between athletics and music. Music education is neither interscholastic nor intercollegiate athletics. In athletics, the game is important. In music, the learning process should be more important than the concert.

- Study the manner in which the physical education discipline has embraced a "lifetime sports" mentality and separated itself from interscholastic and intercollegiate sports. Apply this to "lifetime music" and begin to wave a similar banner.

- Understand that changes such as site-based management, block scheduling, and the elimination of music administrators interrupts the K–12 curricular sequence in music programs.

- Celebrate, point with pride, and study the process used by those school districts with music programs that have demonstrated exemplary results.
- Remember that no truly quality program is created suddenly.
- Be acutely aware of the diverse and multiple cultures that influence the curriculum and content that you present in music education.

It has been in vogue for some time to criticize the educational structure of the schools and colleges in the United States. I am annoyed when the critics of the American educational process advocate the assimilation of more cognitive skills and learning at the expense of affective learning and the affective mindset. Adding even more academic requirements and/or beginning them earlier in the educational process is not necessarily tied to better learning.

Herein lies a great concern. Aristotle declared that excellence is not an act but a habit. I might add that to excel is an affective mindset, a way of life, and a continuing process—not an event. It is quite exciting to observe students when they are involved in excellence (e.g., a fine performing group). Their entire demeanor changes and they begin, in many instances for the first time in their life, to strive for even greater excellence. Students who never experience excellence sometimes mistake mediocrity for excellence. Why is this affective mindset seldom a factor in the development of strongly "academic" educational programs and yet plays a very important role in development of strong music programs? My answer is, "Because the affective sense is not measurable." Therefore, our educational colleagues all but ignore it. And in fact, it contributes to our lack of status in curricular and academic issues. Because we insist on more and more tests, and music cannot accurately test these affective attributes, we are caught in a Catch 22 that we must work to end. Those who *aspire to excel* in the future must find a way to measure both the cognitive and the affective benefits of music.

Excellence is, in fact, not a destination at which one arrives; rather, it is an ideal to which one must aspire, for the job of attaining excellence is one that never ends. I think of excellence as a vicinity, a shifting target that varies from person to person and from ensemble to ensemble by day or by year. Thus, the goal is to get into the vicinity of excellence—and stay there. Excellence can also be shaped or manipulated, by the design and quality of curriculum, budget, policy, instructional competence, and much more.

One discovers that the joy of attaining excellence is a joy that never surfeits. When *aspiring to excel* becomes the norm, we can never let any instance of excellence pass by unnoticed or unappreciated. A continuing commitment to quality will allow us to begin focusing on what is right—not what is wrong—with others and ourselves. What a great journey!

I offer here a potpourri of philosophical thoughts that must also be considered before undertaking the important task of curriculum development. During the course of your educational and musical development, have you ever considered?

- That the performance of music is just as much a curricular matter as is listening to it? Why, then, do we consistently afford more credit to a class in music "appreciation" than a performing group or applied music?
- Why classroom music teachers are often referred to as "vocal teachers"?
- Why "vocal teachers" are more frequently called upon to teach classroom music than instrumental teachers?
- Why it is so difficult to convince many members of the academic team that music is an academic process, not an activity?

- Why classroom music is viewed by some music educators as less important than performing music?
- Why classroom music needs more advocacy than performing music?
- Why the synthesis of the arts into one course offering is easier to sell to administrators than music as a discrete course?
- Why it is easier for a music educator to fall prostrate to the cultural level of a community than to elevate the cultural base of the community?
- Why the quality of a music education program is many times judged on how entertaining the concerts are to the general public?
- Why it appears easier to develop a quality music education program in a suburban environment than an urban or rural environment? I applaud the music teacher, however, who teaches in the urban or rural environment and produces outstanding musical and educational results...and it does happen!
- Whether the arts (music) create or merely reflect the basic culture of a society?
- That the obsession of educators today with cognitive learning to the neglect of affective learning is producing a half-brained approach to the education of children?
- That quantity (large numbers of students) and quality in performance music education are not necessarily one and the same? Quantity usually precedes quality as one attempts to build a student base. This is then followed by the quest for quality. The reverse is far more difficult to attain.
- That music educators have a tendency to spend much more time reproducing music that is already written than

having students create their own music and exhibit their own musical judgments?

- That it might be more exciting for some students to participate in the creative process than to reproduce what has already been created?

- That there is nothing aesthetic, from a musical standpoint, about music notation?

- That hearing pitch and reproducing pitch are two different things?

- That SAT stands for "Standardized Aptitude Test"? Webster defines aptitude as "natural and innate ability." Since the test really does reflect the achievement of knowledge, it really should be labeled "Standardized Achievement Test." Which is correct?

- That the arts truly have reflected and preserved past and present cultures more than any other educational discipline?

- That music is truly a form of communication and, in the case of instrumental music, a non-verbal means of communication?

These considerations (along with many more that you, the reader, could offer) are to me fundamental and basic to a sequential, systematically developed scope and sequence of music instruction K–12.

As one develops a comprehensive K–12 curriculum, there must be a differentiation between what it really means to *understand* music. Though pleasure and enjoyment are important parts of the musical experience, certainly the true understanding of music involves the achievement of a level of knowledge that enables students to derive as much satisfaction from what they *think* about music as they do from what they *hear*. Music learning must involve the mind as much as the emotions. Please remember, however, that the teaching of music reading may be mind expanding, but it has nothing to do with the aesthetic. By engaging the mind, I mean taking an individual beyond the point of "I do not know anything about music, but I know what I like" attitude to an openness that will embrace all types and genres of music as possibilities for additional musical understanding.

To engage the mind of a student, a sequentially based series of conceptual activities needs to be developed from Pre-K through senior high school. Many music education programs flounder haphazardly in this area, with no real direction or feel of continuity within or throughout grade levels. The music program that effectively provides appropriate and sequential learning in choral, instrumental, and classroom music has the greatest opportunity to engage both the musical emotions and the musical mind through a blending of experience, skills, and understanding. The music education curriculum needs to boldly demonstrate the potential for learning through music that which cannot be done through other fields of educational endeavor. It must not fail in the quest to have all children experience music, for music will not fail the children. Music education should give students something worth caring about and something remarkable, special and precious enough to light the fire in their hearts and the passion in their souls. Music education has two central purposes: that of performance and that of reception. Perhaps Charles Schulz says it best:

PEANUTS reprinted by permission of United Feature Syndicate Inc.

Enough philosophy! We must now get to the real nuts and bolts of curriculum development, for it is much more than a series of goals, a scope and sequence, or a program merely on paper. It is the density of the student learning experiences in music that will achieve the desired outcomes. The more density, the greater the total music experience. Even with the same overall goals and concepts, each music education program will be unique, depending on such varying factors as community resources; special ethnic considerations; the imagination, interest, and abilities of the teachers; the amount of team effort expended; and the quality of faculty development, school administrators, curriculum coordinators, and other school personnel.

Blueprint for Success

The following blueprint and sequence was used in the sequential development of the music education program in Williamsport, Pennsylvania. I offer it here as one example of a blueprint that could be successful—and one that worked.

1. MUSIC ADMINISTRATIVE LEADERSHIP – Yes, I know, everyone does not have this luxury! In the passing years, the public schools have seen the steady erosion of the authority and the elimination of music administrators. This has come at the same time that business and industry have eliminated whole layers of "middle managers." The great school music programs of the past were brought about by the likes of Mabelle Glenn in Kansas City, Russell Morgan in Cleveland, Fowler Smith in Detroit, T.P. Giddings in Minneapolis, and Louis Werson in Philadelphia. They were sure of their power and authority, they had the support of the commercial and cultural establishment, they had access to the seats of power in

their city, and they promoted a comprehensive program of music education without fear or favor. Things have changed drastically. Many school districts have lost music supervisors as well as curriculum coordinators in many other subjects.

Only when the managerial myth that music administration is an unessential luxury disappears will the music profession begin to reap benefits from persons who have the clout to effect change. It is one thing to write and speak about what should be in music education, but until doers and producers get into managerial positions that demand the act of administrating as a prerequisite, leadership will be diffused and unfocused—and woefully short of the dedicated leadership that we need. The potential this administrative thrust has for the future of the entire profession is tremendous. The creative and administrative mind, utilized for professional betterment and gain, in conjunction with the art of administration must be allowed to thrive and bring together the learned and the learning. This profession must demand music leadership so morale may soar, music departments may pull together, values may be defined, idealism may flourish, and the music education team may have a quarterback.

The *Opportunity to Learn Standards* recommends that "one music educator in every district or school be designated as coordinator or administrator to provide leadership for the music program." This person is employed on a full-time basis for administration when the staff includes twenty-five or more music educators. The amount of administrative time should be adjusted proportionately when the staff is smaller. Additional administrative staff should be employed at a rate of one-fifth time for each additional five teachers above twenty-five.

The individual who serves as a music administrator is now rarely given the title of director, which implies responsibility for the total program and requisite authority to carry out that responsibility; they frequently bear the title of coordinator or consultant, and their positions are often as anomalous as their title. This is unfortunate! From a curricular standpoint, the ideal structure gives the music administrator and the principal an equal line/staff status on the administrative grid. Should the two not reach consensus on an issue, they must seek counsel with their direct superior. This gives the music administrator the ability to oversee the PreK–12 program along with its sequence of instruction.

2. AN ADMINISTRATIVE ASSISTANT AVAILABLE TO THE ENTIRE MUSIC EDUCATION FACULTY – Yes, I know, that is two out of two impossible dreams—c'mon, Raessler! Read on, because I plan to propose enough cost-saving measures to allow your school district to afford this necessary "luxury."

3. FACULTY COHESIVENESS – I do think I have already stressed this enough for one book; however, one more time: *each of us is only as good as all of us.* Regular department meetings and in-service workshops, PreK–12, should be planned so the entire department gets to know one another, work and plan together, and learn to consider themselves as a complete unit with different divisions rather than isolated teachers responsible only to a particular building. There should be at least two full faculty meetings per year, with the remainder of the monthly meetings divided between the following departmental divisions: elementary

classroom teachers, middle school classroom teachers, senior high school classroom teachers, band directors, orchestra directors, and choral directors. This is very important!

4. DEPARTMENTAL CENTRALIZATION – Herein lies the key element that makes all of the aforementioned "dreams" a possibility. When school districts possess a building-based curriculum structure, not only does it interfere with the curriculum sequence of the school district, but it also creates many unnecessary expenditures. To centralize the music budget under the responsibility of a music administrator saves budgetary expenditures to the point where the hiring of a music administrator as well as an administrative assistant seems feasible in order to oversee the centralization efforts. This is particularly true in middle-sized and large school districts—those in greatest need of a music administrator.

When music materials, be it audiovisual materials, the choral library, the instrumental library, string and band instruments, the student book inventory, or the faculty book inventory are centralized rather than building-based, the cost saving is considerable. The music administrator oversees the resource center, the administrative assistant makes certain teachers receive the materials they need (on time), and the teachers use the resource center to peruse not only a library of books and music but also audiovisual materials and instruments. When all music materials, instruments, and music are removed from individual schools in the school district and housed in one central location, all music faculty have added access to more materials than one school could possibly provide. All music department purchases in the future are made by the music administrator and housed in the centralized location when not in use.

Please know, however, that all music teachers will not initially support this concept because many have worked diligently to secure the supplies for their building, and it becomes difficult for them to give them over to a centralized system. This, however, is essential for this blueprint, and I have found that gradually teachers embrace the idea as they begin to realize the advantages.

5. EDUCATIONAL GOALS FOR CLASSROOM MUSIC THAT ARE CONSUMER-ORIENTED – As stated before, this is an often-neglected area of music education. I believe we must place as much emphasis and curricular development on the teaching of music for future music consumers as we place curricular effort on the preparation of future music performers.

6. EDUCATIONAL GOALS FOR PERFORMING MUSIC CENTERED ON THE SUCCESSFUL PERFORMANCES OF MUSIC – Generally speaking, performing group directors do not hold curriculum development in particularly high regard. The pressures for public performance simply overshadow the true educational mission of the band, choir, and orchestra directors. There remains, however, a great need to compromise this ongoing performance pressure and embrace the genuine need for the development and rendering of educational and musical curricular goals. When a curriculum is successfully executed, the senior high school directors have no need for recruiting concerns because the performing group students simply are transferred, year by year, through the elementary and

middle school/junior high school years into the senior high school groups. Each level feeds the level above it, and directors receiving new students will know the instrument or voice parts along with the ability level of each performer. This sequence will be further explored in Chapter 7: Elementary Music Education and Chapter 8: Middle School Music Education. This may sound too good to be true, but it is not! Read on....

7. COMMUNITY INVOLVEMENT, ENTHUSIASM, AND APPRECIATION – Herein lies the resolution to the notion that success breeds success. Hopefully Chapter 4: Building the Necessary Support and Chapter 5: Relationships will provide the fuel to ignite enthusiasm and appreciation on the part of the community.

8. CONFIDENCE IN THE KNOWLEDGE AND BELIEF THAT STUDENTS WILL CRAVE EXCELLENCE ONCE THEY EXPERIENCE IT – Without having gone through this blueprint and this process, it may be difficult to convince you that this will really occur. To those who question, I say that when you get this far in the procedure, you will understand and experience its merits. Excellence is not only something to which teachers ascribe, for students also share this quest. Have you ever noticed how students truly seek the opportunity to be part of something considered to be excellent? Students will work hard to be accepted into a prize-winning musical organization, while they have a tendency to shy away from groups that do not have the reputation or qualifications that excellence demands.

9. STUDENTS WILL SACRIFICE TO BECOME PART OF SOMETHING CONSIDERED TO BE EXCELLENT – This could mean going to

summer school in order to elect more music courses during the regular academic year, giving up a part-time job, working less hours, or simply giving greater priority to their music study and/or performance. This will happen over and over when this process is followed carefully. I have observed an entire summer school program in a school district progress from a totally remedial emphasis to one that offered more accelerated courses than remedial. The reason this occurred was that music students wanted to take some of their "academic" work in the summer so they could elect more music courses during the fall and spring semesters.

10. PARENTS WILL SACRIFICE IN ORDER TO HAVE THEIR CHILDREN BECOME A PART OF EXCELLENCE – This could include anything from additional carpooling, to subsidizing their children who do not have the time to work a part-time job, to providing the student with an automobile to get to and from additional rehearsals and performances. It also would probably include active involvement in a parent's organization that supports one or all of the performing groups.

11. ONGOING AND EFFECTIVE PUBLIC RELATIONS DESIGNED TO CREATE AND SUSTAIN THE IMAGE OF EXCELLENCE – Understanding and dealing with a wide variety of people is vital for those involved in music leadership, including public relations and departmental image building (see Chapter 4: Building the Necessary Support). Success begins with a small step, and then little by little, as you use your energy as a positive force, you increase the level of communication, and the program gains support.

Curriculum Development

Of equal importance, of course, and working in congruity with this blueprint is the actual curriculum development. This also has a necessary sequence. Please remember that this is a slow and tedious process, beginning in Pre-K and the elementary grades, and working through the grade levels. The steps I recommend are as follows:

1. Carefully review your current program. Articulate your strengths and weaknesses and compare them to your state and national standards and the *Opportunity to Learn Standards*.

2. Develop your own unique Pre-K program philosophy and ascertain just what you want to happen to the total program.

3. Develop PreK–12 program goals in the areas of classroom music, band, orchestra, and choir.

4. Establish the curricular dimensions of the program, along with the extra curricular offerings.

5. Establish musical outcomes for grades 12, 8, and 4, and again compare them with your state and national standards as well as the *Opportunity to Learn Standards*.

6. Build the remainder of the curriculum using a consistent format throughout, similar to the following suggestions:
   - Concept – Keep it simple and singular.
   - Enabling Behaviors – What do you want the students to do to grasp the concept?
   - Materials – State possible materials that could be used to support the concept and the enabling behaviors. List more materials than would be

necessary to encourage teacher creativity in lesson planning.

- Activities – List the activities in which students can engage to support an understanding of the concept. Again, list more activities than would be necessary to teach the lesson so the curriculum does not become limiting to the creative teacher.

- Assessment – How will you know when the students have mastered the concept? Assessment must be built into the curriculum, with the basic goal of the assessment being to gauge the effectiveness of the teacher's work and removing at least some pressure from the students.

7. Identify the resources necessary to successfully engage the curriculum into use. Again, consult with the *Opportunity to Learn Standards*.

When the curricular and extracurricular blueprint is completed, a flowchart similar to the chart on the following page might be developed. The important reason for doing this is to explain to both educators and laymen the importance of curriculum sequence and what happens when this sequence is not followed (i.e., site-based management, block scheduling, intermixing of curricular and extracurricular aspects of the music program, scheduling dilemmas, etc.).

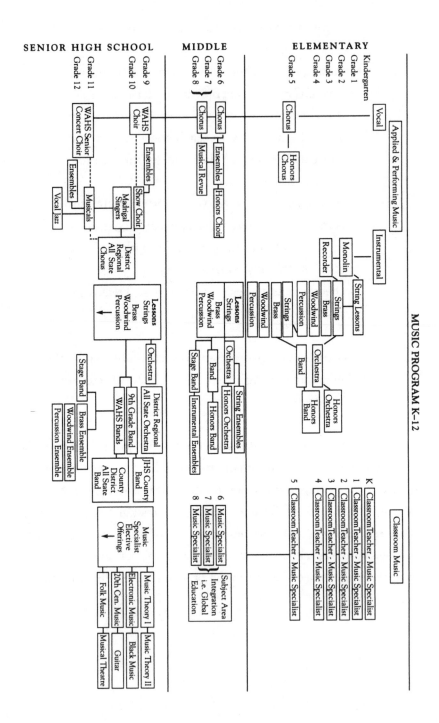

Cautions and Considerations

- The curriculum must be developed by the teachers who teach it, not by the music administrator or curriculum director. When the teachers develop the curriculum, they have ownership and, in turn, can be held accountable for its execution.

- The curriculum document should include ratios of the maximum number of students per teacher. Check the *Opportunity to Learn Standards* for suggestions at each curriculum level.

- Remember the importance of the all-district concerts discussed in Chapter 4 that demonstrate to the public the importance of the curricular flow.

- Students should be able to participate in both choral and instrumental groups at all levels. One does not negate the other! I have seen band directors attempt to upstage the choral director to attract students away from choir and into band (and vice versa). Also, certainly the orchestra program must not be neglected—if there is one! I have known of schools without an orchestra program because the band director did not want to fragment the band program. Thus, a potential orchestra program remained as it was in the past—a good idea.

- Caution—no empires! Do not attempt to rush through the programs. Keep the elementary students doing elementary work, the middle school/junior high school students doing age-appropriate work, and allow the ultimate to occur at the senior high school level. Otherwise, the students will say, "Been there, done that" and drop out of the program.

- Every level of the curriculum must keep the "carrot" in front of the students' faces so they become excited about going on to the next level. By the way, there must always be a next level in performing music; otherwise, why should students elect the same course year after year?

- If areas of your program are not broken, you have no need to repair them. Concentrate on the weak areas.

- Think of the following Chinese axiom as you proceed through the curriculum process:

> I hear, I forget
> I see, I remember
> I do, I understand

Music education is doing!

- Make certain the curriculum does not become limiting and stifle the creativity of the individual teachers as they plan their lessons.

- Once your program commands the excellence ascribed to in this book, be certain to consider the possibility of bringing in an artist-in-residence or commissioning a work by an American composer. Composers will often accept a commissioning for an affordable price when they know it will be performed at a state, regional, or national conference.

- Be careful that your curriculum does not take on a "team sport," extracurricular image while attempting to maintain a curricular reality.

- Proper mainstreaming of students with disabilities is essential for curriculum sequence and success. I have seen improper mainstreaming disrupt classes to the point where the curriculum could barely function. General guidelines for proper mainstreaming are succinctly outlined in the *Opportunity to Learn Standards* cited earlier.[5] They are:

– "When students with disabilities are included in regular music classes:

   a. Their placement is determined on the same basis as placement for students without disabilities (e.g., musical achievement, chronological age).

   b. Music educators are involved in placement decisions and are fully informed about the needs of each student.

   c. Their placement does not result in classes that exceed the average class size for the school by more than 10 percent.

   d. The number of these students does not exceed the average for other classes in the school by more than 10 percent."

– "Music instruction is provided for students receiving special education who are not included in regular music classes. Music instruction for students with disabilities is designed to teach practical music skills and knowledge that will assist the students in functioning successfully in musical environments of the home, school, and community. The amount of time for music instruction is equivalent to that provided to students without disabilities."

   This can readily be established in a self-contained environment.

- "Students with disabilities are given the same opportunities to elect choral and instrumental instruction as other students."

I would caution that the students should be able to accomplish the same musical tasks as the students without disability; however, it is important that they do receive the opportunity to at least make the attempt. I recall an instance where a student in a hearing-impaired class, who was designated "legally deaf," wanted to play the violin. I strongly recommended that this was not really the best instrument for a child with this disability to attempt. After several conversations where I simply refused to allow the child to begin lessons on the instrument, I finally succumbed to the insistence of the future student, his general classroom teacher, and his parents while thinking to myself, "They will find out!" Well, I was the one who found out! The boy participated in the orchestra program through high school, performed in extracurricular chamber groups, auditioned successfully for the All-State Orchestra in Pennsylvania, won the national Itzak Pearlman Award for handicapped musicians, and toured the United States for a year. I certainly learned a lesson about the possibilities of handicapped students.

- "Special experiences should be designed for gifted and talented students according to their abilities and interests."

- The curriculum should be designed to involve students in a recurring cycle of performing, describing, and creating— the three basic modes of musical interaction.

- Be careful not to dwell too heavily on the theory and mechanics of music with students possessing learning disabilities. If they have difficulty learning to read words, how could one hope to have them learn to read music in 30- to 45-minute encounters one or two times per week? Concepts, yes! Facts, no! Use the music to teach music.

- Remember that instrumental and choral teachers need to develop curriculum just as much as classroom music teachers.

- Understand that classroom music teachers get little applause because they have no performing groups. Give them support and at least an occasional pat on the back. Of course, on the other hand, they are not required to put their work on display to the public as are performing group directors.

- Guidelines for student absences (See Appendix C) at all curriculum levels through musical involvement should be established and approved by the upper administration and school board as a part of the curriculum development process. This includes, for example:

  1. Instrumental and/or vocal lessons
  2. Special concerts
     a. Within the home school
     b. Other schools within the school district
     c. Concerts within the community
     d. Exchange concerts

e. Tours

3. County, district, regional, and all-state events
4. Honors rehearsals and concerts (within the school district)

The Role of the Teacher

The teacher's role is critical in the development of this quality music curriculum. I have always had an interest in how music teachers themselves view the areas of curriculum development, goal setting, departmental cohesion, and faculty morale. Here are some responses from teachers about those issues over the years.

- "I truly need to study what makes my colleagues "tick." An objective "stand back and take a look" approach that will hopefully tell me who needs to change, me or them (or both?)—to create not only better working conditions for our music faculty but, more importantly, a better atmosphere for the students we serve and the students who are observing us and, perhaps in some cases, modeling after us/me."

- "Curriculum development is a joke in our district. We simply write up some things and then put it on a shelf in case anyone asks to see it. We all do our own things."

- "We need to strive for more aesthetic experiences for our students and audiences through our choice of music, interpretation, and performance. Working to foster greater emotional involvement and responses will be our best approach in convincing everyone of the place of music in the educational curriculum." (Author's comment: "Really?")

- "We must expand community pride in the school district music program."

- "We need more music faculty attendance at concerts out of our own area of expertise."

- "Develop and encourage more cross support—choral for instrumental and vice versa—between departments."

- "To openly air immediate concerns with cohorts."

- "Make an honest attempt to set our educational values and goals before purchasing new texts and materials. I some-times feel, as I read through the curriculum, that the texts were chosen first and then the curriculum made to fit rather than establishing educational values first and then selecting the appropriate text and materials."

- "To better understand the musical taste of our community in order to meet their desires more effectively and have fewer problems gaining their support." (Author's comment: "Is it better to attempt to elevate the taste of a community or fall prostrate to their cultural level, or attempt to find a happy medium between the two?")

- "I am having difficulty getting my own act together and feel less than qualified to make a critical judgment of the department. I do think we have to be careful that the tremendous push for big shows and exciting performances does not overwhelm the need for a basic teaching of music, especially at the lower levels. I find it difficult to make any cuts into my regular class work in order to put on performances, and I do not seem to accomplish both equally as well as others appear to do. I do not feel that I work well under pressure."

- "We simply need more overall coordination between classroom, choral, and instrumental music."

- "Curriculum sequence means nothing to me. With site-based management in the schools, I have never even met any of the other music teachers in this school district."

- "As a department, I feel that we need to instill a love for music in our students through an understanding of music. Much of our strength lies in the performance areas, but perhaps we should keep in mind that performance is only one means to achieving a love and understanding of music."

- "To achieve a more total awareness of our K–12 curriculum, we should be observing music classes at levels other than the ones we presently teach. This does not mean we should not be observing other teachers in our own area, but other areas should also be included."

- "Perhaps, within the music staff, we could benefit from:
    a. Elementary teachers observing junior/ senior high music groups and classes.
    b. Junior/senior high school teachers observing elementary classroom music teachers.
    c. Instrumental directors observing choral directors.
    d. Choral directors observing instrumental directors."

- "Develop an overall view of the entire department from kindergarten to grade 12. This view should be classroom as well as performance-oriented. This view of the entire department might come about with a better interplay between faculty. Being at one end of the gamut of grades, it sometimes seems that some music teachers actually resent preparing students for further musical experiences."

- "Foster a more deeply seated respect for each other in the music department. This is certainly a talented and capable faculty, but we do not work as a team. It is every person for himself?"

- "I am not sure that I agree with teaching them to be con-sumers of music. I must digest that one more thoroughly."

- "As a department, we need to develop a better relationship with the non-music teachers. We must convince them that music is a worthwhile program rather than something that interferes with their class. Too often we grudgingly give in when the department requests students for lessons or programs, rather than feeling it is justified."

- "It is surely a long hill, but our faculty is still climbing, and the top is getting closer."

I feel certain that most music educators who read this book will readily identify with some and, just possibly, many of these teacher responses. The responses of these teachers are more convincing than I could be. Everyone seems to agree that curricular development and faculty cohesiveness are essential to healthy music programs; however, the attainment is a quest more difficult than it appears.

Based upon the above teacher responses, one might conclude that there are desirable faculty traits and attributes that contribute to the successful accomplishment of the curricular process. Just what are the traits a potential leader would look for that contribute to successful teaching and provide worthy examples for the profession? While there are no truly concise answers to this question, there are certain characteristic behaviors that render success. Some worthy considerations follow:

- Lay down the ground rules to students early, and do not back down or compromise. Project authority.
- Know that students will test you; however, demand their best and be fairly firm and firmly fair.
- Lower your voice for more command.
- Be organized. Know your procedures and what you are going to do and when you will do it. Never have the need to ask a class, "Did we do that last class?"
- Have a lively teaching pace.
- Be consistent in what you demand, and never make a threat you cannot carry through, if necessary.
- Do not ask questions directed to the entire class. The entire class then has a tendency to answer you, thus creating classroom chaos.
- Attempt to refrain from making examples of students in front of the entire class or other children. Handle issues, both positive and negative, in private.
- Remember the value of praise.
- Have seating charts when you do not know the names of your students. It is important to be able to address students by name.
- Know that a quiet class is not necessarily a learning class. Learn to recognize the difference between productive noise and unproductive noise.
- When students give an incorrect answer, attempt to understand their reasoning rather than merely telling them they are wrong.
- Never reprimand an entire class for what an individual or small group has done. Likewise, never punish an entire

class for what an individual or small group has done.

- Think of yourself as an actor or actress on stage when you are teaching. This is a visual age—and by the way, you really are on stage!

- Proper student behavior and good discipline are essential to effective teaching. The teacher is the catalyst for bringing out particular behaviors in students (humor, dedication, respect, silence, productive noise, etc.).

- Celebrate spontaneity as an appendix to your organizational skills.

- Know that finger clicking, "shhh," and "ok" are mannerisms that are useless in the classroom.

- Spend at least as much time telling your students what you like about them as you do correcting their shortcomings...and more, if possible.

- Set yearly goals for yourself. Limit the number of goals to three or four, and choose only those areas in which you would like to see improvement in yourself or your professional environment. Make certain the goals are measurable, and see to it that they are above and beyond the normal expectations of the job.

- Videotape yourself occasionally so you can assess your own teaching, and learn to see and hear yourself as others do.

- Know that the best way to be a leader is to be a model teacher.

- Understand the loneliness of leadership.

It has been nearly two decades since Howard Gardner, an education professor at Harvard University, first promoted a theory of multiple intelligences that offers new insights into the modern-day classroom. His initial 1983 book, *Frames of Mind,* challenges the traditional notion of intelligence and suggests that seven distinct intelligences exist. No book on educational theory or structural leadership would be complete without acknowledging this interesting theory. The seven intelligences articulated by Dr. Gardner include the widely accepted and tested linguistic and logical/mathematical measures of intelligence, but also tests the musical, spatial, bodily kinesthetic, interpersonal, and intrapersonal intelligences. To delve into this theory in great detail is beyond the scope of this book; however, one cannot ignore the favorable implications of the theory on music education. By definition, the seven intelligences include:

1. LOGICAL/MATHEMATICAL – sensitivity to and capacity to discern logical/numerical patterns; ability to handle long chains of reasoning

2. LINGUISTIC/VERBAL – sensitivity to sounds, rhythms, and meaning of words; sensitivity to the different functions of language

3. MUSICAL – ability to produce and appreciate rhythm, pitch, and timbre; appreciation of the forms of musical expressiveness

4. SPATIAL – capacities to perceive the visual/spatial world accurately and to perform transformations from one's initial perceptions

5. BODILY/KINESTHETIC – abilities to control one's body movements and to handle objects skillfully

6. INTERPERSONAL – capacities to discern and respond appropriately to the moods, temperaments, motivations, and desires of other people

7. INTRAPERSONAL – access to one's own feelings and the ability to discriminate among them, and to draw upon them to guide behavior; knowledge of one's own strengths, weaknesses, desires, and intelligence

The recognition of music as a separate intelligence that all human beings possess is indeed significant. In addition, Gardner proposes changing the nature of standardized testing to emphasize a portfolio approach of assessment. Students would submit a collection of their work in the intelligence area being evaluated. In music, that could take many forms, such as an audiotape, videotape, live audition, or presentation of an original musical score. In the music profession, this type of assessment is more common than in many other fields. In the words of Howard Gardner, "Practice is enriched by theory, even as theory is transformed in the light of the fruits and frustrations of practice."[6] (Gardner has many other books since *Frames of Mind* that are worthwhile to read and understand.)

Most importantly, our profession must be willing to address the question of whether music education, as traditionally carried out through general music in the lower grades and almost exclusively large-ensemble instruction in secondary education, is the model that will best serve the learning needs of students in the twenty-first century. When music education consistently speaks with relevance to the fundamental expressive needs of human beings and inspires the musical intrigue that leads to continuing interest, confidence, and skill development for meeting those needs, music will more likely be perceived as essential to the school curriculum.

In closing, I would cite the words of pianist Van Cliburn in his address to the Ft. Worth Independent School Board that Plato said, "Music is to the mind as air is to the body. Music should encompass the body, mind, and spirit of all youth, rural, urban, and suburban. The curriculum vita of all Athenian youth in 460 B.C. included gymnastics, mathematics, and music. Gymnastics to develop the body in order to make the trek through life, mathematics to develop the mind in order to find the way through life, but without music and the other arts, there would be no reason for the trek through life."[7]

1 *The School Music Program: A New Vision.* Reston, VA: Music Educators National Conference, 1994.

2 *National Standards for Arts Education.* Reston, VA: Music Educators National Conference, 1994.

3 *Opportunity-to-Learn Standards for Music Instruction: Grades Pre-K – 12.* Reston, VA: Music Educators National Conference, 1994.

4 *The School Music Program: A New Vision.* pp. 3–4.

5 *Opportunity to Learn Standards for Music Instruction: Grades PreK–12.* p. 4.

6 Howard Gardner, *Reflections on Multiple Intelligence: Myths and Messages.* Phi Delta Kappa, March, 1995, p. 207.

7 Van Cliburn speech to the Board of Directors of the Ft. Worth Independent School District, Music In Our Schools Month, March 1992.

Chapter 7

Elementary Classroom Music Education

The essential building block, the core foundation of a comprehensive K–12 music education curriculum that lies at the heart of every high-quality music program, is the elementary music education program. Indeed, the experiences children have in the elementary school music program are not only formative for students in building musical competence, but they are also paramount in building music *confidence* in their musical competency. The image built and the memories produced from this period in the life of a child will last for a lifetime. For many, fifth grade will be the culminating year in musical education, unless classroom music is required in the middle school.

I am constantly amazed at the number of people who tell me they cannot sing and relate their awareness of this to something a music teacher said to them in elementary school. When people learn that my profession is music education, almost without fail they feel inclined to provide me with a brief—or not so brief—history of their musical experiences in school. Those who had a high school experience will relate to that, but otherwise, they generally relate to their elementary school experiences. We are all aware of their responses.

"I can't sing.......never could."

"I can't carry a tune in a bucket."

"I only sing in the shower."

"My music teacher told me not to sing, just mouth the words. That's how poorly I sing!"

"My music teacher told me I was a blackbird. I really did not know what that meant until I realized that it was the bluebirds who sang well, and the blackbirds were those who couldn't sing right."

Could you imagine a situation where an educational system evaluated students in the fifth grade, and if a student did not have clear potential for becoming a player on the middle school/junior high school or senior high school baseball team, the school and the parents would say that "you are not a baseball player now, and you will never be a baseball player," and that would be the end of baseball for you forever! That would never happen because (1) we think of sports as a lifetime activity essential to good health and (2) we know that young children still have significant physical maturity to experience. We would never think of eliminating physical education at the end of fifth grade for all except those who appear to have talent and great potential. Can you imagine making a decision as to who would continue to pursue mathematics, science, or writing based on fifth grade performance? Or art? My point is simple: *All* of these physical, mental, intellectual, and developmental processes are part of an educational learning continuum that has a significant grounding during the elementary years. So, too, does music.

Yet when it comes to music, that is exactly what we do. From grade six through high school, if you have not been labeled as having a "good voice" or "musical potential," you will label yourself—or others will label you—a "blackbird" for life. You will grow up as embarrassed to be caught singing as to be seen nude in public!

I always thought that singing was as natural to folks as crawling is to babies. I just thought that everyone sang—that is, until I became a music teacher. Then I realized the awful truth! Many people are afraid to sing because some music teacher failed them in the early stages of their musical education. The teacher was so busy teaching them the mechanics of music—time signatures, clefs, the names of the lines and spaces, etc.—that he/she forgot to teach them how to match pitch and sing in tune. Certainly learning to match pitch and sing is the most basic reason to have music class in the elementary school. Children do not even have to be able to read music to be able to sing...more on that later!

If we are ever going to have a large population of people in society who sing and enjoy music, then we must begin when children are very young. Research in the past twenty years is very convincing in establishing evidence that the time between birth and age four is very fertile ground to establish music as a natural activity for young children. Music in early childhood develops abilities and sensitivities that enrich the everyday life of all people. The neglect of that development in younger children causes an irreversible loss of potential, for waiting until the age of five is wasting many valuable years. Edwin Gordon, in his pioneering work on musical aptitude and musical achievement, has stated that a musical aptitude develops to age nine and then becomes stabilized.

Young children love to listen and make music. Have you ever watched small children play alone? They are so incredibly spontaneous and many times "sing-song" while they are doing almost anything, from writing to playing with toys. It becomes a form of language for them. This needs to be recognized, appreciated, and encouraged.

Parents and children used to spend more time together, and music is one way to restore that important element of family life. Even something as simple as a family singing a blessing before they begin a meal establishes music in the home as well as a musical tradition with the family. Unfortunately, children no longer come to school with the musical repertoire and games they used to learn at home before they entered school.

Given the premise that Pre-K and elementary years are critical in the musical development of children, why has the music education profession often given such limited lip service to this initial and basic part of the music curriculum? While there is overwhelming agreement in the profession that budget cuts in the elementary music program are a form of educational malpractice, we have had a tendency to turn our backs when these program cuts do occur—because they don't affect the high school performance program (wrong!). I have not seen many districts where people fought to save an elementary music program as much as they fought to save a high school performing group. Yet without a solid elementary program, it is unlikely there would *be* a quality middle/junior high school or senior high school performing group after a few years!! Would we think a science program or math achievement would be at high levels if the study of math or science were eliminated in the elementary grades? I think not. It is so necessary for "professionals" to observe the educational life from the child's perspective because they cannot speak for themselves with regard to their musical well-being. Certainly the methods books and the methodology are readily available, but in reality, this is the most misunderstood and under-rated dimension of the Pre-K–12 sequence of instruction.

General Observations

Some general observations that have, at times, influenced the direction of my personal leadership follow. Some are valid and others have no validity from a national perspective, but they do represent my experience. You will need to apply the observations to your own experiences and geographical location. One thing is certain: if applicable to your situation or locality, these generalizations are worthy of attention by the profession, both in the positive and negative sense.

Have you noticed that:

- The principle purpose of teaching elementary music is to provide a planning period for the general classroom teachers?
- Elementary music is frequently the first area in music education to be considered for elimination when the budget ax drops—that is, unless someone discovers some reason, usually unrelated to music, for maintaining it?
- One-time encounters by local music groups (symphony, opera, music foundations, etc.), designed to provide the void when music instruction is curtailed or eliminated, simply does not replace a real, live music teacher?
- The lower the grade levels the greater the possibility that the children will not have a certified music teacher?
- Music teachers sometimes have chorus or extra rehearsals at lunchtime to avoid having students pulled out of class? This, in turn, creates "morale" problems because the music teacher is no longer available to take his or her "fair" share of lunchroom duty.
- At times it seems elementary schools have become more "teacher friendly" than "student friendly?"

- Principals have been known to combine two or more elementary classrooms for a music class and assign them to one music teacher for the music period—the rationale for this being that fewer music teachers are required and "the classes would all be taught the same lesson anyway, so why do it three times when one time will accomplish the same goal?"

I hope by now you will realize that these observations are "tongue-in-cheek"…or are they? I would hope that the fallacy of these practices is evident. If not, please re-read Chapter 6. Have you also noticed that:

- In many states, teachers' unions approve a contract that will guarantee the planning periods for teachers? This enhances the odds that music teachers will supply the terms of the union contract and not find their position eliminated.
- Music teachers sometimes think of elementary classroom music as a program that prepares students for performing groups in middle school and high school?
- Some elementary principals require that all elementary classes do at least one performance per year for the PTA? Why would classroom music classes perform? Certainly this exceeds the purpose of classroom music. The purpose of classroom music is to learn about and experience music in a classroom setting, not to perform it in public.
- A music room is available to music teachers if there are extra rooms in the building? However, I have seen classroom music teachers going from room to room with carts, books, CD players, and other equipment, with no piano, etc., while instrumental lessons were being held in the auditorium. The instrumental teacher used a large

124

teaching area while teaching less than ten students who sit and rarely move (unfortunately). So classroom music is less important than instrumental music?

- Sometimes the general classroom teacher will not allow students to attend music class because they have not completed an assignment or are not doing well in their "academic" classes? Is music that unimportant...is it simply a frill?

- College professors in music, outside the discipline of music education (even though they are music educators, their professional discipline is not that of music teacher training), are many times not aware of the importance or significance of elementary classroom music?

I suppose that is enough—and just possibly too many— of my observations. The real meat of this chapter is sequential curriculum development that must occur in spite of the above general observations.

Curriculum Development

In the book *House at Pooh Corner* by Milne, Christopher Robin asked Winnie the Pooh the simple yet extremely complicated question, "Where are we going?" Winnie the Pooh answered by saying:

> "Where are we going, I don't know
> Why does it matter where people go...?
> Out to the wildwood where bluebells grow...
> Anywhere, anywhere, I don't know."

This may have been fine for Winnie the Pooh, but it is the absolute antithesis of a good prescription for the development of a sequence of instruction. As indicated in Chapter 6, it is essential that you know where you are going and how you are going to get there. This is what curriculum development is all about. The blueprint for the journey was established in Chapter 6. Thus, the important thing here is to apply that blueprint specifically to the Pre-K and elementary years. The National Standards have helped to provide the structure for curricular and conceptual cohesion. The sequential music curriculum should be balanced and comprehensive, and should not consist of a collection of unfocused activities. The Pooh curriculum doesn't work! Rather, it needs to be a sequential series of carefully planned concepts leading toward well-defined goals.

How one determines what should be the content of a particular subject area has been a constant source of debate among music educators. To some, content implies the factual knowledge that teachers will impart to their students ("Beethoven bridged the gap from the classical period to the romantic period." "The spaces in the treble clef spell f a c e.") For others, content is defined as the cognitive and behavioral skills that should be attained as a result of the study of a particular subject area. ("Produce a specific pitch accurately with your voice." "Play a major scale on the piano from D′ to D″). For still others, the content of any course should be those essential concepts that define the structure of the discipline. Neither the learning of facts or skills will ensure the ability to apply such knowledge or skill to new situations. Such learning does not embody the potential for further learning.[1] In contrast, by their very nature, the gaining of concepts fulfills this requirement. According to John Dewey, concepts

enable us to generalize, extend, and carry over our understanding from one thing to another. It would be impossible
to overestimate the educational importance of arriving at
concepts. They apply in a variety of situations, are constant

126

in referral, and give standardized known points of reference. Without this conceptualizing, nothing is gained that can be carried over to the better understanding of new experiences. The deposit is what counts, educationally speaking.[2]

For many years, I have had difficulty with a curricular goal that has as its purpose the teaching of music reading. Music reading, as I know it, is interpreting notation in such a way that produces a result called *music*. Music to me is aesthetic. Webster defines the word "aesthetic" as "having to do with the beautiful, as distinguished from the useful, scientific, etc." Notation to me is useful and scientific, but not the aesthetic. Therefore, notation is merely a codifying device to remember what one has composed, or to reproduce that which someone else has composed. When a music teacher spends an inordinate amount of time teaching music notation as opposed to music, the result is scientific, boring, and unaesthetic. Many times I have observed students respond to the teaching of notation in the elementary classroom with, "Why do we have to learn this? I hate music!" How tragic! On the other hand, when music teachers teach the "concepts" of music reading through singing, playing instruments, rhythmic activities, creative activities, listening, and movement, these concepts could combine to lead the students to truly read music—or they may not! Should a student not progress to the point musically where notational comprehension or music reading is necessary, so be it.

The future consumer of music does not need to be able to read music to enjoy it. Music notation is only a means to an end, and that end is music performance. Students in classroom music who do not aspire to participate in the performance of music do not need to learn to read it. Music enjoyment must be the real purpose of classroom music, with notational concepts simply providing more knowledge about the art form. To make music reading the true goal of classroom

127

music is, in my opinion, not only wrong but serves no purpose. As stated earlier, if the true goal of classroom music is to provide students with ongoing experiences in the joy and aesthetics of music, then I could not care less whether or not they learn to read it. On the other hand, those who aspire to perform music individually in band, choral, or orchestral ensembles, or in jazz ensembles, must learn to read the music to accomplish the task. The teaching of the reading of music for performance purposes will be dealt with in Chapters 10 and 11. I hope my emphasis on the differentiation between the education of future consumers of music and the education of future performers of music is becoming evident to you.

Classroom Music Instruction for Special Students

Books and articles written on the subject of curriculum development usually have a section devoted to exceptional students. They advocate that students with physical or learning disabilities and students with limited English proficiency should have the opportunity to participate in music on the same basis as other students. Who would disagree with that? However, there are problems associated with this directive:

- Music students in undergraduate school simply are not given sufficient training in the many facets and faces of special education.
- Curriculum development is rarely created for the self-contained special education classroom. Thus, the untrained music teacher has a tendency to "wing it."
- Mainstreaming of special education students is rarely determined on the same basis as placement for students without disabilities (e.g., musical achievement,

chronological age, etc.).

- Music educators are usually not involved in placement decisions and are generally not fully informed about the needs of each student.
- The mainstreaming of students sometimes results in classes that exceed the average class size for the school by more than 10 percent.[3]

What could a leader do in this situation? The above problems are not only unfair to the students but also to the music teacher. I recall a situation during my career when students were not only improperly mainstreamed in the manners stated above, but they were also never mainstreamed into the same class because the schedule "flip-flopped" every other day. Since the special education teacher's planning period did not "flip-flop," the students would be mainstreamed into different classes each day. In addition, it was maybe a fourth grade one day and a second grade the next day. There was also no regard given to the chronological age of the child with special needs, and the music teacher was not allowed to have knowledge of the type of disability the child possessed because of issues of privacy…not that it would have made that much difference. And yes, it does get worse!

Since the buses for the special students came later than the buses for the regular students, and left before the buses for the regular students, an additional problem was created. The mainstreamed child during first period came late to that class, and the next day left early from the eighth period class. Likewise, the student mainstreamed during the eighth period left early from that class, and the next day arrived late for the first period class. Oh yes, and the teacher's aide did not attend the music classes to remain with the special education teacher for lesson planning. Thus, the music teacher was left alone with students who normally had an aide present. It just seemed like no one really cared about these problems, the students, or the strain it placed on the music teachers.

The most unfortunate part of the situation was the confusion and frustration experienced by the students. I pleaded with the Supervisor of Special Education and the Curriculum Director of the school district for help, but to no avail. The union contract required that every special education teacher have a planning period, and the aide was supposed to plan with the teacher. Thus, there was no option—remember that I stated earlier that public schools have appeared to become more "teacher friendly" than "student friendly"? The special education teachers suggested that the music teachers let the special students come into the music class and just have fun. I insisted that the music department had a curriculum and that, hopefully, music class was fun; however, there was more to a music sequence of instruction than "fun."

At this point, a resolution to the problem seemed hopeless. Out of desperation, I called the State Department of Education and told them of this unbelievable dilemma. Their response was more than I could have hoped for. They were aware of this problem around the state in many school districts. Thus, they decided to create a pilot program in our school district for them to identify the means and emphasize the success of the pilot for other school districts. This was an exciting time for the music faculty. The State Department of Education hired a music therapist to come to the schools to educate the music teachers with regard to the various special education classifications. They also provided the music faculty with curriculum specialists on in-service days to aid in the development of a special education curriculum for the self-contained special classes. The music faculty also received help in dealing with the mainstreamed child. The special education teachers were given in-service training on the music curriculum designed to reinforce the understanding that the music education curriculum was more than "fun."

Music teachers began to be given input in all mainstreaming decisions and were allowed to see the Individual Educational Program (IEP) of all mainstreamed students. Although the special education teachers were not nearly as excited (an understatement!) about the pilot as the music teachers, it was successful in the course of time and remains so today. All music teachers still have access to the music therapist to aid them with the areas in which they feel deficient. Had someone not taken a leadership initiative, nothing would have happened to even improve the situation. You do not know what a difference you can make!

An unfortunate event occurred in the life of my family that brought to light the importance of proper educational care for children with special needs. To be more specific, it occurred in the life of my daughter, who was born with a congenital dislocated hip. Generally this is not a major problem if discovered at birth. Many times correction can be accomplished with only a pillow brace. Unfortunately, both the delivery doctor and the general practitioner missed Laurie's dislocation at birth, and thus, it was not discovered until she began to attempt to walk. At that time, we discovered that she was not only having difficulty walking, but she was also not really crawling in a normal manner. Since Laurie was our first child, we were not aware of any of the signs of abnormality until she reached the walking stage of her development. When her inability to walk became apparent, we immediately consulted with our general practitioner. He quickly sent us to an orthopedic physician, and thus began a journey that continues to this day. This journey has made me particularly sensitive to children with special needs.

Fortunately, my daughter's problem was not life-threatening; however, it did mean that she would spend an undesignated period of time in a total body cast (called a "spica cast") with her legs spread apart to the point where they came out from her body at 45-degree angles. Her confinement in the cast lasted for three years before the doctor felt the hip would remain in place. At this point, she began a series of braces that were designed to bring her legs back to a normal position. Thus, she was in kindergarten before she really began to walk and first grade before she could run and play with the other children. At the end of first grade, she was diagnosed with a reading problem, and it was recommended by the school district that she attend summer school to help with her (cognitive) reading skills. We also observed at this time that her small motor skills were exceptional, but her large motor skills were sadly lacking and coordination in movement was awkward. She was a child with a physical disability and special educational needs. However, her Mother and I decided that she had spent so many years confined in a cast, unable to run and play like other children, that a summer doing this was more important than her attending a summer school for reading deficiency. We would deal with the reading problem in future years. We also took our daughter to a local optometrist to check that her eyesight was not at the root of her reading problem. No problem was diagnosed with her eyesight; however, the doctor also noted that she had severe coordination and perceptual problems. Thus began a much more pleasant segment of our journey.

The optometrist noted that she had not gone through the normal crawling stages in infancy because of her confinement in the cast, and this was the cause of the lack of coordination in her large motor skills. Thus, we embarked on a year-long program recommended by him that was designed to improve her motor skills. Since my wife and I were both music teachers, we quickly realized that many of the recommended activities were similar to those used in the elementary music classroom, especially rhythmic movement and moving to steady beats. We also took our daughter through the crawling process that she had missed.

I had just received a sabbatical leave for music study in Japan from Gettysburg College, where I taught. So we embarked on an exciting year of family music experiences, which included Laurie and her brother. Laurie attended an international school that was flexible enough not to push the reading or workbook activities for a year. At the end of the year, we returned to the United States and the U.S. public school system. We were thrilled to learn that Laurie's reading problem no longer existed. In fact, she was placed in the top reading group in her elementary school. All of this happened without even working on reading for a full year. What the optometrist had predicted really did happen! Thus, there is obviously some relationship between body coordination, eye coordination, and reading ability. As Laurie's coordination and perceptual development continued to develop, so did her reading ability. To this day, she is a fast reader and is also a college graduate (Syracuse University) who had no special needs during her collegiate experience. The hip, however, does continue to present problems.

After this experience in my own family, I visited elementary classrooms while observing student teachers (and later teachers in the field), and I could sense certain physical movements and patterns during movement and rhythmic activities that were similar to those of Laurie's. I would ask the general classroom teacher if the child was a poor reader, and I was rarely wrong. That one could identify a reading problem by the movement patterns and characteristics of children, indeed, seemed revolutionary to me. I have spoken many times to other educators about this experience and have had limited response. I know that one experience does not make a complete study; however, I do believe more research on the relationship between perceptual development and reading skills would be—could be—valuable. I suppose this is merely one more non-musical reason to have music education—one of many. I find these reasons most worthwhile as long as the celebration of the non-musical attributes of music education do not upstage the study of music as a discrete discipline.

International Curriculum Theories

Several noted music educators from the United States and abroad have greatly influenced the direction of music education during the twentieth century.

Carl Orff, from Austria, espoused the concept of creativity through his observe–imitate–experiment–create process; Zolton Kodaly, from Hungary, centered on singing as the basis for music instruction, the use of folk and art music, the tonic sol-fa hand signs, and rhythmic syllables; Shinichi Suzuki, from Japan, initially confined his teaching to that of the violin and stressed rote instruction exclusively in the early stages of musical learning along with family involvement in the learning process (particularly the mother); and Emile Jaques-Dalcroze, from Switzerland, developed an elaborate system of rhythmic training and movement called *eurhythmics*.

In the United States, Edwin Gordon stresses the theory that children have a portfolio of musical intelligences, with the primary ones being rhythmic and tonal intelligence. He introduced the theory of audiation, which asserts that we are able to perceive and create music in our heads. The Manhattanville Music Curriculum Project (MMCP) had as its objective the development of a music curriculum and related materials for a sequential music program for primary grades through high school. The MMCP encourages students to experiment with both environmental and musical concepts in a program where students are expected to become composers, conductors, performers, listeners, and critics in classroom activities. It is designed as a curriculum concept spiral and includes a sequenced series of problem-solving situations for the students to encounter.

It is not the purpose of this book to favor one system over another, or even to delve into the theories in any depth. The music educator must make that decision. The music series available from book companies in the United States favor a more eclectic approach, using bits and pieces from many concepts or theories to teach music. Many music teachers favor the eclectic approach. Teachers who are not certain of their own goals must eventually reach conclusions that present a feeling of philosophical comfort. These teachers must read, study, and make a choice based upon knowledge, understanding, and sufficient training to teach well in the chosen sequence. Music educators who have had a smattering of conflicting methodologies in undergraduate school are in a position to better understand the need for further training. This advanced study, available at the graduate level, is an absolute necessity. The rewards to any teacher willing to spend the time and effort necessary to become truly professional and literate are manifold to both the teacher's colleagues and to his/her students. This ignites the lamp of leadership!

Thus, it must be said again and again that fundamental music learning must take place in early childhood and must be formalized through conceptualized instruction that leads to musical understanding in the elementary and secondary schools. Change is a difficult circumstance to embrace; in fact, the only individuals I know who truly seek change are those who are very unhappy in their present circumstances or a baby with a wet diaper. On the other hand, how can you expect different results if you keep doing the same thing?

On the subject of change, I now introduce a potpourri of thoughts and considerations with regard to common concerns I have noted as I observed student teachers, beginning teachers, and experienced teachers in their classrooms over the past 40+ years. These common practices will hopefully supply a list of common problems to avoid along with general hints for success. Having considered the title "Nut and Bolts," I decided to title it "Notes and Rests" since this is a book on music education. "Notes and Rests" are a combination of recommendations for success and suggestions for avoidance.

Notes and Rests

SINGING

- The true and basic goal of the elementary music education program is to teach students to match pitch and sing in tune.

- Children must initially learn the difference between their singing voice, their speaking voice, and their playground voice.

- In teaching children to match pitch, attempt to have them relax. Take their hands, work to eliminate the tension in their elbows, and with their hands and arms attempt to physically demonstrate to them higher and lower pitches as you raise and lower their arms.

- Research is needed to ascertain whether or not there is a correlation between the ability to match pitches and sing in tune, and whether or not there is a correlation between learning disabilities and perceptual problems.

- The descending minor third is the most prominent and easy-to-match interval in a child's vocal repertoire.

- Always provide some motivation for a song before beginning to teach it.

- When beginning the singing of a song, make certain you do a "ready sing" on the initial starting pitch of the song, even if it is not the root of the chord.

- Do not begin a class with the teaching of a new song. Teach it early in the lesson, but don't introduce the lesson in this way.

- Do not teach more than one new song per lesson, and do not teach the new song late in the lesson.

- The knowledge of correct procedures for teaching rote or note songs is very important, so do not abbreviate them. It is important to teach songs correctly and thoroughly.

- After teaching the song, review it in future classes until it is learned well.

- Do not use a CD or piano to teach a new song; use your voices. The CD may be used to introduce the song (motivation) or to review it in future classes.

- Do not sing with the children when they respond to your initial singing of the phrases in teaching a rote song.

- Children (and adults) respond best to music when they are not hearing it for the first time.

- Be certain your students possess a repertoire of the traditional songs that might be considered major folk songs of the United States and other countries.

- At the end of the lesson, have the students put their heads on their desks, and then sing quietly to them the new song taught in the lesson. This provides a review of the song taught early in the lesson and allows the song to remain fresh in the students' minds.

- The Dalcroze, Kodaly, and Orff methods provide significant suggestions for singing activities.

LISTENING

- Lower elementary students have a tendency to confuse loud and soft with high and low.

- When students are listening to a musical composition, you must epitomize the interested and active listener. After all, that is what you expect of your students.

- Music might well be played while students enter and leave the music room.

- The Manhattanville Music Curriculum Project (MMCP) includes listening as an integral part of its main focus on creativity.

RHYTHM/MOVEMENT

- Students must be taught to respond to the music—not in spite of it. Students have a normal tendency to move (or dance) in spite of the music rather than to the music. They must be taught to listen and respond to what they hear.

- When involving students in creative movement, don't lead by example (i.e., do it yourself). The students will follow you rather than create their own movements.

- The approach and theories of Dalcroze, Kodaly, and Orff involve movement as an integral part of their focus.

INSTRUMENTAL ACTIVITY

- Recorders are the best exploratory instruments because they are fairly easy to learn and have functioned as a valid instrument down through the ages.

- When accompanying a class with piano, do not play the melody. Be sure to provide an accompaniment with no melody line. This is important in the process of developing independent singers.

- Teachers should not sit down when using the piano as an accompaniment device. Have the back of the piano facing the students, then stand and face the students when playing.

- The approach and theories of Carl Orff use instruments as one of their basic tenants.

CREATIVITY

- Creativity is the least understood of the five basic areas of elementary classroom music (singing, listening, playing instruments, rhythm/movement, and creativity).

- Creativity is the least taught of the five basic areas of elementary classroom music.

- When engaging in creativity with students, it is important that you do not lead or model.

- The approach and theories of Dalcroze involve creativity through improvisation, Orff invented his own set of instruments and uses recorder in support of musical creativity, and the Manhattanville Music Curriculum Project (MMCP) emphasizes musical composition in support of creativity.

DISCIPLINE

- To have effective class discipline, you must first win the love of the students and then earn their respect. One without the other is not beneficial. Love without respect can lead to a chaotic classroom, and respect without love provides only a quiet classroom.

- I have observed that men have a tendency to have more difficulty than women in establishing effective discipline in Pre-K and elementary grades. They appear too soft and permissive as they attempt to identify with the young age. Really!

- "I'm waiting!" is not an effective discipline tool.

- If you grasp the students' interest, attention and curiosity, the words "discipline control" are non-issues.

CONCEPTUAL DEVELOPMENT

- Specific concepts must be established for each grade level, and they need to be cyclical. That is, they must return again and again in the curricular sequence through the grades. This is called the *spiral curriculum*.

- Then lessons need to be developed around the concepts, building one upon another, lesson by lesson and grade by grade.

- Rarely teach more than one new concept per lesson, although previously taught concepts might/should be included in each lesson. Too many concepts addressed in a lesson have a tendency to confuse students.

- A short review of the concepts covered in the lesson should occur at the end of each lesson.

Music Learning

- According to the *Opportunity to Learn Standards*, every student in elementary school should receive "general music instruction each week for at least ninety minutes, excluding time devoted to elective instrumental or choral instruction. Music is woven into the curriculum through the school day." Also, "Instruction by music specialists is provided in periods of not less then twenty minutes, nor more than thirty minutes in grades 1 and 2, and in periods of not less than twenty-five minutes nor more than forty-five-minutes in grades 3 through 6. Classes in general music are no longer than classes in other subjects of the curriculum."[4]

- Capitalize on the affective domain as much as possible in the music learning process.

- Each lesson should progress from the familiar to the familiar, with new material or recently introduced material included early in the lesson.

- Be sure to make the music class musical. You have a marvelous tool at your disposal, so be sure to use it. Avoid oververbalization! Do not have a class of facts. Music must be the strong force.

- The attention span of the students must be considered with regard to the length of the class period. Choose the concept to be taught, and use singing, listening, rhythm/movement, instruments, and creativity in support of the concept to provide lesson variety. Be careful not to engage in a particular classroom activity too long if it exceeds the attention span of the students. Look for *teachable moments*, particularly in the lower elementary grades. The mood of the children must match the mood of the activity. You must allow spontaneity to enter the classroom. Teach the young children when their minds are open to being taught.

- Do not attempt to *hothouse* learning. This is the opposite of a teachable moment. Hothousing is when a parent or teacher attempts to get information into a young child's mind as soon as possible, regardless of whether the child is ready or open to learning a particular concept.

- Curriculum should be more than simply the reproduction of a music series book.

- A "mystery melody" in each class is a good motivational tool for approaching the concept of notation. Write the initial phrase of the familiar song on the board at the beginning of each class, and have the class attempt to identify it.

- When students are being taught the concepts about notation or music reading, you must constantly emphasize to the students to look at their books or the music in front of them. Many times I have observed elementary music encounters where the teachers stress the reading concept and the students appear to be looking everywhere but at the music itself. Conceptual understanding about music reading does not come easy, and a great deal of time and effort must be given to the task, usually more time than that allotted to classroom music in most elementary schools.

- Pre-tests and post-tests at each grade level are good assessment tools. Remember that it is just as important to assess the teachers teaching as it is students learning.

- There have been many debates about whether a male teaching elementary music should use falsetto or his normal voice. It is true that with falsetto, a male teacher can match the pitches of the elementary children. The other side of the issue is also worth considering, however. I personally remember that my male elementary classroom teacher, Mr. Caton, was a wonderful music teacher. He was an inspiration to me as I matured musically and embarked on my career as a music educator. I will never forget, however, that during my elementary school years, I discussed with my parents the thought that this huge man (and he was big!) sang with this funny voice. I truly thought he had a problem. It did not seem normal to me. Think about it! I would suspect that a combination of a normal male voice with an occasional use of falsetto, when needed, might prove more desirable and appropriate.

- A professional development program and curriculum instructional planning go hand in hand and should be pursued at the same time.

Hopefully the contents of this chapter have clearly stressed the principle that general classroom music and classroom music in general is essential for a higher development of the aesthetic potential of children. Elementary performing ensembles will be given attention in Chapters 10 and 11. Reform is difficult. It requires a major shift in our thinking and planning. It requires the acceptance of the ever-changing characteristics of children, and it requires the acceptance of a new teaching/learning environment. As music educators, we can bring about an answer to the question Christopher Robin posed to Winnie the Pooh, "Where are we going?" We can provide the structural experiences that will help all young children in this country realize their dreams, develop their musical abilities, and have richer, far more meaningful lives because of their exposure to the musical arts in their elementary school years. [5]

1 Eunice Boardman. "Generating a Theory of Music Instruction." *Music Educators Journal*. September 2001, pp. 45–53.
2 John Dewey. *How We Think*. 1910; reprint, Mineola, New York: Dover Publications, 1997, p. 129.
3 *Opportunity to Learn Standards for Music Instruction: Grades PreK–12*, p. 4.
4 *Opportunity to Learn Standards for Music Instruction: Grades PreK–12*, p. 3.
5 Portions of this chapter are edited from a speech presented to members of the Texas Association of Music Schools by Dr. David G. Woods, April 2000.

Chapter 8

Middle School Classroom Music Education

The organizational structure of American education has undergone several systemic changes. In the early days of our country, most public schools were grammar schools with grades 1 through 6, and later grades 7 and 8, in single buildings and often in one room. Secondary education as a distinct and specialized component of public education started in the 1830s with the Boston Latin School. High schools became a regular part of communities starting in the 1870s and 1880s, but only in the largest cities. Junior high schools as a concept started in the early 1900s, and in earnest after World War I as the student population of many American communities grew large enough to begin to segment. The concept of middle schools came out of the early school reform movement of the late 1950s in California and began to become popular alternatives to junior high schools in the 1960s. By the late 1980s, nearly 85 percent of junior high schools had become middle schools.

As an educational system in this country, we have spent the most time restructuring our education system around students between the ages of eleven and fourteen. Many adults, and many educators, view these years with alarm and despair, for they represent an age group of students undergoing significant changes in adolescence—physical, emotional, hormonal, behavioral, sexual, and intellectual. The middle school was developed to be a more sensitive and developmental transitional link between elementary and high school. However, those who work in middle schools and with middle-level children must be committed to this age group to be successful, and they must with that commitment bring a keen understanding of the philosophical, psychological, sociological, conceptual, and logistical problems these students encounter during these formative years. If those who work in middle school education do not have these understandings, the middle school becomes a middle school in name only. The fact that there are so many different variations of grade levels in middle schools throughout the country (5–8, 6–8, 7–8, 4–8, 7–9) speaks to the confusion that exists about how best to address this part of our educational system, as well as the varying organizational structures that have been adopted more to solve space and financial concerns rather than for the sake of the education and philosophical goals of the program of instruction. In a perfect world, the schools would exist first and foremost for the students. Unfortunately, our educational world is not always that perfect.

Historically, schools with grades 7, 8, and 9 were labeled junior high schools. This represented a certain redundancy, suggesting a hierarchy of similar kinds of experiences, just with different age groups. Indeed, that is precisely what occurred in many school districts and in the minds of many music educators. There were junior high school football teams and, consequently, junior high school marching bands and cheerleaders. There were interscholastic basketball teams and, consequently, pep bands. There were junior high school students doing Broadway musicals with romantic entanglements far beyond their emotional or experiential understanding, especially for seventh and eighth grade students! There were junior high school choirs over-singing so they could sound as close as possible to a senior high school choir. There was little or no celebration of the uniqueness of the middle or transitional years, and no real thought given to the relationship of age, skill development, physical development, or experience unique to this age group. The fact that junior high school music programs mirrored senior high school programs is logical since senior high music programs spent much of their time mirroring college and university music programs. As junior high schools attempted to engage students in a mini-high school experience, it encouraged educators to quicken the educational process to accelerate student maturation.

I remember very clearly the anger of one very well-known junior high school band director who was enraged when his district switched to middle schools and he lost his ninth grade band members to the high school. His concern was not for the students he was going to teach. Rather, he was most concerned that he could not perform Grainger's *Lincolnshire Posy* in the coming year. Thus, the process just seemed to be "do it at the junior high school level and then do it again at the senior high school level." Human beings are living longer than ever, yet there always seems to be that tendency to accumulate more and more knowledge in an increasingly shorter period of time. One must question, "Why the hurry?" Ghandi said, "There is more to life than increasing its speed." I agree!

The middle school concept stressed *transition* rather than introduction and reintroduction. This philosophy provided many opportunities for students to experiment and experience breadth rather than depth in learning, along a conceptual continuum that better matched adolescent psychological, intellectual, cognitive, and physical development. A true middle school philosophy requires a careful analysis of the architectural design of the program of studies, the curriculum, and the grasp of the concept by the administration, teachers, and guidance staff.

Even though middle school performing groups may not perform the level of literature that junior high school groups (with older players) enjoy, it still seems that a 6–8 middle school philosophy is valuable for the following reasons:

- The philosophical base of the middle school emphasizes transition from the elementary years to the high school, where the ultimate of performance and learning should occur.
- Where the middle school is neither a junior high school nor a mini-high school, experience can be open-ended, broad, and encourage continued musical exploration at the high school level.
- The ninth grade "mindset" appears to function better as the younger member of a large body of students rather than the older member of a large body of students.
- The eighth grade student appears to function better as the older "child" rather than the middle child.

There are certain program issues that, in my experience, are critical for a successful and comprehensive music program at the middle school level. As a leader, I suggest you share this list with your administrator, colleagues, or board members—it may just prevent a crisis before it occurs.

- Classroom music should be required for all students in grades 6, 7, and 8.
- A seven- or eight-period day is critical.
- Avoid the outmoded activity period approach to scheduling. Explore the possibilities of a period during the academic day when all student/teacher encounters deal with acceleration or remediation. This helps eliminate many of the usual pullout programs in the middle school and provides for performing group rehearsals on school

time. All students choose eight elective encounters per year. This concept will be explored in more depth later in this chapter, as well as in Chapters 10 and 11.

- Never allow performing music to replace classroom music. The two serve different functions and populations, and an experience in one should not replace the experience in the other. One primarily should serve the future performer of music, and the other the future consumer of music.

- Make certain major performing groups receive academic credit and the students are graded for the course. The large performing groups must be part of the performing music curriculum from the elementary school through the high school (see Chapters 10 and 11) and must be considered as a curricular offering at all levels.

- Avoid the temptation to do too much too soon. Three rehearsals per week are adequate at the middle school level. An overkill in rehearsals and/or performances at the middle school level could create eventual burnout at the senior high school level.

- Remember that the middle school is part of the K–12 sequence of instruction leading to the culmination and commencement at the senior high school level. The middle school is transitional and not an end in itself—no middle school empires, please!

- Work to avoid erratic mainstreaming. These practices, especially in the middle school, create havoc in the classroom. It may be the law to mainstream special children, but it is not the law to mainstream them into an environment where they cannot function. Follow the mainstreaming guidelines established in Chapter 7. Students with learning problems to begin with simply cannot succeed in a planned, sequentially developed curriculum unless they possess the ability to do so. Do, however, make certain all special students have music class, at least in a self-contained environment.

- Marching band (with the exception of occasional street marching for pedagogical purposes) should not exist before the ninth grade.

- Care should be exercised to guarantee that middle school children rarely travel for performance and competitive purposes. A rare exception might be for performances at the state or national music education conference. Hold off on those big trips until senior high school and college. Otherwise, your students may say, "Been there, done that," and go on to some other elective encounter. There must always be that carrot in front of the students' faces. They must want to go on to the next level.

- Separate sixth grade performing groups from seventh and eighth grade performing groups. The musical demands are too wide for all three grade levels to be incorporated into one performing group.

- Provide for class instructional encounters, on school time, for students who do not study privately. Without class lessons, performing groups become split into the "haves" (those who study privately) and the "have-nots" (those who do not study at all). This breakdown many times occurs along socio-economic lines. The rotating, or "pull-out," program is the most satisfactory resolution to this potential pitfall—and has been for many years. This will be discussed in Chapter 11.

- Do not attempt to schedule small performing groups (jazz band, etc.) during the school day. Small ensembles and musical revues should be extra curricular, meeting before or after school.

Now that the philosophical base has been established, one now needs to look into the real essence of middle school: the middle school student!

The Middle School Student

Some refer to it as the "terrible" ages of eleven through fourteen. We were all there for a time as we traveled through the passages of life—and most of us want to forget this short stopover between childhood and young adulthood! The fact that we are all here today is proof that we did survive those trying times, and it is annoying how little we really remember of those years. Given that this period of life is unique, special, confusing, distinct, private, personal, peculiar, embarrassing, bewildering, and perplexing, it takes a very special teacher to turn a music class into an exciting adventure for these students.

My experience has shown that when students of this age are given questions rather than answers, they become better students. Teachers cannot *make* students learn at any age, particularly at this age. They can only plant the seeds, and we all know that it is silly to throw out the seeds until the ground is fertile. When the ground is fertile, we no longer need a "teacher" because we now have a student who is willing to learn. Middle school students enjoy a teacher who is free to become the "facilitator" and guide the students in their self-instruction, in part because these students have become very independent and want to assert some of their own decisions. It is important that these teachers/facilitators have a creative sense about their role. Middle-level teachers must also be tolerant of the tremendous changes that a middle-level student goes through in a matter of months or years. The key here is that the students now become responsible for their own learning, and during the three or four years they are loaned to you in the middle school, they learn to respond to you as the catalyst for their learning. The light goes on in their heads and the fire goes on in their souls.

I would suppose by now you are thinking, "What philosophical hogwash!" This would never work with the middle school students I know. Trust me, it can happen. I have seen it happen, and the results were really quite amazing. In this chapter, I will deal only with classroom music and some curricular issues, because performing groups will be discussed in future chapters.

Classroom Music

Let's begin by renaming this section of the chapter. If we were going to think of the music classroom as a music laboratory, what would be necessary? The first thing would be to get rid of all the desks in rows and replace them with stools. Stools can be moved around the classroom in many different arrangements, depending on the activity to be pursued. Add to the stools, many tables placed around the walls of the room where the students are able to engage in their laboratory experiments. I know this sounds more like science class, but remember that Chinese proverb:

I hear, I forget

I see, I remember

I do, I understand

...Music is doing!

Middle school music programs, like many other programs in the schools, have historically been teacher-oriented. Teaching about music was the norm, and classes were not designed to teach musical thinking by direct interaction with musical elements. But part of the secret with middle school students is to let them discover; just as their parents are finding out, *telling* them to do something just doesn't work!

In this music laboratory:

- No longer will the room be aesthetically stark.
- No longer will the desks be placed in neat rows, with the students sitting in them having little or no active involvement in music.
- No longer will the classes be worksheet-oriented.
- No longer will listening be the predominant musical activity.
- All musical learning will be approached as a "hands-on" activity.
- The middle school music curriculum will reflect the philosophy of individualized musical involvement.
- The *teacher* will become the *facilitator*.

The Classroom Music Laboratory

The purpose of this classroom laboratory will be to nurture student interest, learning, and creativity. Even though a certain amount of creativity is inborn, much of it can be promoted by an environment that supports independent thought, freedom, and choice. By engaging the intrinsic motivation of a child, the pleasure that he or she derives from doing something for his or her own sake emerges. With a "hands-on" approach in the music laboratory, students begin to function as learners about music, performers of music, and composers of music. The most important aspect of this engagement is the process, not the product. *Functioning as a musician* is quite different than *being a musician*, and *learning what it is like to be a musician* is different than *existing as a musician*. Aesthetic values differ from person to person. Children are born with the ability to think, act, and live creatively. The true goal is to bring it to the middle school music classroom.

The middle school music teacher's function is to stimulate and not dominate, to encourage and not control, and to question far more than answer. Discovery may be guided but never dictated. Students should be encouraged to use their brains for imagining and imaging. Thus, the music teacher in this classroom laboratory needs to:

- Share by using language familiar to the children, even if it is not musical or academic.
- Share with students the possibilities, not the right or wrong.
- Present things in steps. When one step is accomplished, students go on to the next step. However, each step along the way must be totally accomplished before the next is attempted. Remember that the carrot always needs to be in front of the students' faces.
- Be as flexible as possible. I personally grew up as a very rigid person. I approached every issue as black or white, right or wrong; there was nothing in between. Flexibility allowed me to enter an entirely new world, and the same could happen to you!
- Keep the material simple, at least in the minds of your students. Know when to introduce concepts, how to layer concepts, and when it is time to go on to the next concept.
- Attempt to make that which is shared with your students as personal to them as possible.
- Attempt to share in a contemporary fashion, even if it means using pop culture. If you are not up to date on pop culture, ask the students; they will educate you (and love doing so!).

- Accept the learning of your students where you find them, not where you think they should be.
- Make sure what you share can be visualized and experienced by the students. The old German manner of teaching by presenting factual information is very limiting. Learning needs to be experimental, not factual![1]

The middle school music laboratory should include the functions of:

- Performing music (in class only, please)
- Learning about music
- Creating music

Taking such a simple formula, however, and placing it in the context of a music laboratory takes some creative thought. Let's begin with some basic management suggestions.[2] Initially the students must be instructed in the definition and understanding of the following acronyms:

LGI = Large Group Instruction = performing
SGI = Small Group Instruction = composing
IGI = Individualized Group Instruction = learning about music

The teacher will have a sign containing one of these acronyms at the door as the students enter each class period. This will allow the students to go to the proper area of the room and, hopefully, prepare mentally for the forthcoming activity. In the instances of SGI or IGI, the students will usually be able to begin work immediately.

Performing Music (LGI)

Performing music in the classroom music laboratory begins with the teacher arranging the stools in a semi-circle in the middle of the open area of the room. Possible activities in this arrangement include group singing, group guitar, and/or group keyboard instruction. No attempts should be made to teach notation or music reading when singing. Singing should be designed merely for the pure joy of singing. Use unison, rounds, canons, descants, etc. The most important part of this encounter is to provide experience in classroom performance opportunities that are group-oriented. Band, choir, and orchestra give elective group musical opportunities beyond this. Interested students should be encouraged to elect these groups over and above the classroom music experience.

At times, students may have difficulty singing and playing guitar at the same time. Therefore have half of the class sing (in unison) and the other half play. Then reverse it. An exceptional class may be able to improvise in parts, but generally unison will bring about the most pleasing musical results. In all LGI encounters, it is important that the teacher maintains a lively teaching pace.

Learning About Music (IGI)

Individualized learning centers were popular in the 1970s but seem to have fallen out of favor in the twenty-first century. The advantage of the learning centers for middle school students is that, in all probability, for the first time in their educational life they are held responsible for their own learning. The students play their own tapes or CDs with earphones, showing themselves the filmstrips, videotapes, or other technologies that might apply. The students follow the instructional grid and do whatever the instructions of the individualized station tell them to do. When a student completes the various musical and academic tasks, he or she notifies the teacher (facilitator) that he or she is ready to pass off the evaluation tool and move on to the next station. The teacher then checks the evaluation tool of the student and allows the student to choose the next station. Grades are given according to the number of stations passed off in the nine-week period. Students are aware of the ratio of the number of stations passed off in order to receive a particular grade (A, B, C, etc.). Thus, the students are not only responsible for their own learning but also for their own grade. Students are free to choose those stations they wish to attempt. Sample stations, designed by the teacher might include:

- Monophonic, Homophonic, Mixed, Polyphonic – see Chart #1
- Up, Down, Stays the Same (Understanding the Concept of Notation)
- All Strung Up (Autoharp)
- A One and A Two (Conducting) – see Chart #1
- Big Mac (Rondo Form) – see Chart #2
- What's the Score? (Understanding Notation) – see Chart #2
- Play Your Axe (Playing an Instrument)
- Let's Move (Movement)
- Music of the People, By the People, For the People (Patriotic Music)
- A Fiddle, A Farm, and A Song (Country Music)
- Hearts and Flowers (Romantic Period)
- 'Tis the Gift to Be Simple (Folk Music)
- Sounds of the Outlets (Technology, Electronic Sounds)
- A Band Is…
- A Choir Is…
- An Orchestra Is…
- Hogaku and You (Japanese Traditional Music)
- Latin American Music
- American Indian Music
- The "Now" Generation (Pop Music)
- Lend an Ear (Listening)

- Name That Tune (Understanding the Concept of Notation)
- La, La, La (Singing)
- What Are You Doing the Rest of Your Life? (Careers)

Chart 1

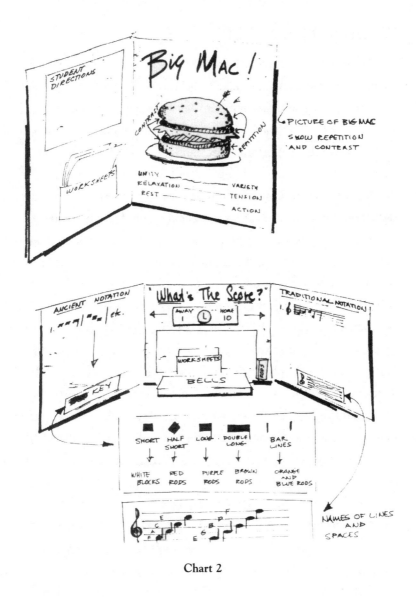

Chart 2

The individual stations should be as brief as possible. The instructions, when brief and simple, may be placed on the poster itself (see Charts 1 and 2). Otherwise, the instructions should be included on an individual sheet and placed on the desk in front of the poster identifying the station.

Creating Music (SGI)

Music content standards in the National Standards, Grades 5–8, include "improvising melodies, variations, and accompaniments," and "composing and arranging music within specified guidelines" as important objectives of a comprehensive school music program. It is, therefore, quite important that music educators provide creative opportunities in the middle school. A creative growth stage appears to exist in children from grades 2 through 4, followed by a developmental plateau that arises between grade 4 and grade 6.

It is difficult to interpret why creativity apparently does not continue to develop between grades 4 and 6; however, it is worth noting that measuring creativity is a relatively new field in music education research and, therefore, becomes problematic to the researcher.[3] Brophy (1998)[4] and Kratus (1985)[5] also identify a leveling or plateau in music creativity among intermediate students (grade 4 in the Brophy study and grade 5 in the Kratus study). The appearance of this developmental plateau may be due to various curricular factors. Teachers working with older students, for example, may not address creative thinking in students as often. Music educators may be concerned with covering material or teaching specific skills that often draw upon convergent thinking at those grade levels. As a result, when working with middle school students, creative activities (such as improvisation) may receive less emphasis.

Once again, the function of the music teacher should be to stimulate rather than dominate, encourage rather than control, and question far more than answer. Discovery may be guided but never dictated.

In retrospect, when one looks back at the Manhattanville Music Curriculum Project (MMCP) that enjoyed limited popularity in the 1960s, it becomes apparent that its initiatives are clearly consistent with current curriculum theory. I could not agree more with Lenore

Pogonowski when she strongly supports the use of the MMCP model and notes that creating, performing, listening, analyzing, and evaluating are mutually supportive behaviors. She notes, however, "some pervasive questions still exist:"

- "How do we think more expansively about how we facilitate student learning, whether they be students preparing to teach or students in the public schools?
- When encouraging teachers to use creative strategies in the classroom, how do we get them beyond their reluctance and fears?
- What do teachers need to construct new knowledge?"

"Until we have some approximation of consensus regarding systematic change, comprehensive music curriculums such as MMCP will continue to exist in the minority of classrooms across the country. Brava and bravo to all of you who have made the leap! You will find yourself at home in this millennium."[6] And to those of you who have not made the leap, consider it for the middle school classroom laboratory.

I would suggest that some of the original intents of MMCP be modified to properly motivate current students as opposed to the 1960s and 1970s students. I have found the following sequence to be quite effective; however, the flexible and spontaneous music teacher may even modify this to meet the dimensions of his/her classroom and the needs of the students.

1. In the LGI setting, students are presented a musical example of a particular form in music (binary, ternary, rondo, etc.).

2. Students are then divided into groups, and each group is given the assignment to compose a musical example using that particular form. The groups may use any sounds they

might invent (found sounds), classroom instruments, their voices (singing and/or speaking), or any instrument they might be studying at the time. Students become composers.

3. As the students realize they are unable to remember what they have composed from one class to another, it becomes apparent that they need to establish some sort of a notational system so they can recall their work from class to class. Since most students cannot notate what they write in traditional western notation, they must create their own notational system. Through this, students learn the true value of notation as opposed to a non-aesthetic, arithmetic exercise. I have found many times that their "invented" notational system takes on the appearance of a work of art. Neither the artwork nor the musical composition would rival the medieval neumes or a Beethoven symphony, but that's fine! When students create, the result is ownership, and with that ownership comes appreciation and understanding—the true purpose of education.

4. When the "composition" is completed, the students then begin preparing the composition for performance. Thus, they must choose their conductor, who rehearses them just as any conductor would rehearse a group preparing for a concert performance.

5. When the group is ready for performance, the entire class is assembled and the performance is given. The teacher videotapes the performance.

6. The videotape is then played for the class as well as the performers for the purpose of evaluation. Either the conductor or the members of the performing ensemble explain

the notation and the form of the composition to the entire class.

All students have the capacity to think, act, and live creatively. Nurturing creative thinking in sound should be a core tenet of the middle school classroom music experience. The mutually supportive behaviors of listening, analyzing, creating, performing, and evaluating produce exciting and amazing results when allowed to flourish in a classroom setting. Consider making the leap!

Scheduling Middle School Music Classes

The music program in the middle school must build sequentially from the music program in the elementary school and provide the foundation for the music program in the high school. Middle school classroom music teachers should be encouraged to identify students who show aptitude and interest that will lead to one or more of the classroom music electives offered at the senior high school level (e.g., guitar, music technology, music theory, world music offerings, etc.). The students must then be encouraged to continue their study at the high school level.

The scheduling of middle school classroom music is always difficult. I agree with the recommendation in the *Opportunity to Learn Standards*,[7] which states, "General music is required of all students through grade 8." I disagree, however, with the recommendation in the same publication which states that every general music course should meet "at least every other day in periods of at least forty-five minutes." I believe a better scheduling format would be a nine-week segment with classroom music meeting every day. When students meet every day, the retention rate is far superior to every other day, several times a week or, at worst, the once-a-week pattern of years gone by. Could you possibly remember how long a week seemed when you were thirteen years old? When students meet every day, even for a period of nine weeks, they look upon the course more as a major encounter rather than something that occurs whenever, or never. Also, the nine-week segments may be combined with nine-week segments of art, industrial, and home technologies to form an arts block. This arts block will fill one period of the school day for one year. This would allow for the exploration of several arts areas during the course of sixth, seventh, and eighth grades.

One of the major concerns of middle school music scheduling is that of performing music. I have counseled and consulted with many school districts about the difficult process of the middle school schedule. It is of major concern to both classroom music teachers and performing group directors. A successful model I have worked with is called the TEEPS model (The Exploratory Enrichment Program). The Williamsport (PA) Area School District has used this model successfully for approximately twenty years, and I recommend it highly.

The school day consists of seven periods plus a TEEPS period. The TEEPS period generally occurs around the lunch period, although this is not essential (see Chart 3). Every teacher in the school proposes a TEEPS course that must support either acceleration, remediation, or exploration. The course must be approved by a group of faculty peers to make certain it does not take on the structure of the traditional activity period of past years. Team sports are excluded from the TEEPS; however, lifetime sports are encouraged.

Every student, except performing music students, takes eight TEEPS per year. Performing music meets during the TEEPS period; however, performing music is a course that students must elect for a full year. Remember that if the performance program has band, choir, and orchestra, it will be necessary to have three rehearsal areas in the school. Since performing music is a course, students will receive course credit and a grade. So that students may be in both choral and instrumental performing groups, preference days, on every other rehearsal day need to be established since directors are now free to trade off their preference days season by season. All groups now meet at the same time. Scheduling now becomes easier for the principal, or other persons doing the scheduling, because all performing group students are scheduled as one group. It is also important to remember that TEEPS are not clubs. They are mini-courses that meet for one-quarter of the school year, and they must either accelerate student learning, provide remediation in areas where students are deficient, or provide an exploratory experience in a new area of learning for students. Don't allow study halls during TEEPS or at any other time in the middle school program.

TEEPS

THE EXPLORATORY ENRICHMENT PROGRAM

MODEL FORMAT

Frequently over the lunch periods, but this is not essential.

	Day 1	Day 2	Day 3	Day 4	Day 5	Day 6
First Lunch	TEEP 1	TEEP 2	TEEP 1	TEEP 2	TEEP 1	TEEP 2
Performing Music	6th grade	7th/8th grade	6th grade	7th/8th grade	6th grade	7th/8th grade
Second Lunch	LUNCH	LUNCH	LUNCH	LUNCH	LUNCH	LUNCH
			OR			
First Lunch	LUNCH	LUNCH	LUNCH	LUNCH	LUNCH	LUNCH
Performing Music	6th grade	7th/8th grade	6th grade	7th/8th grade	6th grade	7th/8th grade
Second Lunch	TEEP 1	TEEP 2	TEEP 1	TEEP 2	TEEP 1	TEEP 2

SUGGESTIONS:
1. Every student, except performing music students takes 8 TEEPS per year.
2. Performing Music students take 4 TEEPS per year.
3. Performing Music meets during the TEEPS period; HOWEVER; performing music is a course which students must elect for a full year.
4. Since Performing Music is a course, students will receive course credit, and a grade.
5. TEEPS are not clubs. They are mini-courses which meet for one-quarter of the school year, and must either accelerate a students learning, provide remediation in areas which the student is deficient, or provide an exploratory experience in a new area of learning for the student.
6. Do not allow study halls during TEEPS or any other time in the Middle School program.
7. Do not allow team sports during the TEEPS period. Emphasize lifetime sports.

Chart 3

165

Discipline in the Middle School Music Program

The etymology of the word *curriculum* suggests "a vision of rapid forward motion toward a finish line." Music teachers possess a vast responsibility for what goes on musically in individual schools, and also for the discipline in the classroom. I have heard many horror stories, particularly from principals, concerning discipline in the middle school music classroom. Curriculum is developed not only to assist all music teachers in the school district with the task of teaching, but also to acquaint administrators, the Board of Directors, interested parents, and all citizens so they understand and realize the function of music education in their schools. Once curriculum is operational, there should be no concern for "keeping the students quiet" or "making them behave." Discipline concerns should no longer be the major topic at faculty meetings. Discipline concerns must be replaced by curricular activity. As long as class discipline, class control, and a curricular organization exist, any type of teaching and learning is possible. It is at this point where teachers are responsible for and obligated to provide this.

An interesting example of the importance of curriculum to class control occurred when an outstanding, successful, and conscientious middle school music teacher (teacher #1), involved in the type of curriculum design advocated in this book, was assigned to monitor a study hall. This true story clearly exhibits the value of a successful curriculum to teacher success. The teacher had never experienced discipline problems until she received the study hall assignment. Her statement to me at the time was "Good teacher I can be, but the role of study hall brute simply does not work for me." Nevertheless, the principal was unbending about the assignment. She went on to say, "When I went to the principal with regard to my discipline concerns in the study hall, it was just assumed that I was a poor teacher. The principal had never visited my classroom, and I was being judged solely on my problems with the study hall." The principal pointed out to the teacher that a fellow teacher (teacher #2) was a very effective study hall monitor and that she might observe his technique. His technique, as it turned out, was to have with him an inseparable paddle.

A good study for any music educator concerned about leadership would be to have observed the exciting music classes of teacher #1, with students actively involved in music learning. Then visit the classes of teacher #2, with paddle always nearby and students sitting quietly and fearfully in every other seat, quite uninvolved in the learning process. Quite a contrast! Teacher #1 was an effective classroom music teacher, and teacher #2 was an "effective" disciplinarian. However, in the eyes of the principal, teacher #1 was not a good teacher because of the study hall problems. Teacher #1 eventually left the profession.

What does this example suggest? First, it demonstrates that a relevant curriculum, designed to meet the needs of the ages of the students it addresses, creates a learning situation involving students to the point where discipline is not an issue. Secondly, it demonstrates that had the principal been wise enough to place teachers in situations where they would be likely to succeed rather than using their failures to judge their effectiveness, there would not have been a problem. The role of a leader is to define reality—and give hope.

Conclusion

The primary aim of music education must be to enrich the human experience. Human experience is enriched in the music classroom when students are able to actually undergo the experiences that music provides.[8] John Dewey made a distinction between "doing" and "undergoing." It is possible to do something without undergoing its consequences.[9] What education at any level seeks is a grasp between the doing and the undergoing, between the musical form and the experience it generates. This is particularly true at the middle school level. Although a certain amount of creativity in students is inborn, much of it can be promoted by an environment that supports independent thought, freedom, and choice.

It should come as no surprise that schools typically put a lid on the creative child. Teresa Amabile, in her book *Growing Up Creative: Nurturing a Lifetime of Creativity*,[10] states that "schools are particularly adept at killing creativity," as they typically use large doses of what Amabile terms "the creativity killers—evaluation, reward, competition, and restricted choice." Music education's major aim must be to design environments that will provide the opportunity for students to engage in creative experiences as a normal and ongoing part of their middle school musical experience. It is well to remember that music, in the end, is not about learning facts about the art form, but it is about the quality of the experience that music makes possible. It is about the experience that moves us, that somehow reaches the deepest part of our soul, that part in which the human spirit resides. Should we forget to attempt to transfer that which music does for us to our students, music education will have no right to exist as an educational and curricular discipline.

---

1 Portions of this list are taken from a clinic presented by Richard Boldrey, Professor of Music at Northwestern University, at the Texas Music Educators Conference in February 2002.

2 Mary Coleman, then music teacher at the Lycoming Valley Middle School in Williamsport, Pennsylvania, designed the Classroom Music Laboratory outlined here.

3 Kiehn, Mark T. *A Study of the Development of Music Creativity Among Elementary School Students*. Unpublished study. Midwestern State University, 2001.

4 Brophy, T. *The Melodic Improvisations of Children Ages Six Through Twelve: A Developmental Perspective*. Unpublished Doctoral Dissertation, University of Kentucky, 2001.

5 Kratus, J. *Rhythm, Melody, Motive and Phrase Characteristics of Original Songs by Children Aged Five to Thirteen*. Unpublished Doctoral Dissertation, Northwestern University (Evanston, Illinois), 1985.

6 Lenore Pogonowski. "A Personal Retrospective on the MMCP," *Music Educators Journal*, July 2001, pp. 23-24.

7 *Opportunity to Learn Standards for Music Instruction: Grades Pre K–12*.(Reston, VA: Music Educators National Conference, 1994), pp. 9–11.

8 Elliot Eisner. "Music Education Six Months After the Turn of the Century," *Arts Education Policy Review*, Volume 102, Number 3, January/February 2001. p. 23.

9 John Dewey. *Experiences and Education*. New York: Macmillan, 1938.

10 Teresa M. Amabile. *Growing Up Creative: Nurturing A Lifetime of Creativity*. New York: Crown, 1989.

Chapter 9

Senior High School Classroom Music Education

One of the outstanding achievements of public school music during the present and past centuries has been the phenomenal development of performance groups. At the senior high school level, these groups have often reached an outstanding level of perfection. As the performance program grew in importance and was accepted by the public, the training of the secondary school music teacher became increasingly dominated by courses that were directly related to a performance-oriented music curriculum. But let me give you another scenario.

Time: Whenever

Place: A typical high school

Scene: The typical high school has a strong band program, a choral music program and, hopefully, an orchestra program. The three directors have been proactive in the development of their programs; however, the choir and orchestra directors feel overshadowed by the band program. No general music program exists at this high school, with the exception of a course in music theory. The course offered at this typical high school is recommended to students intending to major in music in college. It is taught by the choral director.

Situation: The state enacts a high school graduation requirement that includes the fine arts, solidly backed by the state music education organization. The high school administration, needing to fulfill the new requirements, asks the three performing group directors to design new music courses for the non-performing students who must satisfy this new fine arts requirement. The proactive performing group directors suddenly turn into reactive ones, and react they do! These directors have no interest in teaching the non-performing students and no experience in designing courses for them, so they ask the administration where the new teachers are going to come from to teach these students. The administration states that they are going to teach these classes. The performing group directors are upset and never would have lobbied their legislators to pass this new requirement if they had known that it meant they would have to reduce their efforts with performing groups. They forecast a decline in the enrollment and the quality of their performing groups, but the principals have no other choice.

Let me pose some questions for consideration here:

- Should the three proactive performance directors not take a proactive leadership role and fight for the inclusion of performance music as a fine arts requirement rather than a reactive role against classroom music?
- Are colleges and universities training music educators, future directors of performing groups, or both?
- Are music educators proactive with something they are excited about teaching and reactive when it involves areas

they do not know or understand—or do not wish to teach even though their certification is K–12, all-inclusive?

- Do music educators have difficulty embracing the whole because they have worked so hard to make their particular program strong?

- Would a senior high school classroom music program provide competition or enhancement to the performing arts program? (The answer to this one is *neither!*)

- Should music educators be concerned about the overwhelming majority of senior high school students who have no courses to take after grade five, six, seven, or eight, depending on when the classroom requirement for all students ends?

- Should music educators be concerned that less than 15 percent of high school students are enrolled in music, with an even lower percentage in urban and rural school districts?

- Has any research been done to indicate whether or not students enrolled in performing music will, as a result of the process, become better listeners to music and more engaged consumers of music?

- Do we have an obligation to educate performing group students beyond the learning of the notes and the performance of the music?

- Is the learning process for a performer and a consumer of music different? Should it be?

One might assume that a fine arts requirement would be welcomed by music educators everywhere; however, a closer look may find that this is not necessarily true. The fine arts requirements are welcomed by the performing group directors as long as performing group credit will satisfy the requirement and it guarantees the sanctity of their performing ensembles. If, however, the performing group directors, particularly instrumentalists, are asked to teach classroom music, the response is quite different. The negative and predictable response of the performing group teachers to teaching classroom music is brought about not only by the lack of experience and interest in teaching classroom music, but more so by the fear that electives will diminish the quality and size of the present band, orchestra, and choir programs.

My years as a music educator and music administrator have convinced me that the quality of a music program is only as strong as the quality of each of its parts. (It seems I also remember something about this from mathematics.) The development of a string program, for example, does not bring harm to a band or a choir program. It really enhances these programs because it involves students with differing musical interests. The notion that students who sign up for orchestra will lower the number of students in band is inherently wrong, just as the notion that elective classroom music courses at the senior high school level will drain students from performing groups is equally wrong. The performance program addresses performances, and the classroom music program addresses those not interested in performing in large ensembles. We need to also celebrate those students who wish to play individually on instruments (piano, guitar), those who wish to compose music either through technology or the traditional means, as well as those who simply want to learn more about a particular aspect or type of music. In other words, not all children want to perform, but they may have a very deep interest and passion for music.

Since Chapters 10 and 11 will deal with performing music (band, choir, orchestra, and other ensembles), I will limit my writing in this chapter to the overall senior high school music program, along with classroom music.

In order for all of music education to flourish, music educators must be proactive in building the *total* music program, not only the individual specialization of the music teacher. Unfortunately, this is not always the case. Those music teachers who spend so much time "protecting one's turf" expend much energy—valuable energy that could well be expended in developing new musical opportunities for the non-performing students. Again, the sum of the whole is only as strong as the quality of its parts.

High School Music Education Programs in Urban and Rural United States

If the music education program in a school district makes no impact on the community it serves and makes little or no difference in the quality of life of that community, then there is insufficient reason for the music department to exist. If we are to be accountable to the communities that support our music programs, we must find a way in which the music education program is contributing to the cultural health and vitality of the constituents of that community.

The urban environment provides many rich opportunities for music and artistic experiences, from a wide range of professional music organizations to the rich mix of musical cultures. Yet the cost of running a music program in an urban high school can be prohibitive—not just financially, but educationally—because there are such extraordinary needs and deficiencies in math, reading, science, not to mention social issues. For this reason, high school students and urban parents many times assign a low priority to the music experience.

The emphasis on vocational training for the workplace or the increasing concern over urban test scores has led administrators, teachers, and parents to place the arts in a secondary and even tertiary role. The rural environment is often isolated from live performances, and the small size of schools limits large ensemble performance opportunities. Thus, the middle-class, suburban environments have become a haven for active and successful music education programs, the places where families are interested in providing their children with opportunities inside and outside of the school environment. Increasingly, the availability and quality of musical instruction in the United States is uneven and inequitable. For many high school students, opportunities for music instruction, if they exist at all, must be found outside of school. This is only exacerbated further when economic or budgetary hardships force even deeper cuts—and choices. Yet these are the students I perceive to be the most in need of music and the arts.

The great urban music programs of the past are testaments to the vision of individuals who choreographed the K–12 sequence of instruction. I can recall, some fifty years ago, attending the Philadelphia Schools "Music Department on Parade," held in the Spectrum, a large sports arena in central Philadelphia. Louis Werson was the music supervisor at that time. The All City Band, Choir, and Orchestra were outstanding, especially for the era. At that time, the urban school districts provided the model for the suburban districts. Even the classroom music encounters were represented in the All City concert, with many autoharps, movement and dance, rhythm and melody instruments, and all of the musical experiences we still value today. These were presented not as performances but more as "informances." What an exciting evening! School buses moved the hundreds of students to and from the Spectrum as the thousands in the audience thrilled to the accomplishments of the students from the elementary schools up through the high schools. Indeed, the music education department of the Philadelphia School District did make an impact on the cultural life of the community it served. The same was true in the cities of Cleveland, Detroit, Kansas City, and

Minneapolis. As a college student at the time, after witnessing that event I knew I was in the right profession!

But times have changed, and while the value of music in urban education is no less important than it was fifty years ago, there has been a steady erosion in the quality of music education offered to urban young people. In my opinion, the decline in urban school music programs, programs historically taught by Whites and focusing on Western European music traditions, is directly proportional to the increase in urban diversity where large numbers of new urban residents come from many musical cultures. Perhaps we need to think about all-city concerts that celebrate and showcase *music*— instead of bands, choirs, or orchestras, it should also include the great musical diversity demonstrated in the city. The explosion of drumming ensembles, ethnic dance ensembles, gospel choirs, steel drum and mariachi bands all are a testament to the vitality of music.

While rural music education rarely takes the spotlight, this rarely discussed area of our profession is a unique one. In small towns, the music teacher *is* the cultural leader, a teacher, conductor, director of extracurricular activities, church choir director, and director of community ensembles—in short, the embodiment of "The Music Man." This individual carries great responsibility for the musical life of the community and is seen as both an educator and an entertainer. My own personal experience as a rural music educator presented an awesome challenge combined with an overwhelming daily time commitment. In addition to the duties mentioned above, I even directed the yearly minstrel show fundraiser for the Catholic church (minstrel shows were politically correct then!), directed the church choirs in a Protestant church, and taught private lessons in the evenings and on Saturdays. My public school salary was $2,900 for the year, and I saved enough money during the year to spend six weeks in the summer on a Temple University music study-tour, crossing the Atlantic on the SS United States. My how times have changed!

Rural music teachers do, however, learn the value of K–12 sequential learning. They have no one else to blame if their students are deficient when they get to high school. They learn to teach *all* the children. As the only music teacher for grades K–12, they are responsible for building their own program. I directed marching band, concert band, orchestra, choir, and the musical. I taught middle school and elementary classroom music, and the performing groups at those levels. I had no control over my schedule. I was young and was still honing my leadership skills so I could be assertive enough to attempt to take control of my own schedule, even though I did not yet have that invention called *tenure*. I began first period with marching band (concert band later in the year). My second period class was kindergarten, so it was run, run, run from the marching band field into "Little Ducky Duddle."

This experience provided the basis for all I was and all I am in this profession. I learned quickly the vast difference between students at every grade level from kindergarten through senior high school. The strong potential for curriculum sequence, combined with the neighborhood school concept, makes some aspects of the rural school very attractive. Today, the rural school—and the rural music program—is a very thin thread to which the vanishing rural community clings for its cultural vitality. Yet we are having a very difficult time motivating new teachers to even *look* at rural districts.

My point in including a brief discussion on urban and rural music education is that times do change, and the design of curriculum, experience, and opportunities must change with those times. As we look at the potential for a classroom music program at the high school level, we know there are vast numbers of students with many interests, backgrounds, and cultures who desire an experience with and in music. I will never forget the challenges of teaching in urban America, the joys of teaching in suburban America, and the prestige of teaching in rural America.

Multicultural Music in the Senior High School Music Curriculum.

Recognizing the diverse musical cultures of our students and their world is one more key to the survival of music education as an essential element of learning and life. Senior high school orchestra and choral directors seriously explore the great musical literature of Europe as performed for hundreds of years. Bands concentrate mainly on American wind composers in the twentieth century, marches, and a few transcriptions. However, something does seem to be lacking. Senior high school music education programs do not reflect the diversity of musical experience and the multicultural mix of students and their parents. There are those who would argue that this is not necessary. Please allow the educator in me to give a short true/false test designed to reveal your opinions about multicultural education.

1. True / False – Multicultural music education and entertainment should be thought of as one.

2. True / False – It takes a little, if any, education to be an appreciator, an understander, a tolerator, or an audience for another culture.

3. True / False – Multicultural music education is primarily for those students not born in America, and mostly for urban schools.

4. True / False – Multicultural music education is presently addressed in senior high schools of today.

5. True / False – Adding a multicultural dimension to senior high school music education programs as they now exist would probably diminish the quality of our performing groups and raise the cost of music education.

6. True / False – All resources for multicultural music education are vested in school music teachers.

7. True / False – Multicultural music education at the senior
high school level is more akin to what happens in social
studies class than in music class.

8. True / False – Knowledge developed through music education has little or no relationship to knowledge developed
in other subjects.

9. True / False – Multicultural music education should be
thought of more in terms of product than process.

10. True / False – Humanism, just like religion, has no place in
the senior high school, and since culture and religion
are so closely entwined, we best not get involved in
developing any "multicultural chops."

If you indicated that all of the statements above were false,
you have some understanding of the place of multicultural music
education as an important part of basic education. You also recognize
a number of widely held misconceptions that prevent learning
experiences in music from assuming a vital role in the education of
every person. This is particularly true at the senior high school level.

Multicultural music education in the future must focus on the
process, not the product. It must also be adapted to serve all subject
matters of education. We must no longer be self-serving in our
approach to learning. Music needs to be integrated into all subjects,
and music educators must serve as resources and motivators to their
teaching colleagues so the arts may become a basic tool for all learning. We must improve multicultural awareness in performing groups
and concentrate on this area in classroom music—what little there is
at the senior high school level. Placing music into a central position

in the framework of basic education will not threaten the tradition-al role music has played in American schools. Rather, it serves to expand and cement its role. It does not necessarily require the invest-ment of greater funding, but it does require a relocation of teaching priorities and existing classroom resources.

In the final analysis, two contrasting ideas must come into play. The people of the United States today are more concerned with humanistic and cultural matters than ever before, because we are, in fact, more diverse and pluralistic. Yet schools and school music programs seem reluctant to embrace this concern of world music. How much longer can we go on with the obsession of prolonging the life of the heart without also being concerned about the condition of the prolonged heart?

All music educators need to develop their understanding and use of multicultural music education materials, particularly at the senior high school level. It is not only important to education, but it is important to teaching and learning in the twenty-first century, and to tolerance, understanding, worthiness, and well-being—in fact, to the very survival of schools as viable institutions of our multicultur-al society.

Rationale for Senior High School Classroom Music

Music educators must come to grips with the fact that, in spite of the high standards of performance in many schools, the large majority of high school students have no formal contact with music during their high school years. There is also increasing concern that even those students who were active in performing groups, though technically well trained, are sometimes deficient in the understanding of music as an art form.

It is increasingly important that all educators recognize the nature of music in general education. I know this is not a politically popular statement to make; however, the future members of this profession must be ready to assume responsibility in enhancing the general education of all pupils and not exploiting them for public approval.

The School Music Program: A New Vision states that, in the senior high school,

> ...the study of music should contribute in important ways to the quality of every student's life...Because music is an integral part of human history, the ability to listen with understanding is essential if students are to gain a broad cultural and historical perspective. The adult life of every student is enriched by the skills, knowledge, and habits acquired in the study of music."[1]

More specific recommendations brought forth in the *Opportunity to Learn Standards* include:[2]

- The music program in the high school builds sequentially on the music program in the middle school and provides the foundation for lifelong participation and enjoyment of music.
- The music curriculum is described and outlined in a series of sequential and articulated curriculum guides for each course.
- Every music course meets at least every other day in periods of at least forty-five minutes. (I recommend semester-long courses where the classes meet every day.)
- One semester-length course other than band, orchestra, and chorus is offered for each four hundred students in the senior high school.
- Adequate classroom space is provided for the teaching of non-performance music classes.

- Musicians and music institutions of the community are utilized, when available, to enhance and strengthen the school music curriculum. (Consider the possibilities of a performer or artist-in-residence. Often, local foundations will fund this request.)
- Academic credit is awarded for music study on the same basis as for comparable courses.

Classroom music courses can also fill the void of advanced placement (AP) courses often available in music. All departments have "honors" courses; however, historically music departments have had difficulty establishing courses worthy of AP ranking. Students do major in music at universities and, thus, really should have advanced courses available to them.

Classroom Music in the Senior High School.

The classroom music program in the senior high school must be designed to attract that other 90 percent of the school population not involved in performing music. Also, the courses need to flow naturally from the middle school classroom music program so that those whose interest has been stimulated are able to continue to progress. Classroom music, particularly at the senior high school level, has had increased emphasis recently, and many musicians realize that only through general music electives are music teachers able to reach all students.

I am promoting the vitality of a senior classroom music program from personal experience. When I arrived in Williamsport in 1973, I worked to build the elementary and middle school programs first. Then I turned my attention to expanding the number of students involved with music at the high school level. I can recall the reaction of several colleagues in other disciplines when I proposed a set of classroom music offerings to a curriculum committee. An English teacher exclaimed, "You music people have no idea what you are getting yourself in for. You are used to teaching only the cream of the crop, the brightest and the best. You have no idea what it is like to teach some of those lower classes with all their problems." Obviously, the English teacher forgot that music teachers did teach all students through grade 8. Could they possibly be that much different in grades 9 through 12? Also, a science teacher lamented, "The music department has already begun taking our top students away from their learning through those performing groups; now they want to take all students away from the academics. They may as well put harps at the entrance to the high school so people know they are approaching a conservatory of music." I thought that sounded like a good idea (not really)! I responded by stating, "Everyone has a right to sing a song, whether or not they are academically oriented. Students need to become well rounded." Obviously, some of the teachers on the curriculum committee thought of "well roundedness" as "mental ability." The electives, however, did pass the curriculum committee, and up to two hundred non-performance students a semester began electing music offerings.

The sampling of course offerings I propose here were the initial courses offered when the first Williamsport classroom music curriculum was approved. In many states, if twelve or more students elect a course, it must be offered. This provided help in demonstrating the need for added music teachers. There was concern in other disciplines that they could possibly lose teachers if too many students elected the music offerings. Fortunately, this did not happen. I would recommend that all disciplines offer semester elective courses. There should be no big hurry through this thing called life. Intellectual exploration should never cease.

Senior High School
Classroom Music Course Offerings
(semester-long courses)

MUSIC THEORY I (Advanced Placement)   0.5 credit

Music Theory I seeks to develop a thorough grasp of the fundamentals of music through the study of scales, intervals, keys, and triads leading to the writing of simple four-part harmonizations. Strong emphasis is placed on ear training and the improvement of music reading. This course will prove most beneficial to those planning a career in music or music education. Other pupils who want to acquire a good basic musical knowledge would find this course very helpful. Advanced Placement credit available.

MUSIC THEORY II (Advanced Placement)   0.5 credit

Music Theory II follows the general course content of Music Theory I but on a more advanced level. The course will provide deeper insight into the theoretical aspects of music through a study and analysis of the music of various periods of music history with regard to melody, rhythm, and harmony. Sight-reading skills, through the use of solfeggio (syllables), are developed throughout the year. Ear training is an important facet of the course. Prerequisite: Theory I. Advanced Placement credit available.

GUITAR I   0.5 credit

This course is designed to teach beginners the basics of guitar playing. It will include basic picking and chording, tuning, reading chord diagrams, music reading, and mainte-nance of the instrument. Students must provide their own instruments. A rental plan is available through a local music store. Prerequisite: Basic work in middle school classroom music is assumed.

GUITAR II   0.5 credit
This course is designed as a continuation of Guitar I. It will include intermediate picking and chording accompaniments, folk, blues, classical, and rock styles of playing. Barre chording will be strongly emphasized. The reading of intermediate chord diagrams and music will be included. Students will provide their own instruments. Prerequisite: Guitar I or the equivalent.

JAZZ, ROCK AND COUNTRY MUSIC   0.5 credit
This course is designed for the study of the history and development of these three American musical forms. The study of Jazz will include a survey of the evolution of Jazz from the early 1900s to the present. The course will review the evolution of Rock from the 1950s to the present and the social events that influenced the development of the many different existing forms of Rock. Country Music will be studied from the development of country western, bluegrass, and folk to the Nashville sound. Social studies elective credit available.

EVOLUTION OF AFRICAN-AMERICAN MUSIC   0.5 credit
This course is designed to study the history and development of African-American music. The influence of African music on the music of the United States (slave songs, spirituals, rock, jazz, etc.) and the West Indies will be covered.

MUSIC IN TECHNOLOGY I   0.5 credit
This course is designed to provide students with hands-on experience using a variety of media shaping today's music world. Students will receive instructions in the following: 1) basic keyboard technique; 2) basic music theory (scales, modes, chords); 3) practical analysis of the history of music technology; and 4) extensive exploration of contemporary music technology including MIDI (Musical Instrumental Digital Interface)-based music systems (synthesizers, computers, drum machine, sequencers, and signal processors). Previous music theory, musical keyboard, and/or computer skills will be helpful but not required.

MUSIC IN TECHNOLOGY II   0.5 credit
This course is a continuation and expansion of the topics introduced in Music in Technology I. Intermediate and advanced concepts of computer skills, acoustical sounds and techniques, and musical form along with musical improvisation and music composition are topics to be explored. Individual and ensemble performance techniques will also be developed. Prerequisite: Music in Technology I.

FOLK MUSIC (MUSIC OF THE PEOPLE)   0.5 credit
This course is designed as a survey of the many kinds of folk music throughout the world with an emphasis on the folk music and cultural traditions, such as the influence of European and African folk music on American folk music and jazz. Non-western folk music will also be explored along with Latin American music.

MUSIC THEATRE   0.5 credit
American musicals will be investigated historically and
according to categories. Musical elements and techniques
will be explored and demonstrated. Emphasis will be placed
on the visual as well as the aural aspects of musical theatre.
The course will be in four parts: 1) the history of
the American musical and techniques of the theatre; 2)
costuming and make-up (straight and character); 3) scenery
design and construction, lighting, and stage decoration; 4)
stage movement, choreography, and blocking.

PIANO LAB I   0.5 credit
This course is designed to teach beginners the basics of
piano. An emphasis will be placed on improvisation, basic
chording, basic keyboard techniques, and beginning music
reading.

Piano Lab II   0.5 credit
This course is designed as a continuation of Piano Lab I.
More advanced chord sequencing, improvisation, and
keyboard technique will be explored. Prerequisite: Piano
Lab I.

Please know that many other courses could be designed, especially
when they are created to reflect the diverse musical interests, talents,
and cultures of the local school and community.

Conclusion

I would hope that as you read these three chapters that deal with
classroom music—elementary, middle school, and high school—you
would not think of me as opposed to performance music in the

schools. Nothing could be farther from the truth. Band, choir, orchestra, and other performance ensembles are very important to me. This has been the basis of my dedication to this marvelous career. It is my hope that Chapters 10 and 11 will demonstrate my love, joy, honor, and thrill of being a performer of music.

However, we simply must prioritize our educational values for all children and youth to establish a training ground for music through things that last and through the cultivation of the soul, for the rhythm and harmony of life simply cannot exist without these ingredients. Within the discipline of music education, one finds the seed of concentration and the seed of discipline that all young people in the United States need to learn so desperately.

The intense interest in outside stimulation (drugs/alcohol) on the part of so many of our youth should clearly indicate to us a certain need that is not being met in present life and educational encounters. We all know of a wonderful and powerful addiction that can build bridges, unify nations, and heal wounds—an addiction that will never debilitate or bring physical or emotional harm. It can only edify and embrace. That addiction is music.[3]

Will it ever again be "Music for Every Child and Every Child for Music?"

They're easy to do…
Things of no good
And no use to yourself.
What's truly useful and good
Is truly harder than hard to do.

—Dhammapada 7,
translated by Thanessar Bhikku

1 *The School Music Program: A New Vision.* Reston, VA: Music Educators National Conference, 1994, p. 21.
2 *Opportunity to Learn Standards for Music Instruction: Grade PreK–12.* Reston, VA: Music Educators National Conference, 1994, pp. 17–22.
3 Portions of this paragraph are taken from a speech by Van Cliburn to the Board of Directors of the Ft. Worth Independent School District, Music In Our Schools Month, March 1992.

Chapter 10

Instrumental Music Education

At one time or another, every music educator has encountered the following logic of the kind implied in the following situations:

> "Johnny, you have not finished your math so you may not go to music class today!"

> "You are going to have to drop band until you receive a better report card."

> "I don't care if he is your only oboe player. He broke the family curfew last night; thus, he may not go on the orchestra tour."

> "I simply cannot control this child, so the only thing I know is to take something away that he enjoys. Thus, his music must go."

Amazing, isn't it? The thought that "learning should not be fun and since music is fun, it is not valid learning" has permeated American education since its beginning, and it has never really disappeared. We have attempted the curricular approach, the co-curricular approach, and the extra-curricular approach, all to no avail. Educators still support the notion that if Johnny is having difficulty in one subject, he will improve if a subject in which he excels is taken away...and above all, it must be the one he enjoys the most. This is tough logic. Texas has adopted the Ross Perot-initiated "no pass, no play," which has established, in essence, that should an oboe player receive a D or F in an "academic" subject, he or she may not play his/her oboe in band or orchestra outside of school. The law applies to music, athletics, and other selected educational and extracurricular endeavors, and grows in acceptance across the country. Even with all of our sophisticated research on teaching and learning, we still apply the stick and carrot as if trying to get mules to move.

John Adams said, "I must study politics and war that my sons may have the liberty to study mathematics and philosophy...in order to give their children a right to study painting, poetry, and music." He did not add, "That is, unless they are having difficulty with reading, writing, science, or social studies."

Virtually every individual or association that has made a major contribution to Western education since Plato has included the arts among the basics...not the "frills," not the extracurricular, not the co-curricular...the basics! In this chapter, I will make the following assumptions:

- Every school district has an orchestra and a band program that are treated as curricular offerings.
- The large ensembles are treated as a curricular subject, and the smaller ensembles are thought of as extracurricular subjects of the music program.
- Instruction on string instruments begins in grade 3 or 4, and instruction on band instruments begins in grade 4 or 5.
- Group lessons are provided throughout the program in string, wind, and percussion instruments for all students who do not study privately.

- Instrumental groups at the elementary level meet at least two times per week during the school day; at the middle school level, the groups meet at least three times per week during the school day; and at the senior high school level, the groups meet every day and are elected by the students as part of their curricular schedule.
- In middle and senior high schools not utilizing block scheduling, the school day includes no fewer than eight instructional periods.

These assumptions come from my own personal experience and, in my view, constitute requisite minimums in instrumental music programs I have observed that are of good quality and achievement. I believe these assumptions form the basis for a successful and sequentially developed instrumental music program.

The 3 R's of Successful Band and Orchestra Programs

In the history of instrumental music education, there has never been a time when the subjects of student recruitment, student retention, and readjustment for program balance have not been major issues. Since instrumental music enrollments rely heavily on the desire of the students to want to participate, these three topics become absolutely critical and basic to the success of the entire program. Instrumental music teachers are unique in that they recruit their own students, teach them well, and retain them to justify their positions, thus the tremendous importance of leadership in these endeavors. As competition for student time and interest continues to increase, the challenge that is faced in attracting students to band or orchestra becomes more difficult, as does the challenge of maintaining student interest once they are involved. I offer here some "tips" based on personal experience that I consider standard and essential to a successful instrumental music program. It may seem very basic to you, but I can assure you that in my very recent experiences, these kinds of activities are new information to many instrumental music educators today.

Recruiting New Students:

- Present a demonstration of the various instruments available from the school district, through rental or purchase. Using faculty, student teachers, advanced high school players, and advanced performers from the community is the most satisfactory. As long as the musical performers are solid, the range of ages and professions can make for positive student exposure. Music used should be easily identified by the students and/or appealing to them. Be certain to play to the audience. A student assembly may be the best setting for this recruiting presentation, as it allows fellow teachers in other disciplines to hear the music staff perform (something they rarely experience). While there are satisfactory recruiting films available, and many music dealers are willing to demonstrate, nothing can take the place of an exciting live musical performance.

- Some procedure must be followed to establish a predictive rating of potential success for each interested student. Although not always totally accurate, it does give an indication to teachers and parents of those who most probably will succeed. No students should be denied participation in the program because of this procedure, however. An effective predictive rating scheme has been developed by James Froseth in his NABIM Recruiting Manual.[1] Also, many studies have shown a positive and significant relationship between musical aptitude and student achievement, as measured by various achievement tests, the most recent by Richard Holsomback.[2] The positive relationships in this study held up across two academic years.

- A meeting should then be held for the parents of all students who indicate a desire to study an instrument. The busy world in which parents live today dictates the format of this meeting—short, sweet, and complete. Have local dealers present that evening so everything can be completed in one night. Parents will thank you for that.

- Make every attempt to exhibit program quality. Should you have a growing or already successful program, it might be worthwhile to present to the parents a profile of program growth, including the enrollments at each level of the program, growth from year to year, and percentages of school population involved (see Chart #1). Have a TV playing videotapes of the instrumental groups in the hallway for casual observance by parents and potential students.

- A "Fingertips Facts" pamphlet for parents (and community) should be prepared showing recent awards won. The pamphlet needs to market the program and allow the parents to quickly find information about the program, all in one location.

Chart 1
INSTRUMENTAL MUSIC PROGRAM
Population Statistics
2003–2013

_____ School District

Total

YEAR	LEVEL	STRINGS	BAND	INSTRUMENTAL POPULATION	SCHOOL POPULATION	%	COMBINED %
2003–04	High School	48	215	263	2,366	11%	
	Middle School	102	355	457	1,838	25%	
	Elem. School	239	302	541 (1,261)	1,817	30%	21%
2004–05	High School	53	209	262	2,208	12%	
	Middle School	101	359	460	1,845	25%	
	Elem. School	241	266	527 (1,249)	1,600	33%	22%
2005–06	High School	68	225	293	2,154	14%	
	Middle School	97	330	427	1,812	24%	
	Elem. School	237	272	509 (1,229)	1,438	35%	23%
2006–07	High School	69	246	315	2,050	15%	
	Middle School	110	308	418	1,730	24%	
	Elem. School	251	250	501 (1,234)	1,402	36%	24%
2007–08	High School	74	247	321	2,119	15%	
	Middle School	112	306	420	1,580	27%	
	Elem. School	275	269	544 (1,285)	1,374	40%	25%

Retention of Students in the Program:

The key to successful retention throughout the entire instrumental experience is that there is a teacher who cares why students start, cares when they lose heart or interest, and cares even more passionately when students of any age stop instrumental music. A sensitive, caring, compassionate, and motivating teacher is a key to student retention in instrumental music.

The power of the instrumental music teacher is magnified through direct communication with parents on all factors of the program. Quick communication with parents, not only when a student has problems but even more importantly when the student is achieving, is crucial. The parents may be hearing strange sounds at home that are perfectly normal to the teacher but very unusual to the parents. They need to know, not just for motivational purposes but also for pedagogical purposes, that the student is doing well. The longer the student is in the instrumental music program, the more the family has invested in their involvement. They deserve this communication.

When a student develops problems at any level, communication is also another prime factor that contributes to retention. This communication is fostered by teachers who are sensitive about students, can sense frustration, provide the appropriate kinds of motivational comments, know when to offer individual help, and do so in a personal and appropriate manner. There is a direct relationship between students who want to quit, peer pressure, and the ability of an effective teacher to meet their individual needs with respect and a sense of commitment.

If it becomes clear that a student may drop the program at any time, elementary through high school, after frequent communication with the parent, a "drop-out letter" should immediately be sent to the parent acknowledging the request and seeking a final intervention of help to see if the child should continue (see Appendix A). In many programs, parents are often not aware of their child's loss of interest until it is too late. A proactive stance by the music educator will keep them informed along the way. Included in this letter should be an "Instrumental Music Survey for Parents" (see Appendix B), which should include questions to determine knowledge about the child's lack of interest, the success of the program itself, and the parents' opinions with regard to the situation.

Every director should keep a record of the retention rates from year to year. If a dropout rate exceeds certain limits (I recommend 30 percent for elementary students, 20 percent for middle/junior high school students, and 10 percent for senior high school students), there is a problem with that teacher/student rapport that needs to be carefully evaluated. Likewise, program size statistics should be maintained from year to year in order to assess growth or reduction patterns (see Chart #1).

An individualized instrumental music curriculum from elementary through senior high school needs to be developed and consistently maintained throughout the district. Participation guidelines need to be recorded in a document and signed by both the student and the parent to be certain everyone understands program expectations early in the year (see Appendix C). Note that this is only an example of a document establishing guidelines for participation. Every director needs to adapt these guidelines to his/her own situation. All students have musical, academic, and social needs and abilities. A quality program must be able to serve all three as one, as well as separate, and address individually those three significantly different components of a student's school life.

All-district band and orchestra (separate them!) concerts should be presented each year involving elementary, middle/junior high, and senior high school students. This gives both parents and students a total perspective of the complete program in one evening. Remember that it is just as important to motivate the parent as it is the child.

Readjustment (for program balance):

Student population charts must be developed to show precisely how many instrumentalists exist at each grade level and on each instrument (see Appendix D). To accomplish this, the total staff (regardless of district size) must be committed to holding frequent problem-solving sessions to assume a continuous balance throughout the program. These meetings should occur at least one time per month, and the results should incite decisions regarding alternate instrument choices for students as well as future recruiting needs.

When the audience rises to its feet and gives the ensemble a five-minute ovation, when you see the excitement, pride, and happiness in the eyes of your students and their parents...then this attention to the three R's will have been worthwhile.

Teaching Instrumental Music

The instrumental music teacher today has many commercial methods books from which to choose. These include books on pedagogy, theory, improvisation, and jazz. However, we all know there is more to teaching instrumental music than a single methods book. As a former professor of music pedagogy, I hold strong opinions about the importance of productive procedures of instruction in instrumental music. They are as follows:

- Larger groups (than ten) of students can be taught together in classes of like instruments at similar levels of proficiency throughout the entire 4–12 instrumental music program.

- A sequentially developed curriculum, individualized so students may progress at their own rate, is essential for every instrumental program. This curriculum needs to flow naturally from elementary school through senior high school.

  Lessons need to possess variety and include more than pages of material from a commercial instrumental music lesson book. Lesson variety may be achieved if the following lesson components are adhered to:

a. Scales

b. Sight-reading/ear training

c. Work from the sequential district curriculum, spirally conceived (material repeated several times throughout the curriculum) by the music staff of that particular school district

This material should be organized by ability levels, not grade levels, thus producing an individualized curriculum where students may proceed at their own pace. Typically, this curriculum would have approximately twelve levels. See Appendix E for examples of Level I for woodwinds and brass, percussion, and string instrument curriculums, along with a checklist for recording individual student progress (see Appendix F).

This spiral curriculum is referred to as a rubric. A rubric is a well-articulated set of statements that are used as publicly visible criteria for the judgment of student music responses and performance behaviors. A rubric identifies the qualities a teacher expects to observe in performance behaviors at several points along a scale. Numbers are assigned to correspond to the levels of increasing performance capability/achievement (Level I, Level II, Level III, etc.).

A checklist is a written inventory of skills or behaviors to be checked off by the teacher as a record of student attainments. Checklists provide a record of behaviors/skills that were attained or not attained in a performance task.[3]

d. Two-, three-, and four-part ensemble literature.

    e. Band or orchestra music. It is permissible to include music from band or orchestra rehearsals as long as it includes only those segments to be rehearsed during the next large ensemble rehearsal. (This not only saves valuable time but requires the director to plan rehearsals carefully and immediately after each rehearsal.)

    f. Appropriate listening experiences designed to provide students with an opportunity to hear a master performer playing the instrument.

- Lessons should proceed from the familiar to the unfamiliar, gradually moving back to the familiar.
- Students should be grouped by their ability on a particular instrument not by age, type of instrument, grade level, or combinations of the above. (For example, a typical class would be Level I, flutes; Level II, violins; Level III, trumpets; etc). I firmly believe that small group lessons of this kind, even in high school, are critical to the development of advanced performance skills and musical knowledge.

I believe that when these guidelines are followed, students will learn to play instruments more quickly, easily, and with greater musical satisfaction. This can only lead to a more musically capable large ensemble.

One aspect of the instrumental music program remains problematic. The small class lesson continues to be in jeopardy in our nation's schools. Classroom teachers at all levels, even elementary, are becoming increasingly frustrated with "pull-out" programs. We know there are tremendous pressures on teachers to raise student achievement. The billy club of testing programs looms over their heads in a constant manner that is intimidating for everyone.

Yet I maintain that to adhere to the small group lesson concept remains critical to the teaching of instrumental music. I recognize that this approach, especially at the high school level, is not common across the country. The extreme differences in techniques between the various instruments of the band and orchestra necessitate individual attention that is impossible to provide in an ensemble rehearsal. Schools that do not provide lessons to students also create inequities among students based on their socio-economic status because, in such schools, only students who have the money to pay for private lessons receive quality instruction. School administrators, therefore, need to be persuaded to develop a schedule that addresses the needs of instrumental music students by providing for small group lessons. Research has consistently indicated that students who are pulled out of other classes for instrumental music study perform as well as those who remain in class—and often perform better.[4] The best scheduling system will vary from district to district, and possibly from school to school; however, some form of pull-out instrumental lessons during the school day is the only system known that produces quality results. Research has demonstrated this. Potentially, the most successful approach has been the rotating pull-out program, where students would only miss the same class every seven or eight weeks, depending on the number of instructional periods the school has in a day.[5]

In addition, the proper scheduling of the large ensembles is critical. At the elementary level, band, choir, and orchestra need to be scheduled on school time when the least interruption will result to other classes. Let me also add that as students mature into the secondary instrumental music program, there are two simple but important rules for the successful scheduling of large ensembles:

1. Schedule music first, along with any other classes that cross grade lines.

2. Do not schedule the music ensemble during the same period as a singleton. A singleton is any course offering that involves only one section.

As new methods of teaching and scheduling are studied, it must be understood that no methodology was ever intended to be permanent or inflexible. Changes and reforms in education should offer opportunities, not threats. As new, carefully researched commercial method books continue to appear and school reforms place renewed emphasis on teaching and learning practices, I can envision a future where this developed craft turns into a teaching art. Hopefully, accepted once and for all, it can remain a valid part of the educational program for all students in American schools.

When adequate scheduling is in place, the instrumental music teacher then has an obligation to produce a quality program. The reading and playing ability of the students must increase. Good time management practices must be utilized, and the levels of programming difficulty should reflect the skills and concepts the students have experienced in the lesson situation. If not, the teacher is then required to spend an inordinate amount of time in rote teaching the music—both in rehearsals and in lessons. I have no difficulty with the thought that carefully chosen performance materials can also constitute acceptable lesson material, but if the concert is produced as a largely rote learned effort, I have difficulty labeling it as "music education."

The rote performance, however impressive as a finished showpiece, cannot be considered a substitute for a carefully planned, carefully taught, carefully evaluated instructional course of study. The problem can become self-perpetuating: the following concert will need to be even more dependent on rote learning since the young musicians have been "taught that they can play acceptably without developing reading skills, and even those skills they already accumulated will begin to atrophy with lack of use. The students get caught in a downward, spiraling trap...with some parallels to a drug habit, and the instrumental music teacher, alas, is the pusher. I have observed situations where the great effort to produce prize-winning bands and/or orchestras has tended to not encourage the individual students to aspire to greater achievement as musicians. Good performing groups must result from the constant development of the musicianship of the student.

The Band Program

A tutor who tooted a flute
Tried to teach two young tooters to toot
Said the two to the tutor
Is it harder to toot, or
To tutor two tooters to toot?

—Anonymous

Concert Band:

Bands have been a powerful musical force in this country since the Revolutionary War. Most of the early bands were associated with a military purpose. The first official military band in the United States was the United States Marine Band, organized in 1798. The band movement accelerated as more and more military outposts had bands associated with them. The Civil War saw an explosion of bands, which were viewed as an important part of patriotic ceremonies in every town.

After the Civil War, with many instruments now available and musicians to play them, town bands began to grow in popularity. One must understand that there was no cultural infrastructure except in the largest cities on the East Coast. For many communities, the town band was the beginning of a cultural community. This led to the golden age of the town band, 1870–1930. I remember playing trumpet in the Liberty Band, a town band in Middletown, Pa., as late as 1947. I was the youngster in the group, but those guys could really play those Sousa Marches. We even marched in parades. In Williamsport, Pa., The Repaz Band was established in 1831, and is one of the oldest non-military town bands in continuous existence in the United States. The school district music program continues to affect the cultural base of this community by encouraging post high school participation in this band. The Repaz Band March remains a popular march today. In 1889, there were ten thousand adult and juvenile bands in the United States. There were town bands, circus bands, family bands, ethnic bands, industrial bands, and orphanage bands. Bands were all-American. Famous bands lead by John Philip Sousa and Patrick Gilmore criss-crossed the country performing concerts to standing room-only crowds. My first trumpet teacher during high school, George Reahm, was a retired member of the Sousa Band. He fed me a steady diet of Herbert L. Clarke solos. With the heavy use of bands in World War I, musicians returned ready to recruit young students into bands in the period of the 1920s. College bands began to appear during the final years of the nineteenth century.

An important factor leading to the promotion and expansion of the public school band movement was the band contest. The first national band contest was held in Chicago in 1923. Beginning in 1926 and continuing until 1940, a system of regional and national contests was organized. After World War II, band contests were organized by independent band "leagues," or state music education and/or interscholastic league organizations. The rise of professional organizations for every level of the band world began in earnest after World War II. They include:

- American Bandmasters Association (ABA), established in 1929. The primary objective of the ABA during the early years was working toward the standardization of instrumentation.
- National School Band Association (NSBA), 1926–1952. The NSBA was originally formed to organize the national band contests.
- Phi Beta Mu, 1939. Organized to recognize outstanding bandmasters.
- College Band Directors National Association (CBDNA), 1941. Formed by William D. Revelli, a primary objective of this association has been to encourage the composing of original works for band.
- National Band Association (NBA), 1960.
- American School Band Directors Association (ASBDA), 1953.
- State band and music education associations.

One important by-product of the American band movement was the role bands played after World War II in the stimulation of new wind music. The emphasis placed on new compositions by new, emerging composers energized the composition world of this country and really began to give American composition a distinct feel different from that of old masters and transcriptions played before. The American band movement gave voice to an entirely new generation of composers in this country.

Competition:

It is inevitable that a book on music education would address competition since it has become such an integral part of the music education profession. Competition abounds, for chairs; district, regional, and state band, orchestra, and choir competitions; solo competitions; small and large ensemble competitions; flags; winter drum lines; and marching band competitions. Some believe that competition is the behavioral equivalent of gravity, a natural and inevitable force, something akin to the "survival of the fittest" part of the genetic make-up of animal and human worlds. Some believe that as people vie for a prize, honor, advantage, space, position, sex, or whatever, excellence is rewarded, and in the process, the best people win and rise to the top while the less able lose and sink to the bottom. How often have you heard that this is the "American way," a kind of strange logic used to justify social inequity? It is doubtful that competition is going to go away. It is a force in American business, industry, education, sports, and even the arts.

Could it be that if competition is so "natural" among the human species so, too, is cooperation? In fact, just possibly cooperation is more critical to human progress than competition and a more valuable by-product of music participation. A musical ensemble composed of competitive individuals without teamwork and cooperation is, by definition, quite ineffective.

Parents instill competition in their children at a very young age. Some parents enter their children in beauty contests, baton twirling contests, and the like. The athletic team sports activities begin at this age and are pursued by the parents with vigor in the hopes that their child will hit the home run, make the touchdown or goal and, above all, be on the winning team that leads to a sports scholarship.

At the elementary level, there are spelling contests, selection of soloists or actors based on tryouts, ability grouping based on test performance and, of course, Little League and other athletic contests that reach a peak frenzy before team sports begin in middle school and high school. During the middle school/junior high school and senior high school years, youth are exposed to even more competition. At school there is grading on a curve, trying out for athletic teams, cheerleading, debate, acting roles, art exhibits with prizes, theater and music competitions, competing for valedictorian and acceptance into top colleges, etc.

Competition can have serious side effects, however. The pressure to compete and win has led many people to make unethical judgments to achieve at the highest levels, to win, for fame, to make more money. We see this in sports, in the American economy, in cheating on tests, and the list goes on.

Obviously, in a competitive society, coming in second is tantamount to losing. When winning becomes the only thing, the joy of participation is lost. If ten marching bands enter a competition and the average band size is 100, there are 1,000 students competing. If the winning band has 100 members, and being #1 is all-important to each group, then 900 students are losers. Directors need to carefully circumvent the #1 philosophy by concentrating on other goals, such as the attainment of a particular score, correct musical or marching executions, competing with themselves to place higher than the last competition, etc. This way the attainment of #1 becomes the icing on the cake rather than the cake itself. It must be the process that is the driving force, not the outcome. The question must be asked, "Did you get better?"—not "Did you win?" Those who learn to *aspire to excel* know how to teach for and ask the former question.

I am not naïve enough to think that we can eliminate competition in American society. I must admit, too, that I like competition. I thrive on it! I love team sports of all kinds. Golf, however, has taught me to compete with myself and has also taught me that my high handicap will still allow me to play and compete with the very best golfers. All I need to do is play my game, and if the other golfer has a bad day or does not play his/her normal game, I will win the match. In short, it is not the competition that bothers me. Rather, it is the problems inherent in the competition—the by-products—that bother me. Music education must not be a win-or-lose encounter.

Making music needs to be an enjoyable experience, not an athletic contest. The actual competitive world of music ensembles takes on many forms and shapes, and creates the potential for many trophies to be taken home and displayed amidst the athletic team trophies. Awards are possible for marching band, concert band, symphonic band, wind ensemble, wind symphony, and jazz band from various size schools. One has difficulty at times distinguishing between the many possible combinations of competitions. Select ensembles at times compete with non-select ensembles—and just when does a concert band become a wind ensemble, and what is the real difference between a symphonic band and a concert band? Other awards are available for various small ensembles, jazz band, guard units (rifles, flags, dance, etc), majorettes, best brass, best woodwinds, best percussion, best drum major, best soloist, and on and on ad infinitum. These competitions frequently emerge as a publicity event at an amusement or theme park, or some other entertainment spot during the spring of the year. Some high schools even revive their fall marching band show in an attempt to accumulate more trophies.

I personally prefer the adjudication concept with notable directors, often from the university level, as adjudicators. In this venue, the students are able to play the music for the sake of the music rather than for the purpose of winning a competition. I hope there is a difference. I hope the real reason we hold these "music in the park" competitions isn't just to fill up the amusement parks with high school students who spend money, therefore making the parks profitable!

"Winning gives birth to hostility,
Losing, one lies down in pain,
The calmed lie down with ease,
Having set losing and winning aside."

—Dhammapada, 15,
Translated by Thanissaro Bhikkhu

Strengths and Challenges:

The Gemeinhardt Company recently issued its *Gemeinhardt Report 4*[6] as part of its ongoing research project to provide program leadership support to U.S. music educators. The company found that the top program strengths, in the opinion of directors, band parents, band members, and music dealers, are brought about for the following reasons:

The program has:
- Dedicated directors
- Enthusiastic directors
- Directors who understand the blending of sound (ensemble development)
- Directors who teach the fundamentals of music thoroughly
- Exposure to quality music
- Directors communicating well with students in band
- Good classroom management
- High performance standards

Among the most important challenges band directors face in attempting to avoid program weaknesses are:
- Insufficient funding from the school
- Class schedules conflicting with band
- Inadequate practice facilities
- Students participating in sports conflicting with band

- Total program not committed to team teaching
- Other school activities conflicting with band
- Lack of encouragement from parents
- Low parental appreciation of the benefits of beginning band
- Parents not persuasive with school and community about band needs
- Lack of good participation in music by students following graduation
- Unable to raise sufficient funds from sources outside of school
- Beginning students have low appreciation of the benefits of band

Many of these strengths and challenges may also be applied to orchestra and choral programs. The concert ensemble is the basis of a good band, choir, or orchestra program. This concert ensemble is never better than its director. In the simplest terms, directors need to know where they are going, get up and go, and in the process take a little more than their share of the blame and a little less than their share of the credit. They make music happen, despite the odds.

Marching Band:

It is September! The marching band, football, band competitions, pomp, and pageantry all blend to create a wonderful time of the year. They bring back to me many memories of years gone by—memories of playing trumpet in my first halftime show when I was in fifth grade at the Highspire (PA) high school football game (it was a small school district and the band needed players); memories of being chosen drum major of the West Chester (PA) State University marching band—one hundred men and a drum major (certainly wouldn't happen today!); my years as a high school band director; and my year as a college band director (including marching band) replacing a sabbatical leave.

Historically, the marching band began as a collegiate support group shortly after intercollegiate football began in American colleges. It was only natural that marching bands would follow when high schools began playing football in the 1920s. When college marching bands began doing field shows during the halftime of football games, it was again only natural that high school bands would begin to emulate their college counterparts. Band and music education became parallel with interscholastic athletics because to the fans, and eventually "the person on the street," marching band *was* music education rather than one segment of a comprehensive program. In their naiveté, band directors thought they were creating a new audience in support of their music education program. In reality, band directors were allying themselves forever with competitive athletics and creating the nemesis they fight today.

Our "curricular art form" became a team sport. So here we stand with the basic premise that music is a curricular subject (sometimes extracurricular and sometimes co-curricular) but deeply allied with the athletic complex in American education. How do we *really* explain this to the masses? I truly believe the American marching band is an original American art form that needs to be celebrated. *I'm serious about this!* The purpose of this art form is for entertainment, and as it matures with the quality of music performed, it will have every reason to be considered educational if there is a balance between the teaching process, the literature performed, and the aspect of competition. Certainly, in my opinion, a good marching band is nothing more than a fine concert band on the football field. Why do they need to compete?

My personal middle-of-the-road philosophy regarding marching band, and eventually band competitions, will indeed catch up with me at some time. On the one hand, I find myself defending and even advocating marching band activities and competitions, and on the other hand, it seems I am constantly criticizing them. The truth is I love marching band and the competitions that drive the sport. Wait—that is it!! Marching band is a team sport, and since I love team sports and I also love music, therefore I love marching band. WOW! I finally have it all figured out. As long as I think of marching band in this context, I am comfortable. Even when the marching band is a non-competitive group at football games, it still attempts to be better than (beat) the band of the opposing school.

When I attempt to justify marching band as a curricular subject, I have difficulty. Obviously, it is not a black-and-white issue, but let's face it, it is here to stay. So let's enjoy this original American art form. I have published two "tongue-in-cheek" articles about marching band (see Appendices G and H). These articles have enjoyed more reprints than any articles I have published. May you enjoy the intended humor, and may my true love and understanding of the marching band become apparent.

This leads to an all-too-brief discussion of whether or not students should be given the option of playing only in concert band and not marching band, playing only in marching band and not concert band, or both. Beyond the exception of fall athletics, I fear that the quality of the total band program would be in jeopardy if options were given to students. Therefore, I continue to embrace the thought that a band is a band, and sometimes it presents concert literature and other times it marches. I know this is a controversial subject that is multilateral and invites much debate. However, my thoughts are centered on the following:

- Bands have historically marched and they have performed in concert. Even the John Philip Sousa band did these two things, and the members where not afforded the privilege of deciding whether they would only play when sitting

213

down, or only play when marching, or both.

- When students are provided these options, fragmentation of the basic ensemble occurs. If a marching band is a live concert band on the field, it is difficult to achieve this when the ensemble has no consistency. A serious fragmentation of the basic ensemble occurs. This seriously jeopardizes the director's control of the functioning of the group. Unless there is a physical problem, students in courses are not provided the option to decide in which parts of the course they will or will not participate. For example, students in mathematics are not afforded the opportunity to decide whether they will learn addition skills, or only subtraction skills, or both.

- When this group fragmentation occurs, a lack of cohesiveness within the group develops because the director is basically working with three groups: those who march and play, those who only sit and play, and those who do both. This makes the development of ensemble that much more difficult. Also, it is in this environment that "prima dona's" emerge, thus further negating the cohesiveness.

- These three fragmented groups within a group create a scheduling nightmare. What would happen to the students who only play on the concert stage when the other students are marching, or vice versa? Obviously, additional staff would be necessary to be assigned to take change of whatever group is not rehearsing on a given day.

- As indicated earlier in this chapter, the band staff must work very hard, beginning in the elementary school, to develop a balance of instrumentation within the groups so the high school is assured of balanced instrumentation when the students get there. To provide students the three options in question (to march, not march, or both) would greatly hamper these efforts to develop proper instrumentation balance in any of the groups. Marching band, then, could possibly be the first ever curricular team sport. The complications seem endless. Obviously, each school district will have to find its answers; however, whether or not they compete, the playing part of marching band must be curricular when quality music is performed.

While focused on controversy, some attention must be given to those students who are made fun of or discriminated against because of their involvement in band. What a tragedy! As stated earlier in this chapter, the band has had a history in its own quest for recognition and not only as a support group for athletic teams. This is a difficult tradition to balance, however; the hours spent in support of athletic teams (only to be made fun of by athletes, coaches, and fans) has brought about the mentality that if you cannot play sports you can always play in the band. Any group suffering discrimination will, in this age, rise up and insist upon the recognition it deserves. Certainly, we do not need to embrace this or even foster it; however, we do need to recognize that it exists and understand the reason. I am hopeful this will diminish in time.

The Jazz Program:

Jazz is also an original American art form, which has every right to be an integral part of the music program of every school district. Participation in jazz contributes to Content Standard #3 of the National Standards: Improvise melodies, variations, and accompaniments. All too often, however, the jazz program involves only the brasses, woodwinds, and percussion. Certainly vocalists deserve to have equal opportunity to perform and improvise in the jazz idiom, and string players should also have the right to experience the studio orchestra concept.

Scheduling the jazz program is not easy because to schedule it during the school day interferes with large ensemble scheduling. Also, the practice of scheduling jazz groups during the school day has a tendency to prohibit instrumentalists from participating in choral groups and singers participating in instrumental groups. A third disadvantage is preventing brass, woodwind, and percussion players from having time to also perform in orchestra. Thus, it would seem advisable to schedule jazz ensembles as an after-school, extracurricular activity. I know this is not necessarily going to be a popular recommendation in the minds of jazz-oriented instructors; however, there are only so many hours in a school day.

The jazz musician must be musical, creative, and have passion for the art form, and thus, he/she will go the extra mile to attend after-school rehearsals. I would caution that it is important for the jazz program to flow from the large ensemble, with the exception of piano and guitar. The musical "jazzer" is quite needed in the large ensemble, and jazz should not replace the classical endeavor. Rather, it should enhance it. J. Richard Dunscomb and Dr. Willie Hill, at the 2002 MENC National Conference in Nashville, Tennessee, articulated a "Director's Checklist for Building Your Jazz Program." I think it worth including here:

- Evaluate your strengths and weaknesses for teaching jazz. This should be ongoing as you continue to grow. Begin with one group and concentrate on quality, not quantity. Rehearse in a square seating arrangement, and perform in normal concert seating.
- Do not be intimidated by jazz—jump on board and learn!
- Create jazz listening as a priority for yourself and your students.
- Encourage your students to buy selected CDs.

- Create a three-year set of goals. Follow them and adjust them as necessary. Create a secure base to build upon.

Bottom line, jazz is here to stay and should be a part of any comprehensive music education program.

The Orchestra (Strings) Program

String education as we know it today had its roots in England in 1898. At that time, there were considerable differences in approach concerning the teaching of string instruments in classes. The conservatory system had small classes where the students played individually. The public school instrumental classes were larger, perhaps sixteen or even as many as thirty, where the students played together. The conservatories used method books most often from their European counterparts, while the public school classes used books especially prepared for the public schools, in addition to some conservatory methods. Public school class instruction became a mainstay of string teaching.

The event in England in 1898 that was destined to help change the course of string education was brought about by the Murdock Company, dealers in musical instruments. They began violin classes in the All Saints School at Maidstone, England, as an experiment in developing a love for orchestral music. The Murdock Company of London supplied instruments, music equipment, the organization, and the teachers. The classes were held under the supervision of the school, and payments were arranged in small weekly amounts so the poorer children could afford lessons. During the first few years of its existence, almost a half million violins were sold by the Murdock Company in some five thousand schools. Massed performances were presented periodically to provide an outlet for the students, to promote the program and, presumably, to stimulate additional business for the Murdock Company.

Albert Mitchell, Paul Stoeving, and Charles Farnsworth observed this system prior to World War I and carried it to the United States. All three wrote, taught, and lectured on the technique they observed in England, and thus began the class instrumental instruction in the United States as we know it today. In 1913, Boston became the first city in the United States to introduce string class teaching into the public schools during the school day.[7] In 1918, Albert Mitchell published a violin method for use with his classes.[8] Also, in 1914, Paul Stoeving reported his ideas and opinions to the Music Teachers National Association (MTNA) at their convention in Pittsburgh. His writings concerning the efficacy and procedures to be used for teaching stringed instruments in class are still as pertinent today as when they were written.[9] They are still carried on and promoted by the American String Teachers Association (ASTA) and the National School Orchestra Association (NSOA). After World War I, school orchestras blossomed across the country.

I have had great concern for many years about an endangered species in our profession: string programs, be it public school or university. Frightening statistics emerge when one analyzes the number of string programs in the public schools of the United States in comparison to the number of choral and band programs. Naturally, this cannot help but affect college and university programs that continually work to recruit string players from throughout this country.

Various studies show that the larger the school or school district, the stronger the chances that the school or district has a string program. The smaller school districts are more inclined to concentrate on choir and band, and ignore the thought of a string program. It also becomes apparent in the smaller school districts that although they may offer string instruction at the elementary level, few of them offer orchestra at the middle school level, and even fewer at the high school level. The program size just seems to diminish the higher the grade level. I continually ask the question, "Have string programs that support Western European art music traditions diminished over time as the cultural diversity of our communities has grown?[10]

It is my conviction that talented, energetic, and well-trained teachers hold the leadership key to nurturing and building our nation's string programs. Certainly a major component of the building of these string programs is the existence of universities and schools of music with strong commitments to the training and nurturing of string teachers. Public schools and universities must form partnerships to train qualified string teachers and provide these prospective teachers with the proper education they need to be effective. University professionals must understand their role in this relationship and the need to remain committed to foster the training of competent string teachers as well as fine performers. We must be certain that we do not merely pay lip service to the idea of educating quality string teachers, for far too few universities have faculty string education specialists. Also, all too few offer the necessary courses to prepare students adequately for teaching as well as offering scholarships for students majoring in string education. The scholarships are mainly designed to attract those planning to major in performance or those who have outstanding performance abilities. There appears to be more interest in developing the university orchestras than in educating potential string teachers. The shortage is, indeed, acute. Experts in string education have long recognized those problems, but the scene remains constant.

There is, however, some hope. The emergence of the Suzuki concept throughout the United States has injected new life into string education and interest in string performance. String enrollments in many areas are increasing, especially in suburbs, university communities, and areas with high concentrations of Asian Americans. Technology, fiddling, jazz improvisation, mariachi, strolling strings, and other ensembles culturally relevant to a local constituency have emerged throughout the United States, stimulating new interest in the value of string education in the schools. However, the zealous allegiance to band and choir as the primary form of performance-based music education has excluded all too many students from discovering the treasures of string playing and the orchestral experience. As band directors and choral directors go about their day-to-day pursuits, the survival of the fittest becomes the rule. Precious little time remains to "save our strings." This has served as a challenge to all of music education, coalition groups, and concerned citizens who are attempting to save music education from devastating exclusion in current educational thought. Indeed, what good is it to win the battle to "save our strings" if we lose the battle to save music education?

Some universities have initiated string projects that provide hands-on teaching experience that undergraduates receive during all of their college years. The American String Teachers Association and the National School Orchestra Association have collaborated in a university string teacher education project to stimulate the number of new string teachers in this country, currently facing a serious shortfall. By the time they graduate, they have had four or five years of practical training and experience in many of the activities of a professional teacher, from recruiting to lesson planning, from teaching private and group lessons to coaching chamber music and conducting orchestras. We have long known that a good performer is not necessarily a good teacher, but we seem to fail to convince our performance-based colleagues that we need to train string teachers who have the expertise necessary to teach children and rebuild public school string programs.

Suffice to say, as we continue in our quest to make music education an essential part of a total education, we must also be certain to include string music education as an integral part of music education, both in process and product. Our profession must not contribute further to the deprivation of string programs in the United States, for they are already an endangered species.

Strolling Strings:

The strolling strings movement, modeled after the United States Air Force Strolling Strings, has become more and more popular throughout the United States. The "strollers" have, for the first time, given string educators the opportunity to compete with the "marchers" of the marching band. There we go with competition again! High school orchestras no longer need to sell hoagies, candy, or magazines to raise money for the spring trip. They earn it by "strolling." The music ranges from classical to semi-classical to current pop and country tunes. The stereophonic sound provided by string players throughout the dining area never cease to bring audiences to their feet. The joy of the recipient is quickly apparent when one of the male "strollers" kneels on one knee and plays especially for one of the pretty ladies in the audience.

Even at the university level, the strolling strings have had a tremendous impact on fundraising. Although some have grumbled that the strolling strings are far too commercial for a good university orchestra program, the outcome is overwhelmingly positive. First, it is good for the students who are classically trained to also have a commercial outlet and to have an opportunity to earn money for themselves and/or their ensembles. A good violinist is always in demand as a strolling violinist. Secondly, it provides positive exposure for the orchestra program of the school district or the university. Actually, due to the popularity of the groups, many times directors must turn down more requests than they take because of the time factor. One disgruntled music professor lamented after a dinner that featured chamber music followed by strolling strings, "Everyone chatted at dinner over the chamber music, but no one uttered a word when the strolling strings entered...no one even moved. This is but one example of the lack of culture in the United States today." By the way, the audience was a group of university music school administrators at their annual conference. On the other hand, Dr. William Tucker, then Chancellor of Texas Christian University stated, " I like to showcase some of the fine performers of TCU, and the Strolling Strings knock people over every time. They are my greatest fundraisers."

Strolling Strings are here to stay!

Notes and Rests

- In lessons, teacher modeling matters, especially in the beginning and ending phases of the learning of a piece. If you cannot demonstrate on that particular instrument yourself, use a CD to demonstrate correct tone quality, articulation, etc. Also remember that there is a difference between demonstrating and "playing along."

- For the grading of lessons at the elementary level, consider:
  ☺ –Has Mastered
  😐 –Working On It
  ☹ –Not Yet

- Curriculum is an ongoing process year after year, not a seasonal encounter. It must begin in the elementary school and build, year after year. Any periodic interference with this development severely impairs, if not totally destroys, the intent and the worth of the curriculum.

- There is a difference between three people sitting in a class lesson each receiving a private lesson, and three people receiving a group lesson. In the first situation, two people are always sitting passively while one person plays.

- School districts need to adopt a uniform instrumental music series throughout the school district so instruction is cohesive.

- Establish uniform sticking for percussionists.

- It has become a common practice for school districts to provide two instruments (one for home and one for school, commonly referred to as twofers) to students who play large instruments (euphonium, tuba, and string bass). School bus drivers are reluctant to transport these larger instruments. The students with only one instrument must be able to take it onto the school bus themselves.

- When possible, have students stand for their lessons for purposes of breath control and posture.

- In rehearsal, do not spend an inordinate amount of time "getting ready to get ready." Eliminate the beginning clutter; this is the time when your students are most alert, so rehearse.

- The pacing of your rehearsal must be steady, not necessarily fast.

- Rarely give group approval because there is usually some who are not doing it accurately.

- Plan the first beginner concert right before the first rental agreement runs out. Plan a middle school "in progress" concert in January right before the eighth grade students begin to establish their high school schedule for the following year. Encourage the parents to come back in May to hear the finished product.

- Think about the possibility of providing a second ensemble, particularly at the high school level, for students who merely want to make music without the desire to necessarily excel on the instrument. These students also need to be encouraged to participate.

- In rehearsal, don't just identify problems. Show solutions.

- Know the score well, study the music, and predict problems.

- It is not the director's job to teach the notes; the students learn the notes. The director makes music out of the notes.

- A group is never better than its director. Rather, it is reflective of the ability of the director.

- The director needs to teach, not preach.

- Uniform bowing in orchestral ensembles is a must. When possible, the concertmaster will establish the bowing.

- Middle school bands should rarely march, except for pedagogical reasons (i.e., teaching students to march and play at the same time). This can frequently occur in the spring, following the final concert of the year.

- Music must be polished after it is learned.

- Homophonic warm-ups are the best (Bach Chorales, for example). Why not have the group also sing their parts? Even though hearing a tone and producing a tone are two different things, singing parts develops better intonation through ear training.

- Foot tapping is a "no-no" in rehearsal and in concert.

- When asking an ensemble to repeat a section, there must be a reason—not just a "play it again" from the director.

- Do not over-program. Choose music according to the ability level of the students.

- Allow no more than two students to a stand.

- Tape record ensemble rehearsals as much as possible for self-evaluation and program cognition.

- All too often directors spend more time than necessary on matters that are not right with the student or the ensemble, such as discipline, lack of practice, forgetting music, etc. Think about a merit/demerit approach, where students and ensembles are credited just as much for what they do correctly as what they do wrong.

- If students cannot play the music slowly, they cannot play it, whether in a lesson or an ensemble.

- At the high school level, schedule orchestra and band during the same period so selected woodwind, brass, and percussion players from band may rehearse with the orchestra occasionally.

- At the middle school and high school levels, never schedule a class that crosses grade lines against a singleton (a class with only one section). Schedule music groups that cross grade lines first.

- Parents' organizations are important for band, choir, and orchestra. Some have one group called music parents. I prefer separate organizations because the groups do not generally need equal funding; however, the one group concept has worked well in many school districts. In short, if it is working, it does not need to be fixed or changed. The director, however, must always be in charge and let the parents know that their main functions are to chaperone and to raise funds.

- Parent groups should not be asked to raise funds for equipment, uniforms, or music. These are the responsibility of the school district (unless, of course, the parents of athletes raise money for athletic team uniforms). Parent funding should be above and beyond those items that a school district budget would generally absorb.

- The most effective way to convince the administration to hire more staff is to establish the need.

- Directors must not be in competition with one another.

- Director modesty is a disservice to a program. A director who is boastful and arrogant is also a disservice to a program. There must be a happy medium.

- Expectations are sometimes the most difficult thing to communicate. There needs to be the option to reach beyond the goals. Directors can bring this about.

- Never put students in the middle between two teachers.

- Attend other departmental performances in addition to your own. Make it a goal to attend one concert of every K–12 music colleague in your school district during a certain period of time. Naturally, the time period will vary based on the size of the school district and the number of music colleagues.

- Consider having the school board support one music dealer by board action after all interested dealers have submitted bids on rental plans and repair policies to the music faculty. The music faculty then recommends to the school board the bid that best meets the needs of the program and the pocketbook of the parents. It must be made clear, however, that parents are free to use whichever dealer they prefer.

- Auditoriums are rarely good rehearsal rooms. Hopefully they are good performance areas when people are assembled in the audience, for then the acoustics change.

- What if all teachers needed to recruit students in order to have students in their classrooms?

One vexing problem remains as we look forward to a curricular future for performing music that is based on musical values and results and is accepted on its own merits as an essential part of education. John Goodlad, many years ago, perhaps stated it best when he said:

...to those school board members, and others who often sound as though they would deprive children of access in school to performing music in order to assure attention to reading, writing, spelling, and mathematics, let me say simply that the sacrifice is unnecessary. It will just be necessary for the principal and teachers of some schools—perhaps most—to become more efficient in the allocation and use of time.[11]

Instrumental music education plays a significant and defining part of the complex of music education found in America. The performance of instrumental music adds to cognitive learning in the same way as the study of philosophy or religion or psychology. As instrumental music educators face a tough national climate—in school reform and restructuring, competition, changing student and family values—leadership will be required to transition this vitally important asset of our communities into the coming decades. Those who *aspire to excel* in instrumental music will be rewarded if they can keep their eye on the prize: the balance between performance, comprehensive music learning, and competition. From time to time, all of these subjects influence the economic body and practical affairs of communities and nations. Indeed, they are all important only if the soul of man is important!

---

1 Froseth, James O. *NABIM Recruiting Manual*. Chicago: GIA Publications, Inc.,1974.

2 "Musical Aptitude and Student Achievement of Beginning Instrumental Music Students: Results of the Second-Year Study," A study by J. Richard Holsomback, Jr. Longview, TX, 2002.

3 Curriculum rubric developed by Albert Nacinovich, then Coordinator of Instrumental Music, and the band and orchestra faculty of the Williamsport (PA) Area School District.

4 Schuler, Scott C. *Effects of Instrumental Pullouts and Other Arts Opportunities on Students' General Achievement*. Hartford, CT: State of Connecticut, Department of Education, 1991.

5 Schuler, Scott C. *Scheduling Alternatives for Instrumental Music Lessons*. Hartford, CT: State of Connecticut, Department of Education, 1991.

6 Brown, Joseph D. *Opportunities and Solutions for U.S. Instrumental Programs*. Elkhart, IN: Gemeinhardt Corporation, 1994, pp. 4–5.

7 Keene. *A History of Music Education in the United States*. pp. 281–282.

8 Mitchell, Albert. *The Class Method for the Violin*. Boston: Oliver Ditson Co., 1918.

9 Keene. *A History of Music Education in the United States*. p. 282.

10 Goodlad, John. *A Place Called School*. New York: McGraw Hill Book Co., 1984, pp. 134–136.

11 Ibid

Chapter 11

Choral Music Education

The woods would be very silent
if no birds sang there except
those that sing the best.

—Henry David Thoreau

During the twentieth century, choral music education in the schools of the United States has grown from modest beginnings to an important curricular program. Many statements in Chapter 10 (Instrumental Music Education) also apply to choral music education, especially the assumptions on pages 192–193. The review of those assumptions that apply to the choral area follow:

- Every school district has a choral program that is treated as a curricular offering.
- The large ensembles are treated as a curricular subject, and the smaller ensembles represent extracurricular offerings of the music program.
- Choral instruction begins no later than grade 5.
- Choral ensembles are offered during the school day and are scheduled so all members of each ensemble meet as a unit throughout the school year. At the elementary level, the choral groups meet at least one time per week for an

equivalent of one hour; at the middle school level, the groups meet at least three times per week during the school day; and at the senior high school level the groups meet every day and are elected by the students as a part of their curricular schedule.

- In the middle and senior high schools not utilizing block scheduling, the school day includes no fewer than eight instructional periods.

- There is a place for all students who wish to sing, and there must also be a select/auditioned group for the purpose of choral music program development.

- All interested elementary students are admitted to the choral program after they have learned to match pitch.

These assumptions form the basis for a successful sequentially developed choral program.

History of Choral Music Education

Singing was the initial activity in music education in the United States. As stated in Chapter 3, the colonial singing schools and Lowell Mason established vocal music classes in the Boston public schools. F. Melius Christianson established the *a cappella* tradition at St. Olaf College in Northfield, Minnesota. Actually Peter Lutkin is credited with establishing the first *a cappella* choir in 1892 at Northwestern University. However, it was the touring program of the St. Olaf Choir and the resultant national acclaim received that moved collegiate, high school, and church choirs around the country in the direction of *a cappella* singing. This influence has continued through the years. Presently, the *New York Times* in an article dated April 25, 2002, stated, "From the Ivy League to Berkeley, groups are multiplying, even on campuses that have football teams and fraternities. Some institutions, like Yale, Cornell, and the Universities of Pennsylvania and Michigan, now have a dozen or more *a cappella* groups each, including graduate and professional school groups like the Harvard Law School's Scales of Justice (Motto: "Because justice is blind, not deaf"), the Yale Law School's Habeas Chorus, and the Ambassachords from the Fletcher School of Diplomacy at Tufts."

The uniqueness of the St. Olaf concept included singers memorizing their music in sectional rehearsals, as no copies were permitted in full rehearsals or performances. A few members of the choir had pitch pipes, and at their performances, between pieces and during applause, the pitch of the next number was quietly passed around the choir. At the end of each year, all singers in the choir resigned to be auditioned at the beginning of the following year. Many factors were considered in the audition, from vocal overtones to personality. A carefully designed straightness of tone without vibrato in all vocal registers was considered important. Christianson's ideal of a straight tone excited a controversy that claimed the attention of all choir directors, to which no director could remain neutral. Opponents of the straight tone called Christiansen's ideal "flat and colorless." High schools around the country also began to assimilate *a cappella* techniques, and by the middle of the 1930s, the tradition had reached its peak of popularity.[1]

In the late 1930s, Robert Shaw assessed:

When I was in college in Pamona in Southern California, there were four major and influential choral traditions. There was the Christiansen–Lutheran–St. Olaf tradition, which brought a vibratoless pseudo-Gregorian tone to a pseudosacred literature located somewhere between folk song and "The Rosary." There was also the Williamson–

Westminster–Wasp tradition, which brought a convulsive operatic vocalism to every piece of music it touched, from folk songs to Bach cantatas. There were leisurely, lively, good humored, and all-but-improvised folk and student songs of Marshal Bartholomew and the Yale singing group. And there was the tradition planted—so far as I know—only by Archibald T. Davison and nourished (at that time) by G. Wallace Woodworth, the focus of which was the extraordinary polyphonic literature of the Medieval, Renaissance, and early Baroque periods transcribed for male voices and sung for purposes totally other than credit, recruitment, profit, or prizes.[2]

The Westminster Choir, under the direction of John Findley Williamson, was not as influential as the St. Olaf group; however, a weekly radio broadcast from 1932 to 1934 did provide national notice. Other than this, the principal focus of the choir was in the direction of church music. Most of the Westminster Choir College students went into church music. The college, now part of Rider University, did not add a music education program until 1961.

In the 1940s, the mainstream of American choral music made a dramatic change. The choral philosophy and techniques of Robert Shaw attracted national attention. Fred Waring hired Mr. Shaw in 1938 to conduct the Fred Waring Glee Club. Waring's career had begun in Tyrone, Pennsylvania, around 1916, when Fred, his brother Tom, and two high school cronies formed a combo called "Waring's Banjazzatra" to play at local dances and parties. Although Fred Waring began what he called his "tone-syllable technique" of enunciation, some attribute the tone syllables to Robert Shaw. Shaw did spell out the words to the pieces for his Collegiate Chorale in "tone syllable" fashion:

"bray-ee kfo-uh tho-oo bee-oo-tee-uh sev- n-lil lah-eet, an duh-shuh rin thuhm mo-uhm-neeng." bah bshaw.[3]
(Break forth oh beauteous heavenly light, and usher in the morning. Bob Shaw)

In 1945, Shaw left the Waring organization to develop his own ensemble, and it was his work with the Collegiate Chorale and The Robert Shaw Chorale over the next two decades that best exemplifies his approach to choral music.

In the meantime, Fred Waring extended the Pennsylvanians' operations into the educational field and became known as the "man who taught America how to sing." He established a publishing company, Words and Music, Inc. (which later became Shawnee Press, Inc), to meet the demand for the choral arrangements made famous by Fred Waring and the Pennsylvanians. The rest of both Shaw and Waring is now, of course, famed choral history.

Like orchestras and bands, the choral movement in American schools followed and modeled those college, university, and professional organizations. Even though virtually every church had a choir, the high school choir movement did not grow all that quickly until the 1930s, and then exploded in the 1950s after World War II. The reasons were evident in many ways. The high visibility of the Waring groups, the rise of the American Broadway musical, increasing fame of college choral organizations and, by then, emerging generations of children who had had the benefit of choral music in elementary school. The founding of the American Choral Directors Association (ACDA) in 1959 has also influenced the mainstream of American choral music. ACDA includes over 15,000 members and provides an important state, regional, and national forum for the discussion of choral music concerns. The organization has assumed an important role as the foremost advocate of choral music in the United States.

Choral Program Leadership

Choral music educators at all levels, like all effective music educators, must be competent leaders. In addition to their teaching and musicianship skills, the effective music educator—and certainly choral music educator—must be knowledgeable about public relations, student recruitment, budgeting, fund-raising, scheduling, music and equipment maintenance, apparel selection, purchase and maintenance for the various ensembles, and numerous other administrative tasks. The complexities of a sequential choral program that includes elementary school, middle/junior high school, and senior high school are great. Important aspects of a successful program include, but are not limited to the following:

- The program must include leadership to attain overall program coordination from grade 5 to grade 12. There must also be communication at the horizontal level from school to school, and at the elementary, middle/junior high school, and senior high school levels where there is more than one school at a given level.
- The entire choral staff must meet and plan together on a regular basis...at least monthly.
- The choral music program, just like band and orchestra, must establish an image of excellence. The program must not appear less important and less successful than the band or orchestra program. The program must not acquire an inferiority complex. Remember that God provides a free instrument to singers. Parents will appreciate this.
- An overall sequential curriculum needs to be developed from elementary through senior high school, which includes common warm-ups, literature selections representing a variety of styles, composers, periods, foreign languages, and common pronunciation guides. This

curriculum must be a smooth and continuing process rather than a leap into the unknown at each level.

- Curricular decisions should be made through a collaborative effort, resulting in a curriculum that draws on the full resources of the choral faculty of the school district.

- The choral faculty needs to remain cohesive, non-competitive, and collegial.

- An emphasis must be placed upon the retention of young male singers as they proceed through the awkward voice change.

- The high school program should include small choral ensembles meeting after school on a regular basis as an extracurricular encounter. Groups such as Show Choir, Vocal Jazz, Madrigal Ensembles, Barbershop, and Male and Female Choir's are but examples of what might be included in the extracurricular offerings.

Organizational Hints

Some helpful organizational hints designed to enhance the success of this comprehensive choral program follow:

- Organize an up-to-date, single copy file for all choral music stored in the central location described in Chapter 6. This file should contain information on the number of copies available (revised after each use), a performance record of when the music was performed, and perhaps a comment sheet. This helps to eliminate duplication, maintain an accurate accounting of all music, save teacher time when searching through the library, and assist in program planning.

- Establish a Choral Cumulative File, which includes information on every student and their graduation date (Class of "date"). These files are then passed on from elementary school to middle/junior high school to senior high school. This enhances the student flow throughout the district. Include information on the file such as dates of entry into the program (and exit and/or re-entry, if appropriate), attitude, basic ability, reliability, etc.

- Proper scheduling is essential for the health of the program. Scheduling needs are as follows:

  a. Revisit the scheduling recommendation in Chapter 10.

  b. The seven- or eight-period school day remains essential.

  c. Attempt to schedule a select ensemble during first period; however, do not schedule both a select instrumental ensemble and a select choral ensemble during the same period. This prohibits singers from also performing in an instrumental ensemble. The advantage of first period is that it will allow the scheduling of meetings or rehearsals from time to time before school. Also consider offering to take the ensemble as a homeroom, thus giving one even more access to the students. Then rehearsals can run directly into the regular rehearsal period. Also, both teacher and students are generally more alert at this time.

  d. The last period in the day also provides the opportunity to occasionally extend the rehearsal; however, there are many more conflicts after school than before school, and

this is probably the time of day when the fresh-
ness of morning is long since gone.

e. Lunchtime is probably the least desirable time
for a choral rehearsal because hunger sets in
before lunch and lethargy sets in after lunch.

f. However, good choirs have evolved out of
rehearsals occurring during any period of the
day. It is the choral director who makes the
difference.

- Revisit the "Performing Group Participation Guidelines,"
Appendix C. These guidelines include both choral and
instrumental music.

- Recruitment is a critical issue in choral music—not just
the recruitment of bodies but also an appropriate female
and male balance. Also, the development of pride,
tradition, and the quest for excellence referred to in
previous chapters is an essential element in successful
recruiting.

- Finding the fine line between successful student
interaction, humor, and socialization issues and commanding the respect and admiration of the students is not an
easy task. It varies from situation to situation and teacher
to teacher. It is an essential quest, however, in which every
successful choral director needs to find success.

Choral Program Organization

The basic principles of a sequentially developed choral music
education program are the same from level to level; however, each
level has its own unique differences that need to be considered.

At the elementary level, there must be a place for all students who wish to sing. Elementary classroom music should provide this, and one of the main goals of this experience must be to teach students to match pitch. In grade 4, it might be worthwhile to establish a non-select chorus so students have the opportunity to assess the experience and the choral director has an opportunity to assess the desire, attention span, musicality, and social skills of the students. However, in grade 5, when the true "choral" experience begins, a prerequisite for membership must be tone matching ability and the meeting of teacher expectations for behavior and musicianship. Otherwise, the experience would be that of group singing, and general music class provides that.

I am aware that many principals do not want chorus to be selective; however, one cannot begin part work when every student does not match pitch in the first place. Prior to fifth grade, it has been the duty of the music teacher to develop the child's singing voice so that he/she can produce a healthy, in tune, and musical tone. When the choral experience begins, it becomes the choral director's obligation to model, in body and voice, what a singer looks like, sounds like, and rehearses like. This sequence of instruction will provide not only a chorus that sings well but also growth in musicianship. Repertoire must be chosen that is proper for the voices, the age, and the rehearsal schedule.

The middle/junior high school poses an entirely new set of considerations. The effects of a successful elementary music program can be quickly negated when the middle/junior high school program does not retain the students who began in the program. As stated in Chapter 8, middle/junior high school students are highly enthusiastic and motivated; thus, the key is to channel the energy and direct their motivation toward positive ends. If these individuals become lost to the program at this age, there is a strong chance they will never return.

The major concern at this age is the voice change of both males and females as they move from childhood through adolescence to adulthood. The more obvious change occurs in the boys as they lose the treble quality of the unchanged male voice and make the transition to the mature male sound. This makes the selection of appropriate music with a limited tessitura particularly challenging but acute. In the pre-voice change, the boys should sing alto for a period of time in mixed groups since they must learn to sing parts when their voices change. Throughout middle school, boys should have opportunities to sing alone without the girls...and in parts! SATB is possible, but at least aim for SAB. The female voice change is far subtler than the male voice. The main symptoms are pitch insecurity, breathiness or huskiness of tone, change in speaking voice, change in range capabilities, and the development of register breaks.[4] There are many theories with regard to the male changing voices. The men whose thinking greatly influenced American thought regarding the male changing voice during the twentieth century were Frederick Swanson, Duncan McKenzie, and Irvin Cooper.[5] For a full explanation of each theory, consult the writings of each man.

Suffice to say, choral directors at the middle school/junior high school level must possess all of the qualities of any fine choral music educator, but even more, they must possess tremendous enthusiasm for and love of this age group. The senior high school choral program is the most complex and time consuming of all levels. This level requires dedication and devotion beyond the norm.

Every choral program should include smaller elective ensembles that meet after school and flow directly out of the primary, curricular choral ensemble. Students who wish to participate in the specialized ensembles should be required to participate in the primary ensemble before they are allowed to audition for one of the specialized groups. In this way, the primary ensemble(s) retain the correct educational priority and emphasis. Types of ensembles vary from school to school, community to community, as well as by ethnic concerns and interest. Examples follow:

- Show Choir – This is probably the most popular of all extracurricular choral ensembles. The combination of music and movement is very attractive to both students and audiences; however, it is important that the group not receive undue emphasis. I raise some cautions about show choir because it has the same tendency to overwhelm a comprehensive education in choral music that marching band has for instrumental music. John Hylton, in his book *Comprehensive Choral Music Education*, gives some basic suggestions for the development of the show choir. I paraphrase them here:

  1. Be sure to create a choir that is choreographed rather than a group of dancers who also try to sing.
  2. Unless you have strong talent in the area of choreography, engage the services of someone to design and teach movement. The movement must enhance the music rather than the other way around.
  3. Costumes for the show choir should be dramatic, showy, and comfortable.
  4. Smaller is better. The larger the group, the harder it is to choreograph. Twelve to sixteen students are ideal.
  5. The better the quality of the sound system, the better the ensemble will sound (assuming they sound good when not amplified).

6. A good show choir can be in great demand. Keep the goals and objectives of the total choral music curriculum in mind, and do not over-schedule the show choir.[6]

- Vocal Jazz – Vocal jazz, a very distinct ensemble different from show choir, requires not only strong musicians but also creative musicians. Many of the elements of jazz such as improvisation, spontaneity, creativity, and what is not on the page are often lost in stock arrangements. Of course, how many choral directors have never been involved in vocal jazz? Quite a few! Unfortunately, jazz in the public schools all too often constitutes a totally instrumental involvement. The choral music education program must include jazz as a part of the program. The vocal jazz direc-tor must stress listening to jazz, teach improvisation (espe-cially skat singing), liberate the students from being a slave to the page, and be willing to listen to his/her own musical instincts. Instincts lead to passion; passion leads to per-formance, believability, and attitude. Vocal jazz often attracts a different type of student than the show choir, and it is important to reinforce the creative pursuits of these students as they learn to skat and celebrate the jazz idiom and ideals through vocal performance.

- Madrigals – Madrigal ensembles and madrigal feasts have achieved great popularity in recent years. This vocal chamber music ensemble is just another way to build student musicianship. It, however, will not enjoy the same type of student popularity as the show choir or vocal jazz, should it be offered. Again, this group should be available to students as a supplement to their primary choral experience. The classically trained choral director should have no difficulty feeling qualified and capable of conducting this group.

- Barbershop – This specialized vocal ensemble requires unique knowledge to create a fine quartet or an ensemble using barbershop harmony. The Society for the Preservation and Encouragement of Barbershop Quartet Singing in America (SPEBQSA) has many resources for choral music educators. Although this medium has had a male-dominated history, women, too, enjoy participation (The Sweet Adelines). However, this has not yet attracted a great deal of interest at the high school level.

- Men's and Women's Chorus – These groups may be curricular or extracurricular. They should be curricular only when the members do not sing in another curricular choral ensemble. Women's choirs are more prevalent than men's ensembles. Because a larger number of women than men participate in a choral ensemble, a treble (female) choir is sometimes established to accommodate those who do not participate in the mixed ensemble.

Attire becomes a critical decision for choral directors. Many times, attractive and quite presentable outfits can be made by the students themselves or by their parents. Basically, wearing apparel falls into the following categories:

- Some type of uniform dress, assembled from the student's current wardrobe
- Choir robes
- Tuxedos and gowns (black)
- Blazers and dresses

Choral directors are just as tempted to involve their groups in competition as their instrumental counterparts. The same rules apply from adjudication and evaluation by qualified adjudicators to winning a "sweepstakes trophy" that might involve many endeavors. There are many pros and cons to competition, which were articulated in Chapter 10. It is wise to view competition in light of its impact on the personal and musical growth of the student participants. Don't allow competition to be the end-all of the program. The program must stand on its own feet.

Broadway musicals—and, to a much lesser degree, opera—have enjoyed increasing popularity in public schools today. If, however, the "show" ever becomes more important than the choral program itself, there is a problem. When a successful choral program produces a musical or an opera (and I do not recommend this for every school, and both must be carefully chosen so as to not overtax the young voices), this can be very exciting. I have personally experienced the joy of watching and hearing a high school choir in Williamsport, Pennsylvania, produce the Mozart opera, "The Marriage of Figaro." It was a delightful production that attracted a great deal of media attention (including television) and enjoyed five nights of sold-out performances. Another year, the same choir presented the Carl Orff "Carmina Burana." In both performances, the high school orchestra (the advanced group) provided the accompaniment, and student performers sang the solo parts. Again, great caution must be exercised that young singers do not overuse their voices or attempt to sing out of their comfortable range. Adult soloists need to be used sparingly, and if they are used, there must be a reason, such as an extended tessitura being too great for the young voices, bringing in a faculty soloist from a local university, or bringing in a particularly talented and/or notable soloist from the community.

Rehearsal and Performance Hints

Effective choral rehearsal and performance technique is critical to successful choral directors. The information contained in this section is based on the advice I have given to teachers and student teachers throughout the course of my career. Many of these "hints" were given over and over because the shortcomings and/or problems are common ones to many, especially beginning teachers. They follow:

- Proper posture is an important element in both rehearsal and concert. I suggest that all choral groups from the elementary level through the senior high school level stand when they rehearse. There are several advantages to this:

  1. It is more difficult to have poor posture when standing.
  2. When groups always stand to rehearse, the thought of sitting does not occur to the students. This is simply something they have always done.
  3. Having groups rehearse on risers takes up less space since no chairs are involved. Frequently, rehearsal space is at a premium.
  4. Fainting becomes less of a problem when choral groups are accustomed to standing.

- In addition to normal vocalizing, begin rehearsals with some two-part (elementary), three- or four-part (middle/junior high school), or four-part (senior high school) homophonic warm-ups. Bach chorales are very good for this. It helps to develop a sense of ensemble.

- The choral groups must be taught to support the tone, sing with ease (do not push the voice beyond its normal capabilities), and carry the phrase out to the end. These are the three greatest errors I have observed in young choirs.

- Rehearsals must possess variety and be planned carefully, both short term and long term. Rehearsals should be planned in this way:
  1. Familiar music
  2. Least learned music (just segments of the work(s))
  3. Medium learned (again, stressing just a certain section)
  4. Polishing of learned music (entire composition)
  5. Familiar music

- Consider having students sing something familiar or something they particularly like as they leave the room at the end of rehearsal (just for the fun of it). They must be instructed to stop singing as soon as they get to the door leading to the hall. The students depart with a good feeling.

- Don't hand out or collect music during rehearsal time. Valuable time is lost, and it interferes with the intensity of the rehearsal. Have a music folder for each student with all the music being rehearsed in the folder. The students pick up their own folder upon entering the rehearsal hall and put their own folder back upon departure from the rehearsal hall.

- Don't use the piano as a "crutch" in rehearsal. Keep the choral rehearsal choral. Play very little piano in rehearsal other than to:
  1. Introduce the song.

2. Give starting (initial) pitches.

3. Accompany the choir after the composition is learned.

The piano is not a good model for vocal production. It is important for the choir to learn to sing independently of the piano. Never use the piano to teach notes, only to enhance. When introducing a new composition, don't play the melody line along with the choir as they sing. If it is necessary to use the piano to establish accurate pitches and intervals, play it for the choir and then have them sing without the piano. This develops true music reading, choral independence, and ensemble in a much more effective manner than using the piano as an essential crutch. Even young choirs are able to do this if the practice is always followed. All rehearsals should be conducted *a cappella* until the composition is learned; then, if there is an accompaniment, it may be added.

- Don't sing along with the choir you are conducting. You must hear the choir and not yourself, and you cannot assess their sound when you are singing yourself. You must be listening for balance, blend, diction, and tone quality, not exercising your own vocal chords.

- If ensemble development and preciseness of notes is directly proportional to the amount of time you remove yourself from the piano, when does a good choir become an ensemble? I think it happens when the music is mastered. However, what is the definition of mastered? I have learned that mastered is when the group is cohesive in attack, release, blend, and ensemble, and when the total group performs and thinks as one.

I recall, with appreciation, that one time during my choral conducting years when some choral directors I respected—namely, Fred Waring, Earl Willhoite of Shawnee Press, John Raymond of Lafayette College (Choral Director), Tom Waring (Fred's brother), and Wally Hornibrook (of The Pennsylvanians)—spoke with me about choral polishing and ensemble development. This was the greatest critique I ever had! In essence, they said, "Your choirs are so very, very good and you are so talented" (pride, sigh, oh how I love it!). "BUT" (the bubble burst), "you do not finish your work. They perform before they are ready. They are not yet a choir; they are one hundred people with voices who are singing. They know their parts, but it is still group singing." They helped me to understand, as a conductor, this great difference.

Ensemble development occurs only through careful rehearsal planning along with knowing when the work is completed and ready for performance...and it is not ready for performance until the choir has developed a sense of ensemble. This sense is very important in the development of any choir, and possibly the real test comes when the director and choir feel secure that the notes are learned and in place. The director then spends the rest of the rehearsal time concentrating on balance, blend, phrasing, and group cohesiveness. A choral group is no different than an instrumental group with words, and they both require the same nurturing when developing ensemble. Possibly this is why Robert Shaw was equally at home in front of a choir or a symphony orchestra. Bottom line...there is a difference between a group singing and a choir, and it is important for the choral director to understand this distinction.

- This issue of polishing and finishing the artistic product needs further clarification. The first two weeks at the beginning of the year, or after a concert, will certainly be all "rehearsal and reading," but from that time on, every rehearsal should have a time devoted to "polishing and finishing" so the repertoire always includes some numbers basically ready to go. This eliminates "panic time" right before a performance and helps make the performance enjoyable for the singer, the director, and the audience rather than one of anxiety, where all are merely hoping they will just make it through the performance.

  Polishing occurs during all rehearsals, not just at the end. Every rehearsal must be carefully planned so students get to the point where they perform "over their heads" musically because the director is asking for or demanding it. In the end, the road to success lies with the director.

- The issue of memorization is, I think, an important element of the polishing and finishing aspect of choral development. Naturally, in the case of oratorio and other major works, an exception exists. It is without music that the choir leaves the domain of a certain number of singers and becomes an ensemble that can be honed and polished. It is at this point when the choral group is truly able to work as one with the conductor, without the interference of having to look at the printed page. The oneness of the conductor with the group intellectually, musically, and emotionally is a precious occasion. Don't fail to pursue it!

- When conducting, make certain your body movement, size of beat, and independent left hand reflect the music and how you want it to sound. I have observed many variations on this theme, even to the point where one director did not conduct. This person held the music in one hand and occasionally beat time and pointed with the other. Conducting should be very much like dance. It must reflect the music, draw the musicality out of the notation when it is learned, and develop the cohesive, tight ensemble. When good conducting style is not present, the end result is equally as unmusical.

- I have developed a rather "tacky" document entitled Choir Rules and Regulations (see Appendix I); however, it does appear to appeal to the adolescent mind and gets the do's and don'ts of choral singing across in the manner of a spoof. It is not presently all-inclusive, and should be added to or subtracted from based on the priorities of the individual choral director. I hope that at least the concept will prove useful.

Copyright Laws

The illegal photocopying of copyrighted music has become a major problem for all music educators—not just choral directors. I include the warning in this chapter because it becomes particularly tempting with choral music, where all students receive the same music. The easy availability of high-quality photocopying machines combined with budgetary concerns make the situation even more enticing.

In addition to the issue of illegal photocopying, there are other copyright restrictions that have an impact upon the profession. These include the right to perform copyrighted music under certain circumstances, to sell recordings of concerts for profit, and to broadcast performances on radio or television. Jay Althouse has published a comprehensive booklet on the subject that should become a part of the library of every music educator...and be adhered to.[7] It is the law, and the violation thereof is a criminal act.

Religious Music in the Schools

Over the past thirty years, we have become extremely sensitive to the issue of the teaching and performance of sacred music in choral music programs. I have found this increased concern somewhat related to our over-sensitivity about many issues in American education. It seems that discussing choral music without teaching the relationship text is like talking about architecture minus the cathedral, or a religious painting without the scriptural themes. More than anyone, I am always concerned about imposing or proselytizing any viewpoint—political or religious—with students in schools. Yet there is a vast repertoire of the world's choral music that we must recognize and understand from both musical and cultural viewpoints.

There are several emerging positions, both ethical and legal, about this issue.

Position of MENC:

It is the position of the Music Educators National Conference that the study and performance of religious music within an educational context is a vital and appropriate part of a comprehensive music education. The omission of sacred music from the school curriculum would result in an incomplete educational experience.[8]

Position of ACDA:

It is the position of the American Choral Directors Association that sacred music should be included in public school education on the basis of aesthetic education, artistic performance, culture, and heritage, not to mention that it is also a form of entertainment. Also, all significant choral music composed before the twelfth century was religious in nature.[9]

Lowell Mason may have been the first to approach the controversial subject when he was successful in convincing the Boston Public Schools to include music as a regular subject in the curriculum for the purpose of improving singing in the church. For over a hundred years, the issue was relatively dormant. The Bible was read out loud every morning in school, followed by the recitation of the Lord's Prayer and the Pledge of Allegiance. Religious music was sung freely in schools, and there were Christmas and Easter programs. Gradually, students began refusing to say the entire Lord's Prayer or to say it at all. They claimed it violated certain religious beliefs. In 1962, the United States Supreme Court ruled prayer in schools unconstitutional. It became clear that religious freedom had limits in public education. (For a listing of the important landmark decisions regarding religious content in education, see Appendix J.)

In addition to the position statements of MENC and ACDA quoted on the previous page, these organizations have also stated that the study of religious music is a vital and appropriate part of the total music experience in both performance and listening.[10] Choral music educators should eliminate any religious pageantry, prayers, clergy participation, or religious symbols that might be involved when teaching or performing religious music. If it is possible to study another form of government without indoctrination or saluting another flag, and if it is all right to examine the ills of contemporary society without promoting the seeds of revolution, then one should be able to study religious music without religious indoctrination. But the key word is *study*!

It all seems so simple and logical, but is it? "To study" is defined as "an effort to learn by reading or thinking." There is no particular emotion involved. The study of music can be quite academic; however, when one performs it or listens to it, a new element is involved...that of emotions. This brings me back to the issue discussed earlier in this book, the issue of education vs. entertainment. When one teaches music in the schools for educational purposes, having lesson plans, objectives, and a curriculum, one is educating. When one performs the music, however, there is an audience, the choir has perfected the music to the point where the emotions become involved, and the goal is to project those emotions to an audience. When does an audience become a congregation?

Audience   = concert hall = people applaud
Congregation = church   = people do not applaud
                                   (usually)

But sometimes they do applaud. When they applaud, do they do so because they are being entertained, or are they being moved in a religious way?

Certainly, by nature, the affective or emotional response brought about by music could, indeed, be considered to further the cause of a particular religion for both performer and listener.

Is the purpose of a band or pep band at an athletic event to affect the spirit of the fans to cheer for a particular team? At least, it is supposed to!

Music has long played a crucial role in social, political, cultural, and patriotic contexts, not to mention religious ones. In World Wars I and II, music was used to influence public opinion and create a sense of patriotism among people. Songs such as "The White Cliffs of Dover," "Waltzing Matilda" (Australia), "Let's Remember Pearl Harbor, As We Did the Alamo," and "God Bless America" (sung by Kate Smith) were written to influence public thought. This was not an isolated instance. Music has influenced thought, relaxation, stimulation, communication and, yes, even revolution.

In the 1960s and 1970s when revolt and destruction of the so-called "establishment" was the theme of the day, "We Shall Overcome" became the song identified with rebellion. I was in Japan at the time and attended a Japanese student protest rally in the Shinjiku Station, an underground subway station in Tokyo. The Japanese students were joining their American counterparts in protest. The subway station had tremendous acoustics that any choral group would love. The Japanese students did snake dancing around the station to "We Shall Overcome" to the accompaniment of many guitars. They also sang "Hey Jude" (Beatles) and the folk song "Michael Row Your Boat Ashore," believing that they, too, were protest songs.

The Taliban in Afghanistan outlawed all music unless it was patriotic or religious due to a feeling that music influenced thought and attitude. They, like the Church of Christ, outlawed the use of instruments, thinking they were not God given as voices are and, therefore, not pure but created by man and, therefore, sinful. If music has such power in patriotism, revolution, society, and religion, why should it not be studied in schools to understand that power? Again, the key word is *study*. It is important to ask, as we prepare and sing music that is either political or religious in nature, do we teach our students why this music has the power that it does?

Since September 11, 2001, we have heard, "God Bless America," "America the Beautiful" (God shed his grace on thee), "Amazing Grace," "The Lord's Prayer," etc., in many ceremonies attended by government officials, from the President on down. Were these ceremonies government-sponsored? Was this a separation of church and state? Did the religious music performed have an effect on you? All religions seemed to have been represented by the spoken word, but what about song?

Thus, I get to my final question: Does the music of a society create its culture, or does it reflect its culture? History has shown that the arts and music of a culture are used to study that culture—that is a given. Thus, the real issue or question is: What power does the music of a culture have in the creation of that culture? Or what power does religious music have in the creation of religious belief?

Presently, some parents and even some celebrities are leading movements against the lyrics of the present-day rock music. It is their position that the music and the lyrics affect youth in negative ways, despite the fact that the youth seem to already know the meaning of the words. Therefore, the question still remains: Does the music reflect or create the culture? The answer is not a simple one. Perhaps each person will need to supply his or her own answer to this one!

A letter written to the principal of Williamsport (PA) High School by a dissatisfied parent clearly demonstrates that not everyone understands, or even cares about, the separation of church and state. Also, this parent truly does not understand the difference between education and entertainment. The letter follows:

Mr. Principal:

I'm writing in regard to the past Christmas concert (choir). You offered the opportunity for all parents, grandparents and friends to be present by having it on a Sunday afternoon. The only problem was, no one understood a word the kids sang. What horrible music. Most of the parents can't even speak a foreign language. We thought we were going to get an afternoon of good old fashion Christmas carols presented by our kids. I certainly was shocked. That was awful to sit there through a couple of hours of this foreign music. It was pure suffering. We are the older generation and at Christmas time enjoy good old fashion Christmas music. Is the solution to go to a foreign country to hear Christmas music done in the English language? I counted at least 5 people that left during the concert and there were probably 100 more that wanted to.

A suggestion for concerts, if our children can't be taught to sing in the English language, then don't offer it to the public, because we certainly didn't enjoy it. Maybe another solution would be to get rid of the chorus teacher. This may be impressive to someone, who I can't imagine—not the parents. Maybe a foreign language teacher.

Let's get some good old Christmas carols in a language we can understand and be proud of what our students are being taught. Everyone I talked to thought the concert was awful and we would like to know if something can be done about it? I would like my child to be taught English songs.

—Very dissatisfied parent

(Note: A great deal of the concert was *The Messiah*, in English, of course. The audience that the "very dissatisfied parent" did not speak with closed the concert with a standing ovation—after the *Hallelujah Chorus*, of course. Some German carols were also sung, as I recall, in German, of course. The incorrect English and misspelling in the letter were not corrected, of course.)

The principal sent the letter to the Associate Superintendent (and Curriculum Director), who sent the letter to me, the Supervisor of Music Education, with the following message:

Ken–
Although this is only one letter and it is anonymous, our choral people must be aware of their audience when they select music for a concert.

I know you have already discussed this with them, but you may wish to share this letter.

Associate Superintendent

Once again, the issue of entertainment vs. education rears its ugly head. Apparently, even the Associate Superintendent and Curriculum Director don't really understand the issue.

The choral directors (there were two because there were seven choirs, plus five non-performance classes to be taught) shared the contents of the letter with the choir members, and several responded in writing. I have chosen one particularly poignant response to include here:

Dear "Chorus Teachers,"

Let it be known that if you are unhappy because of the opinions surrounding you, I, for one, am most satisfied and grateful for the education you have given me. Although praise is voiced far less than criticism, it is still existent, and you are more than worthy of compliment. So fret not the administrative surveillance you must endure, and do not allow Philistine parents the pleasure of slowing the progress you have worked so hard to create.

William Shakespeare once wrote:

"Now this overdone, or come tardy off,
though it make the unskillful laugh,
cannot but make the judicious grieve;
the censure of one must not in your
allowance o'er weigh a whole theater
of others."

—Hamlet, Act III, Scene 2

But what "very dissatisfied parent" would bother to comprehend the words of a man who wrote in such a confusing way. The choirs of Williamsport High School's stature should not be forced to degrade its learning and its talent for an uncultured audience. I enjoy the music performed by the WAHS choirs and I would consider any regression in difficulty to be a "step down" in the quality of music education in the schools of Williamsport. So, for the student's sake…keep up the good work!

Sincerely,

Paul "Cotton" Mayer

President of the Senior Class Executive Board

Wow! Somebody got it! Someone understood that the business of a music educator is to educate. And the most thrilling part is that IT WAS A STUDENT!

A simple conclusion to the religious music issue, regardless of whether it is a Christmas carol or an oratorio, might be:

- Study religious music—don't practice religion in rehearsal.
- Expose students to religious music—don't practice religion in rehearsal.
- Religious music should be instructional—don't indoctrinate.
- Educate about religious music—don't convert.
- Religious music can be academic in schools—not devotional. Understand the difference.
- Study what people believe—don't teach what one should believe.
- Be aware of the music of all religions—not just that of your own.

Suffice to say, this issue continues to raise its ugly head, and many school districts around the country are taking the "do it and don't ask, don't tell, and hope for the best" approach. But for others, the sounds of silence are more reassuring than voices and/or instruments that do have the power to move, persuade, and protect.

And the debate goes on, with "Christmas Concerts" becoming "Holiday Concerts," "Easter Programs" now "Spring Programs," and religious music removed from music textbooks And yet gospel choirs, particularly in urban schools and universities, seem to be flourishing. Indeed, it seems that music is everywhere, and it is difficult to silence it or its power.

I close this chapter with the words of Robert Shaw. As the great communicator he was, he wrote to his choirs on a regular basis. The dialogue to me is very meaningful...I hope you concur.

Dear People:

...Someone asked me later Wednesday night what I meant by saying "music is the most moral of all the arts." At least two things come to mind at the justification of the instinct. The first is that the making of music is the everlasting and inescapable act of creation. With the visual arts, a work is completed. It may be viewed by men of succeeding generations, usually singly. But the life of music is reborn with every singing. It actually doesn't exist on paper, but in time and sound. It has existed in the composer's spirit—but at each singing it seeks a new life. And the performer, though his craft is that of representation and his proper approach, that of humility, cannot escape the responsibilities of creation. And this has some moral references.

The second thing that comes to mind is that of all the arts, music is the most linked with the community of expression. This meaning of music is somehow most open to the amateur musician, and nowhere does it find its expression so fully as among the people who sing together. It rests upon a common devotion to the composer's utterance and a mutual respect for the personal dignity of fellow workers. And that has moral references. The words are hard to find, and they come out colder than they go in—and much too pompously.[11]

...We cannot import creativity—we cannot buy the produce of the human spirit, nor can we exchange it for political, religious, social, or economic advancement—without selling it into slavery or stunting its growth. It is not a question of whether we shall have "culture." Every community has its culture. Culture is not an ivory-towered cult, but the total spiritual environment and product of community life. And in this area, none of us can perform by proxy.[12]

...I suppose the first scriptural enigma any of us memorize as a child is "God is love...." In my case, it was some years before I realized that there was a possibility that it said exactly what it meant and meant exactly what it said. Not, "God is to be loved," or "God loves," but God is love...G = L.

At least by analogy (I would say by absolute coincidence), music is love, and so is a chorus, and so is singing together....

I now invite you to realize, with appropriate wonder, that your participation and your "chorus" are not extra baggage, addendum or post-script, but provide an involvement and commitment which furnish the only light there is. There is no other meaning.

Certainly not in words.[13]

RS

With Love for a Chorus,

KRR

1 Hylton, John B. *Comprehensive Choral Music Education*. Englewood Cliffs, NJ: Prentice Hall, Inc., A Simon and Schuster Company, pp. 258–9.
2 Mussulman, Joseph A. *Dear People…Robert Shaw*. Bloomington, IN: Indiana University Press, p. 4.
3 Mussulman, Joseph A. p. 23.
4 Hylton, John B. *Comprehensive Choral Music Education*. p. 85.
5 Hylton, John B. p. 82.
6 Hylton, John B. p. 245.
7 Althouse, Jay. Copyright: *The Completer Guide for Music Educators*. East Stroudsburg, PA: Music In Action, 1984.
8 *Religious Music in the Schools*. Pamphlet. Washington, DC: Music Educators National Conference, 1996.
9 "ACDA Policy Statement." *Choral Journal*, December 1993, p. 52.
10 "Christmas Without Carols." *Music Educators Journal*, November 1968, p. 43.
11 Mussulman. p. 108.
12 Mussulman. p. 123.
13 Mussulman. p. 246.

Chapter 12

Music in Higher Education

Somehow, as I began the task of developing and writing this chapter, I sensed a personal feeling that it is good to be shifting to a new "country." I have, it seems, explored every possible aspect of the pre-college/university experience in music education. Now as this exploration advances to higher education, one finds a totally different situation where leadership takes on a new face. Academic life is intensely political, and tact and diplomacy are necessary even though they many times are difficult to distinguish from deception and cunningness. College professors are covetous of their independence, proud of their specialized competencies, afraid of losing their turf, not easily led, and suspicious of being told what or how they serve.

There are reasons why college faculty act the way they do. They have tenure, which gives them an autonomy and independence that is a very different relationship between faculty and administrative leadership than that found in K–12 education. They are expected to become specialists in their fields and, therefore, tend to have a narrow focus on the profession. In fact, their salaries depend on how specialized and well-known they really are. It is difficult for administrators to help a faculty member narrowly focusing on early music to see the broader picture of a comprehensive school of music—let alone music education! The nature of decision-making (discussed in earlier chapters) is a holdover from the British system of faculty leadership and governance. The process of dialogue and consensus is a difficult one to negotiate as a leader in higher education; it rarely exists in K–12. Those of you reading this book who are K–12 music educators must understand that the nature of higher education is very, very different than K–12.

Leadership in Higher Education

Robert Greenleaf[1] has devoted his book, *Servant Leadership*, to the many complexities that reside in leading and serving in the academy of higher education. His concerns are "for the individual in society and his seeming bent to deal with the massive problems of our times wholly in terms of systems, ideologies, and movements" and "for the individual as a serving person, and the tendency to deny wholeness and creative fulfillment to oneself by failing to lead when there is opportunity." He states that "the great leader is seen as a servant first." At the heart of that statement, it seems, is that within the soul of the potential leader at the university level must be a responsiveness to service, a willingness to lead, a capability of taking care of details, a firmness in holding to higher goals, an ability to marshal successfully one's own energies, and an ability to compliment the work of others.[2] Leadership at any level of the academy must be a way of life. It would appear, at times, that the faculty's job is to think for the university, the president's to speak for it, and the provost's to make certain the faculty does not speak or the president think. The dean, unfortunately, does not fit into the picture because he/she is an individual too dumb to be a professor and too smart to be a president.[3] (Please pardon the attempt at satirical humor.)

Like people and plants, schools of music have a life cycle. They have a green and supple youth, a time of flourishing strength, and a gnarled old age. Faculty many times have more of a tendency to look back than to look forward, and when they do look forward, it is more from the perspective of what is being done at competitive institutions, or for them personally, rather than from the perspective of what their institution should and could be. A school of music may go from youth to old age in two or three decades, or it may last for centuries. It also may go through a period of stagnation and then be revived. In short, though, decline is not inevitable. Organizations need not stagnate given proper nourishment. They need to renew themselves continually because there are certain rules that are important for the prevention of departmental dry rot and the commencement of departmental renewal. As higher education is changing at a faster and faster pace, the life cycle of schools of music is changing, too.

When I came to Texas Christian University, I brought with me experience in the administration of both higher education and public education. As I watched the school of music faculty grapple with challenges in enrollment, quality of performing groups, in stature and reputation, in discourse and civility, and in quality of facility and operations, I believed a new set of "rules" were important for the future of this—and really any—school of music. They follow:

RULE 1 – The School of Music must have an effective program for the recruitment and development of talent, both at the professional level and the student level.

There must be the kind of recruitment policy that will bring in a steady flow of able and highly motivated individuals, and it cannot afford to allow these people to go to seed, or get sidetracked or "boxed in." There must be a positive, constructive environment of career and department development.

RULE 2 – The School of Music must be a hospitable environment for the individual.

Organizations that kill the spark of individuality in their members greatly diminish their capacity for change.

RULE 3 – The School of Music must have built-in provisions for self-criticism.

There must be an atmosphere where anything can be asked, and the only way to do this is to create an atmosphere in which anyone can speak up without fear of retribution but with respect for the institution and the process of dialogue.

Rule 4 – The School of Music must find some means to combat the vested interests that frequently grow up among faculty.

Some rise above the vested interests, but the average school has a faculty that hold dear, like a grim death, to its particular piece of the musical terrain as though the elevation of another part of the school would bring about their eventual downfall. The issue here must be cooperation rather than isolation, and excellence rather than mediocrity.

RULE 5 – The School of Music must be more interested in what it is going to become than what it has been.

It is true that we learn from the past, as it gives us a sense of perspective; however, the major part of the time must be spent looking forward, not backward. There is only a four-year turnaround in an undergraduate student body, and even less in the graduate population. One only need retire to realize how quickly the student body is regenerated. In this short period of time, the very best musical education possible must be available to the students. They care little about the future of the program (at least at this age), and they care even less about the past. They are here now!

On another thought, it is important to be able to look to that collective department of the future with an open mind and without fear of failure. Failure does not mean incompetence. Failure is often equated with wrong, bad, lesser, unworthy, etc. In essence, failure is merely an incompletion of the task at hand. It offers the opportunity to regroup and seek another solution. Music is perfected through a series of failures (wrong notes, missed key changes, bad counting, unseen accidentals, etc.), so why not apply this to all that is done? The lesson is simple: the way to become more proficient at anything is to be willing to fail and continue to work on improvement. The visionaries are simply those who do not quit.

RULE 6 – The School of Music must run on motivation, on conviction, and on morale.

It is necessary to strongly believe that it makes an important difference whether the school does well or poorly. The faculty has to care about the unit as a whole. They must believe that their efforts as individuals will mean something to and be recognized by the entire school. Caring is the poetry of the heart and the music of the mind.

RULE 7 – The School of Music must thrive on trust rather than suspect and the positive rather than the negative.

Trust in the administration must be earned, and once established it will develop a stronger bond of trust in each other as colleagues. This must be affirmed. There must be belief that the collective purpose of the school is to help each member of the faculty be as good as he/she can be, for only then can the cohesive whole of the school feed and nourish itself. A lofty goal, true, but when this occurs, the process simply continues to get better. Success breeds success.

What could a faculty member do to help with this process? One important proviso at the onset: colleagues need to be trusted friends and cooperate willingly with one another. There are always some who are versed in petty faculty intrigue and vindictive backbiting. From cutting remarks, the road inexorably descends to unpleasant acts such as initiating students to take sides in personal squabbles and creating disruptive factions within the school. This simply must not occur. By training and temperament, musicians/professors are inclined to quibble and argue points. Faculty "authorities" are sometimes hypersensitive, intellectually arrogant, and obsessed in their self-concern.

As you deal with the musician/academic, it is important to be sensitive to the fact that when you put anyone in a no-win situation, you do precisely that—lose! If academic colleagues and musical professionals cannot behave with generosity toward colleagues, how can students or anyone else view the professional ranks any more kindly? To become mature in relationships is a part of being educated, as distinguished from being merely knowledgeable in a particular field. Remember that everyone is only as good as each of us, and tenure does not replace that responsibility.

RULE 8 – The School of Music must have some means of combating the process by which people become prisoners of their procedures.

By the same token, programs and procedures must be constantly reviewed for potential or existing dry rot. Otherwise, the rule book will grow fatter as the ideas grow fewer. Faculty compete, for example, for limited promotions and salary raises. At one of the universities where I served, the administrator for each school or department had to rank the faculty from "best" to "worst." For example, if there are twenty-five faculty in the school, each faculty member must receive a number from 1 to 25, with no "ties" allowed. The yearly raises are then divided accordingly.

In another large research university, the dean must rank faculty from most competent to least competent three different ways: by discipline, by rank, and by overall faculty worth to the institution. One year, the Philosophy Department refused to participate in this exercise, arguing that its faculty was uniformly excellent. The upper administration insisted that the faculty must be ranked or else no monies for faculty raises would be allocated to the department.

This process for administrators is complex and means one thing: an unhappy and disgruntled faculty. We must find ways to evaluate colleagues and account for ourselves in ways that are effective but that do not destroy either the nature of our own art form or the profession of activities that support it.

RULE 9 – The School of Music needs to be certain there is fluidity of internal structure.

Jurisdictional boundaries tend to get set in concrete (band, choir, theory, musicology, applied, etc.) within the school, and pretty soon no resolution to a problem is seriously considered if there is any danger that it will threaten any other jurisdictional lines. This, at times, leads to difficult, disagreeable, or disgruntled faculty. As more and more schools of music look at interdisciplinary connections within the school of music, and as technology and media blur lines of the disciplines, the internal organizational and governance structure of music schools must change, or it will decline.

Those faculty whose horizons are limited to their own discipline or program cannot be allowed to limit the flexibility, growth, or innovation so desperately needed in higher education today. The leader in higher education who can balance this transition in faculty governance and program innovation is a true leader because this is difficult work given the current structure of higher education. But it is starting to happen. Colleagues must co-exist and learn to work together for the good of the whole.

RULE 10 – The School of Music must have an adequate system of positive internal communication.

This communication needs to center on the building and strength of the school rather than a defensive dialogue attempting to defend a turf that is not being threatened. In short, the cup must be half full and not half empty. A top-down administrative structure, with its inherent micro-management, creates the unfortunate environment where acceptance appears more appealing than creation, and status quo more desirable than fighting the odds. There is an air of intimidation and stagnation that occurs when faculty members find themselves caught in this administrative style. I would rather enjoy a style that leans more to consensus and involvement in decision-making, even though it must be understood that administrators, at times, must make decisions on their own.

It is valuable to train the mind to stand apart, and to study and examine the workings of the school of music. That, to me, is the definition of a liberal educator—the ability to examine the total program of the entire music unit as opposed to the program in which the individual is personally involved. Without this freehanded view of the whole, the mind closes and narrows; thus, assumptions underlying the totality are made without adequate information. That is why it is so important to read and expose oneself to great minds. The goal here is to have the faculty reach consensus and speak with one mind. (OK! I have never experienced a university faculty speak with one mind; however, it is a noble goal.) After all, too many feel that the profession of "university professor" may be the most enjoyable and highly paid (considering hours worked) job in the world.

(Much truth can be imparted through humor. Appendices K and L explore life in a university school of music through "tongue-in-cheek" humor. In Appendix K, the satire on Mr. Wolfgang Mozart explores the difficulties this man might have had in acquiring a university teaching position today. I am not certain of the author. Appendix L, which speaks to the relationship of the band director and the band department to the Director of the School of Music and, in essence, the school as a whole, is actual.)

Communication

When you work you are a flute through whose heart
    the whispering of the hours turns to music.
Which of you would be a reed, noisy or silent,
    when all else plays together in unison?

Life is indeed darkness save when there is urge.
And all urge is bland save where there is knowledge.

And all knowledge is vain save where there is work.
And all the work is empty save when there is love.

Work is love made visible.
And if you cannot work with love but only with distaste,
  it is better that you should leave your work and sit at
  the gate of the temple
  and take alms of those who work with joy,
For if you sing though as angels and love not the singing,
  you muffle man's ears to the voices of the day and the
  voices of the night.

Your soul is oftentimes a battlefield upon which your
  reason and your judgment
  wage war against your passion and your appetite.
Would that I could be the peacemaker in your soul, that I
  might turn the discord
  and the rivalry of your elements into oneness and
  melody,
But how shall I, unless you yourselves be also the
  peacemakers, nay,
  the lovers of all your elements?

—From *The Prophet* by Kahil Gibran

College professors have not been known to be the great communicators. Most talk of the necessity for it, but few communicate well. Within the academy at large, communication tends to be bureaucratic, fitful, and seldom concerned with teaching and learning but much more with career and performance or research. Reason, passion, and love simply must overrule negative energy.

In a meeting with the music faculty during one of my recent consulting visits, we attempted to identify items of communication that might be of help in avoiding future conflict within the School of Music. I feel this group came up with quite an inclusive list. It follows:

1. Scheduling – Inform colleagues of planned rehearsals, master classes, extra rehearsals, etc., in *advance* so discussion may ensue should a conflict occur.

2. Never put the students "in the middle" between any faction, such as the voice faculty vs. the choral division, professor vs. professor, or student vs. student.

3. Communicate with one another. Attempt to work things out before anger sets in, not in retrospect.

4. Respect the notion that each faculty member is doing his or her very best to do the job well. They are not attempting to "do their colleagues in."

5. Know that students will be tired at the end of the semester. Realize how tired the faculty is. Why would one expect students to be otherwise?

6. Plan ahead! Avoid last-minute changes that affect others negatively. Do not schedule master classes, rehearsals, concerts, etc, without regard to the departmental calendar that has been scheduled for an entire semester, even though in your mind your "event" is the most important one.

7. Openly support your colleagues. Animosity occurs when colleagues down colleagues, be it to students or to other faculty. It frequently gets back to the person being criticized, and cruelty results. It is nearly impossible to move forward together as long as there is internal strife.

8. Remember that your area is not the only one in the department. When "extra rehearsals" or "makeup lessons" or "master classes" are scheduled during faculty or student recitals or other events students are expected to attend, collegial harmony diminishes and the students are placed in the middle.

9. If something is not broken (if there is no problem), don't attempt to fix it.

10. Observe line/staff protocol. If someone does not get what he or she wants at one level and then goes up the administrative chain to do so, the erosion of faculty morale becomes significant. Granted, this scenario would demonstrate an administrative weakness in line/staff protocol; however, when faculty observe this very basic rule, respect for authority and respect for colleagues increases.

The report closed with the following paragraph:

We must all remember that we are not in competition with one another. Rather, we must support one another with full knowledge that the totality and cohesiveness of this department is the strength of all its parts working together like clockwork. Consequently, it is the hope of this committee that no one attempts to "overcome" the other in order to survive themselves—we must all survive or we will all fail. Kindness has been described in many ways. It is the needed chain that binds us all together. Everyone knows the pleasure of receiving a kind look, a warm greeting, and a hand held out in the time of need. Such gestures can be made at so little expense, yet they bring such dividends to the investor. It is our hope that none of us lose this as we continue our quest for excellence... and survival.

I have found, again and again, during my many years of consulting that lack of communication and mutual respect are among the greatest weaknesses of Schools of Music.

Combining Leadership and Communication

One year during my higher education years, it seemed that communication, faculty cohesiveness, and cooperation seemed to have disappeared. I was forced to deal with some terrible issues: moral impropriety, some crime, and even violence had surfaced. I felt devastated and at a loss for what to do to "fix things." When frustration sets in, I frequently put my feelings onto paper where I can deal with them more objectively. Sometimes I share what I write with others, and other times I just keep it for future reference or throw it away. This time I shared it with the faculty because there was no other way for us to solve our problems without the faculty being aware of what they were and working together to fix them.

All who are in higher education in music may well face a challenge such as this. The key is that this is not the time to isolate oneself so that factionalism and faculty are left to their own desires and devices. Communication is critical, and you must find a way to bring faculty together if common problems are to be solved. In my case, this was communication at its best, or worst, depending on the perspective of the reader. But it was communication, and there was no question about my feelings at the time. And it did bring the desired responses—communication! And we were a stronger school as a result of that effort. I hate to think what would have happened had I chosen a different and less open path.

What is important to learn from my experience is that leadership does not mean going into your office and coming up with a solution—or no solution! Effective leadership requires you to communicate the issues, bring people together to solve them, and work collectively for positive change. It is not my job (although some faculty would tell you it is) to solve all the problems of the school. In a collective, shared-governance format, there is as much responsibility to share the *problems* as there is to share the *solutions*.

Admissions

The admissions process is directly responsible for many of the historical highs and lows in the music school. This is a critical area because the recruiting and eventual admission of music students is truly the future of the music school. It is quite easy to generalize about admissions because of the many variables that admissions present to the music unit. There are many types of admissions structures in higher education. The largest schools have independent admissions and recruiting offices that make the eventual decision for admission to the music school. Smaller institutions, and certainly liberal arts institutions, will share duties with the university admissions office. My experience has been with all three kinds of admissions processes, and they raise questions that I feel are important to survival, growth, and stability.

I think, however, that admissions depends on the music unit having established precisely what kind of music school it is, or wishes to be, and then recruiting accordingly. It is quite important to both the prospective student and the music school to recruit appropriate students in an honest way and with integrity. Music units generally break into the following generic types (with many variations):

1. Liberal Arts – pre-professional
2. Liberal Arts with a professional emphasis, meaning a bachelor's degree could be considered the terminal degree either in performance or in music education
3. Conservatory – professional with a performance emphasis (and sometimes also with a music education major)
4. Teacher training emphasis, where music education is the major thrust in the music unit

One must then think about the admissions department of the university:

- Is there good communication between admissions and the music unit?
- Does the admissions unit understand the type of a music unit housed in the university?
- Is there a dual admissions process—one where different standards are applied to students entering the music unit than to those entering the university at large?
- Is the university a state or private school? Many times a totally different admissions philosophy exists between these two types of schools.
- Is there an open admissions policy where a large drop-out or failure rate is anticipated, or is it a closed admissions policy where the university supports the notion of a dual responsibility of retention, embracing both the student and the school?
- Does the admissions department consult with the music unit during the admissions process? What is the level of communication? Is it a "left-brained admissions department" recruiting "right-brained students"? Obviously, this could create an academic and musical mess. On one hand, this could be considered discriminatory, but on the other

hand, students must be able to compete academically with their counterparts in other departments of the university.

- Does the music unit have its own admissions department, or is admissions generically apportioned throughout the university?

- Is a music audition required? Is it acknowledged or considered by the admissions department? It may amaze some to know that there are music units that do not require or acknowledge the music audition as a part of the admissions process. Students merely elect music as a major, much as they might elect history, languages, or mathematics.

- Does the university charge the admissions department with the responsibility of providing diversity throughout the student body? These diversities might include, among others:

  a. Ethnic diversity
  b. Cultural diversity
  c. Geographic diversity
  d. Religious diversity
  e. Artistic diversity
  f. Diversity by sex

- What is the charge of the university to the admissions department with regard to music admissions versus a self-designed generic philosophy of admissions? Questions that must be addressed include:

  a. Should all potential students be treated as one and the same?
  b. Should artistically talented students receive special consideration?
  c. How important are SAT scores?

   d. How important is rank in class?

   e. How important is the academic Grade Point
      Average (GPA)?

   f. Is the proposed idea of the seven intelligences
     of Howard Gardner an admissions possibility of
     the future?

- Is it possible to "piggy-back" scholarships? That is, could a music unit scholarship be combined with an academic scholarship? Could two or more academic scholarships be combined?
- Is it possible to award scholarships above financial need?
- Does the admissions office assign a particular person to serve as liaison to the music unit?

The admissions process is a complex one, complimented by many issues beyond those cited above. Some of these ancillary issues follow:

- Realities of the job potential – Parents speak of their concerns with regard to their children making a living after graduation from the university with a music major. To pursue a career in performance is probably a dead-end street unless the musicians were one of the two or three hottest players on their instrument in their state when they were eighteen years of age. A career in composition might be fruitless unless the budding composer has a harmonic language all his/her own by the time he/she is thirty years of age, and a career in musicology is barely possible without a Ph.D. I am not attempting to be negative here; I am attempting to be accurate.
- Once again, this question must be raised: Should music education be thought of as an alternative to music

performance? Is music education still the ultimate insurance policy it once was?

- If students are undecided with regard to a major, should they be encouraged to begin as a music major and then drop out if it proves to not be the major for them, or should they enter a pre-major program with the knowledge that if they eventually choose music as their major, it will probably take a longer period of time to graduate due to prerequisites.

- Is music a valuable pre-professional liberal arts major that could lead to graduate work in medicine or law? There are many statistics that would indicate that this is a positive option.

I would be remiss if I did not encourage every person in a leadership role, real or self- appointed, to be proactive in communicating with the admissions office so a satisfactory and mutually beneficial music admissions philosophy may be established. Both entities must be educated to the needs and guidelines under which the other must work. I would also suggest that you make friends with the admissions office, offer to go on admissions recruiting trips, and invite an admissions counselor to accompany you or members of the music unit on a recruiting trip. Finally, I recommend that the admissions office appoint a certain person to deal specifically with music admissions decisions so this person may act as a liaison between the two areas, understand the uniqueness of the music unit and the music major, and be able to speak knowledgably about both on the campus to prospective students, to the School of Music, and to other members of the admissions office.

Standardized testing with regard to university admissions has been debated over and over in this country (see Chart #1). Recently, the president of the University of California, Richard Atkinson, made a speech proposing dropping the SAT as a test for college admissions. This proposal has since been instituted. On the other hand, George W. Bush began his first major address as President by proposing an enormous federally mandated regime of standardized tests for public school children, with every student being tested in reading and mathematics every year from third through eighth grade. This proposal increased the scope of testing by far more than Atkinson's proposal to reduce it.

Chart 1

The SAT began its life as an intelligence test; an assessment of aptitude that its makers believed measured innate mental ability. Carl Brigham, the test's inventor, was part of the team that developed the Army intelligence tests during World War I; the first SAT was an adopted version of that test. Henry Chauncey, the founding president of the Educational Testing Service, and his boss during his previous job as an assistant dean at Harvard University in the 1930s and 1940s, James Bryant Conant chose the SAT as an admissions test because he saw it as an IQ test. Conant wanted to accomplish two goals: primarily to make sure the best minds go to the top universities so the nation could make use of them, and secondarily to make the student bodies of Harvard and schools like it more academic and more national.

The SAT now has become a national fetish. A large portion of the high school student and parent population believes it is the main determinant of admissions to a selective college which, in turn, is the main determinant of one's future socioeconomic status. High school students and their parents also believe that scores on this all-important test can be raised by spending hundreds, even thousands, of dollars on courses that teach you tricks for outwitting the tests (the test makers deny all of the above).[4] Would it not be better for all students to reliably acquire basic education skills and, therefore, a meaningful chance in life? By the way, the Educational Testing Service who compiles and sells these multifaceted tests has turned into one of the larger corporations in the United States. (Should you be interested in one more political satire, Appendix M contains one entitled *Standardized Testing of Dentistry*.)

My concern about standardized testing and music admissions is that the quality of musicianship continues to be important and must not drift further and further outside the decision for admission. As I consult on various college campuses around the country, I am seeing instances where admissions offices are having fewer relationships with music schools. This is dangerous and really speaks to our future in crucial ways. I hope that leaders in music in higher education will strive for a better balance in admissions involvement.

Music Teacher Education

The shortage of music educators in the United States today is a major area of concern. The long-term solution, obviously, would be to recruit more music education majors to our universities; however, it is not that easy. Once students arrive at the university, they many times lose the perspective they once held of their basic goal of becoming a music educator. How does this happen? What frequently happens is what James Kjellan calls "performance elitism".[5] He notes that this refers to "an attitude engendered by those who view music and performance through a survival-of-the-fittest paradigm." Essentially, this attitude serves to prevent a needed balance between the producers, consumers, and teachers of music.

This "performance elitism" is not unique to any one university in the United States. Even though the largest number of music majors in higher education today are in "music education," our colleagues at times have a conservatory mentality, even when the goals of the institution may not be congruent with the conservatory philosophy. Taking a closer look, one may even find that a number of music teacher education programs today train musicians first and music educators second. The curriculum for music education majors all too often is weighted toward applied and ensemble music offerings and methodologies geared mainly toward large performing ensembles and elementary school general music.

The music education faculty continues to be a political minority in many schools and is in no position to make curricular changes in either the school of music or the school of education. In fact, many have difficulty speaking to their colleagues about what public school music is really all about. Why? In defense of these colleagues, they have never been there...they have never experienced the demands, expectations, and problems that a career in public school music education demands. Thus, their goal is not necessarily consistent with either the important goal of training music educators or the priority of the university that centers on a balanced liberal arts education. Future employment options are not the issue. It should not be surprising, then, that today's teachers entering the field feel ill equipped to handle many issues, including a growing demand for general music courses geared to non-performing students? The "keep the best, shoot the rest" mentality addressed earlier in this book is not going to serve the music teachers of tomorrow very well.

As stated above, many music educators do not want—nor are they prepared—to teach general music to the general student population of a school district. For example, all too few music teachers are comfortable at the piano or with guitars as an accompanying device, or the methods to teach with a keyboard or guitar laboratory. Alas, too few feel well prepared to enter the middle school/junior high school general music class or the senior high school general music class, should it exist.

I have spoken several times in this book about those university music faculty who think of public school music education as what to do when a professional career in music seems an impossibility. It bears repeating one more time. I neither consider the profession of music education a "back-up, just in case," nor do I consider it "second best." I am frequently intrigued with the number of applied music instructors themselves who entered university teaching because they eventually realized they would not have a successful performance career. Thus, they live their would-be career through their students. The music education faculty, leaders though they should be, assume the role of an insurance agent who provides some sort of employment in case a professional career does not materialize.

All of this has a "Catch 22." When music teachers arrive in their positions as an alternative to something else, their students sense this, and fewer and fewer become excited about music or music education as their first choice of a career option. The emulation of music teachers is quite common, and it is these professionals who need to encourage and guide students into music teaching.

Performance graduates who do "fall back" on teaching must frequently learn, at the expense of their first generation of students, that a performance degree is not automatically a license to teach. A recent study of 197 public school band directors that investigated their habits and feelings toward the importance of continued performance after joining the work force (the "real world") concluded that "playing during college creates the band director (music educator?) of the future, but it does not necessarily create a lifelong instrumentalist."[6] Practice time becomes minimal, and it becomes very difficult to maintain those once well-developed performance "chops." As a former trumpet major, I can attest to this.

The music education profession urgently needs talented and motivated music educators who are not in music education by default but who are strong musical individuals capable of inspiring students to learn through their own personal example. Applied music instructors, music theorists, musicologists, and performing group directors working together with the music education faculty must inspire this individual. The mission and influence of this cohesive group must better meet the needs of a broader array of future music educators who must compete for employment in a very different world than their instructors encountered upon graduation. It is long past time that all university music faculty acknowledge teaching as an essential performing art.

If the National Standards for music education are to have an impact on practice in general education, teacher education must respond. Pre-service music teachers must themselves meet the benchmarks set in the Standards. For example, it would be expected that pre-service teachers could sing and play musical instruments (Content Standards 1 and 2), since most college music programs for admission require those abilities. However, it is less common to find in those same students the ability to improvise (Content Standard 3), unless their pre-service teacher education program requires that competency.[7] The inability to improvise is a deficiency frequently identified by college faculty and undergraduate pre-service music educators. At many schools of music, improvisational skills are taught to majors by the department of jazz studies. Often, pre-service music teachers do not have room in their already crowded program of studies to include a course in jazz improvisation in their schedule. Also, they probably would not have the background to audition successfully for the jazz band(s). The piano faculty frequently teaches improvisation skills in piano, a necessity for any future music educator. Unfortunately, few piano professors are able to improvise themselves; thus, they teach functional piano in a non-functional way. They teach from a pedagogical base rather than an improvisational one.

In addition, some states are capping the number of credits a school may offer education majors as well as the number of credits a discipline may require for graduation. Therefore, many students are not permitted electives outside the music department, or the bachelor's degree sequence takes five years to complete and takes the student beyond the number of credits permitted by the state for an undergraduate degree. Neither of these options is desirable. This must change if pre-service teachers are ever going to meet all nine content standards of the National Standards.

Samuel Hope, Executive Director of the National Association of Schools of Music (NASM), writes:

> Each teacher preparation program will need to consider relationships between what it is doing and larger goals for public competencies. Each will need to find its own solutions, thinking through all aspects of its current and prospective situation. Such efforts are critical because the Standards do not require standardization; they require competence.[8]

Since teachers are reluctant to teach what they cannot do them-selves, and because teachers naturally emphasize those areas of the curriculum where they claim expertise, it becomes the responsibility of educational institutions to provide training opportunities for faculties so methodology may reflect that which pre-service teachers will eventually teach. Methods courses come in many different sizes, shapes, and forms. Future performance directors must be schooled in band, orchestra, and choral methods, especially when the certification is a K–12, all-inclusive certification. (I will deal with certification issues later in this chapter.) Future general music teachers (especially at the elementary level) have tough choices to make, determining whether to adopt a particular methodology or pedagogy (Orff, Kodaly, etc.) or choose to be an eclectic music teacher. We must accept both and not face music educators shunned by purists. Unfortunately, there seems to be all too few guidelines and methods for teaching general music at the middle/junior high school and the senior high school.

Instrumental methods teachers are a breed unto themselves, however, and they frequently refer to their methods classes as "technique classes." Sometimes these classes are taught by professional musicians or applied music professors who have not taught in the K–12 public or private schools and rarely, if ever, have taught beginners. Thus, the budding instrumental teacher is given techniques for teaching adults rather than effective techniques for teaching children to successfully play an instrument.

As we continue to study new "methods" of teaching, we must realize that no methodology has ever been intended to be permanent or inflexible. These methods must change with the times. Changes and reforms in education, such as the National Standards, should offer opportunities rather than threats. As new, carefully researched commercial method books continue to appear, and school reforms place renewed emphasis on teaching and learning practices, I can envision a future where the teaching of methods (methodology) turns into a teaching art. Hopefully, accepted once and for all, it can remain a valid part of the educational program for all pre-service students in the colleges and universities of the United States.

Student Teaching and Field Experiences

Student teaching should be one of the most valuable experiences in the music education learning sequence. This is the time the novice spends functioning and behaving as a teacher—still supervised and guided—but a teacher nonetheless. Is this the way the student teaching "experience" is viewed by university officials, cooperating teachers, and even the students? I am afraid not!

Assuming sufficient knowledge and understanding are prerequisites, a person learns to teach by teaching. The prospective music educator needs to begin contact with actual teaching situations as soon as possible. The freshman year is not too soon. There needs to be repeated contacts with actual teaching situations (under the guidance of an experienced music teacher) so coursework can be closely coordinated with the actual experience. It is simply not possible to divorce pedagogy from experience. No matter how many courses a music education student may have taken, the meaning of that instruction does not become evident until experienced in a teaching situation.

Methods courses by themselves are incomplete. They must be closely coordinated with actual teaching experience with students. This is a major boost in the development of a novice teacher. Growth in teaching ability closely follows the pattern of growth in any other endeavor—it is achieved through practice.

The great debate of subject area knowledge and its relationship to teaching effectiveness is particularly evident in music education. As teacher shortages loom on the horizon and pressure is placed on states to develop temporary or "shortcut" certification, those with musical experience (but without methods classes and required student teaching) will continue to decry the requirements of general methods courses to achieve quick certification.

Indeed, there may be some fine musicians who are "natural" teachers and perhaps might not need a formal program of teacher training. Yet even these individuals, given the rapidly changing nature of schools and a probable lack of firsthand experience with today's students, would be more effective educators with added experience. A musician not versed in the fundamentals of teaching, insensitive to the needs of children, and lacking classroom experience cannot possibly make up for these deficiencies by "on-the-job training." This is not an either/or situation. Good teaching requires both musical ability and teaching technique. Again, the key is linking classroom experience with methodology.

If music student teaching and field experiences are to assume a position of more importance and viability in the training of America's future teachers, new goals must be formulated. Each goal appears quite logical in isolation, yet greater debates will rage regarding their practicality when presented with potential obstacles.

Goal: Students should have pre-service teaching experiences in the schools every year, beginning in the freshman year.

Obstacle: At times this interferes with attendance at scheduled classes in the student's schedule.

Goal: The student teacher should be freed from taking other courses during the student teaching semester.

Obstacle: University ensembles need their most mature musicians all four years of the student's time on campus, particularly in smaller colleges. It is difficult to lose a senior for one-half of the senior year. Also, the scholarship student not performing in the ensemble is taking up a scholarship that could be used by someone else who is available to perform with the ensemble.

Goal: The student teacher should have experiences at every level (elementary and secondary) and area (instrumental, vocal, and general music), especially when certification reads K–12, Vocal, Instrumental, and General Music. Otherwise, hypothetically, a piano major in undergraduate school could elect to do his/her student teaching in elementary school vocal and general music, and accept a position as a high school band director. This may sound absurd, but similar things do happen and not only with beginning teachers. I know of experienced teachers whose teaching assignments were changed because of certification factors, against the will of the music teacher. A limited number of students do gain experience in both the elementary and secondary levels, and even fewer experience both vocal and instrumental music, however. They are all richer when they experience all areas of their certification.

Many times, the designation of where a student teacher teaches is a matter of chance, depending on where the individual cooperating teacher happens to teach. The chances that a student teacher will get a position that matches that of his/her cooperating teacher are somewhat slim. It would seem that his/her experience would be more valuable if assigned to an entire school district where he/she could have the opportunity of working with more than one cooperating teacher.

Obstacle: Although it seems I have already presented obstacles and resolutions to this goal, there are more. Where a state offers broad certification areas, the depth of experience in each area for the student teacher may become superficial. Forty-three states offer an all-level certificate for music instruction. Twenty-nine states offer *only* all-level certification. Thirty-one states consider music a single subject area, while fifteen of the remaining states differentiate between vocal and instrumental music. Thirty-four states issue provisional certification for entry-level teachers. Five states currently offer lifetime certification. Forty-three states require testing in basic skills, professional knowledge, music content, or a combination of these areas. Eleven states administer their own tests, while the remainder use PRAXIS Series Tests (Educational Testing Service). Most states offer some level of reciprocity to out-of-state applicants, although required testing is waived only for experienced teachers in most instances. Alternate certification programs, implemented to address the increasing teacher shortage are available in thirty-nine states.[9] Obstacles to this goal abound, but the goal remains important.

Goal: Student teachers and pre-service teachers should be observed and guided by certified music educators experienced in teaching in K–12 schools, preferably those who have also taught the required methodology courses.

Obstacle: Many universities have student teachers in subject areas observed by faculty members from the Education Department, not a teacher in the specialized area. They ask why music should be different? (Because music requires special talents and understandings that are not generic to other subject areas.)

Goal: Outstanding music educators must be identified and encouraged to serve as cooperating teachers. Some method of payment or tuition credit should be awarded as an incentive.

Obstacle: Many outstanding music educators become "burned out" from having helped poorly prepared or unmotivated student teachers. Many are also very protective of their performing groups and afraid that the novice teachers will harm programs or damage classroom discipline. Also, little or no remuneration is offered to cooperating teachers for their efforts.

Goal: Music student teachers should be placed only with certified music teachers.

Obstacle: Certain geographic areas of the country do not have comprehensive K–12 music education programs with K–12 certified music teachers. Some districts have K–8 schools, and then the students go to a regional high school.

Goal: Music student teachers should only be allowed to teach music courses during their student teaching experience.

Obstacle: Some music teachers, especially in rural areas, teach courses other than music, especially if they possess dual certification.

Goal: Student teaching should be full-time for a semester, receive a full semester of academic credit, be off campus, and if possible, the student teachers should live in the community in which they teach.

Obstacle: Students are often needed in the performance ensemble on campus. Living away from campus may also produce economic difficulties for some students. In a four-year program, there may not be enough time to devote a full semester, if not mandated by the state.

When pondered collectively, these goals demonstrate that both student teaching and pre-service classroom encounters are orphans in need of adoption. The time has come for a stronger position to be taken on these issues. Much more is presently being written and talked about regarding this subject; however, the pre-service experiences need more "clout" in the total program of music teacher education. It must become a priority.

Perhaps it might be wise to look at other professions that require a series of residencies and internships following college (e.g., medicine, law, etc.). Possibly the idea of an internship is an idea whose time has come. Placing student teachers in schools for a semester or a year, with some sort of remuneration, would force a partnership between school districts and colleges or universities that would be healthy for everyone and, in particular, the future teacher. There will be those who cry "too expensive." However, major reforms generally cost money. At stake is the creation of an adequate supply of well-prepared teachers for our profession. Unfortunately, until we take steps in this direction, the dilemma will continue. As teacher salaries improve—and they must—the internship might prove worthy of the added experience.

James Froseth writes that "it takes a whole school of music to educate a music teacher."[10] Policy makers, music education program heads, deans, department chairs, and faculties working together with state departments of education and national accrediting bodies must share the responsibility for the recruitment and preparation of music teachers. When more schools of music assign priority to their music education programs and take hold of the National Standards, the promise of a musical education that is comprehensive, sequential, and of high quality can become a reality for all children and their future teachers.

Notes and Rests

- Unlike the public schools, higher education recognizes the study and performance of music as an academic encounter worthy of credit toward graduation. However, the unusual practice is that more credit is afforded to the analysis, listening, and understanding of music (i.e., music appreciation, music theory, music history) than the performance of music (i.e., applied music and performing groups).

- There must be a constant attempt to achieve program balance in the School of Music. No one area or department should overshadow another. This quest is a constant one; however, every offering in the school needs to have academic and musical quality.

- Admissions, Advancement (Development), and Alumni Departments need to work together with the School of Music in a three-pronged approach—that of regulating the number of music majors as well as increasing the number of non-music majors participating in ensembles.

- Admissions, Advancement (Development), Alumni, and the School of Music need to work together to develop a marketing plan to enhance the image of the school and successfully advertise it to the desired constituency. It is important to clearly and succinctly delineate the uniqueness and strengths of the music unit.

- The former preparatory division of Schools of Music has now become community schools. The dated preparatory school no longer provides the future music majors in the home university. Historically, that was the purpose of the preparatory school. Music units will now need to decide whether they wish to continue this venture as a "money-making" program and as a community outreach, or simply abolish the program.

- When possible, it is desirable to have the music library, including listening stations and technology units, in the music building.

- It is many times advisable to develop an advisory committee for the school of music consisting of, perhaps, five alumni, five faculty, five students, five outstanding music teachers from the general recruiting area, and five prominent members of the community. These numbers may be adjusted downward depending on the size of the music unit. This group should meet one or two times per year on a Friday evening and Saturday morning. The members should experience the campus and hear various performing groups on Friday evening and then have group discussions on Saturday morning.

- The marriage of music study to the college curriculum can often become difficult. Music, at times, seems like a round peg in a square hole when it comes to a college curriculum. Attempting to balance general education requirements with music requirements and attempting to make it possible for students to graduate in four years is becoming increasingly difficult. Music may be the most expensive offering of a university (excluding athletics) because of one-on-one teaching and the need for extremely expensive equipment.

Why would a university desire a music program? Music was historically in the conservatory rather than the university. The universities sought to take over the financially troubled conservatories during the last one hundred years to bring this highly regarded institution under their umbrella. The university system's confusion as the music's place and pedagogy has seemed to cause the universities to think of the program more in terms of public relations rather than the true, basic, and creative role of musicianship and scholarship development.

- If it were not for graduation and football, some universities would not want a School of Music.

- Technology makes it possible for students to do many things musically. However, the popularity of electronic keyboards and computer programs has created a sense of paranoia among professionals and performance faculties at the university level for fear they will lose students to technology.

- Assessment is here to stay! It is not the purpose of this book to address assessment; however, every School of Music must go through the process of developing what to assess, determining the appropriate assessment response mode, selecting appropriate materials for assessment, developing a strategy, and developing scoring guides.

- Every School of Music should have a student forum composed of students from the various areas or departments of the music unit (e.g., musicology, choir, theory, music education, etc.). This forum should meet on a regular basis, with the administrative head of the unit who reports the proceedings directly to the music faculty, who have the opportunity to respond, if necessary.

- Sometimes it is better not to give students all they want but rather to help them understand what they ought to want.

- The School of Education and the School of Music must work closely together as equals in developing an exciting music education program and curriculum.

- A simple thought or a carefully orchestrated series of thoughts has a significant impact on our mind, our body, and our emotions. Positive thoughts (joy, happiness, fulfillment, achievement, worthiness) have positive results (enthusiasm, calm, well-being, care, energy, love). Negative thoughts (judgment, unworthiness, mistrust, resentment, fear) produce negative results (tension, anxiety, alienation, anger, fatigue). Where there are good things happening, there is a positive feeling, and where there are problems, the negative vibes abound—simple, logical, and true.

I know I have wandered through many topics requiring leadership in higher education. Yet the whole of the School of Music is required to prepare the whole person in music performance, scholarship, applied teaching, and music education. The leader in higher education becomes a statesman when the transition is made from the singular, discipline-based focus to a comprehensive program of institutional leadership in *all* of music teaching and learning. I am convinced that this is an idea whose time has come. I am convinced that college faculties, unusual as they are, do not resent leadership if it is open, candid, visionary, strong, reasoned, and collegial. Higher education cannot fulfill its expectations in performance and teaching without leaders who inspire confidence through their largeness of mind, inspire trust by developing mutual goals, and develop competence by helping others attain their goals.[11]

1 Greenleaf, R. K. *Servant Leadership*. New York: Paulist Press, 1977, pp. 5–7.
2 Eble, Kenneth E. *The Art of Administration*. San Francisco: Jossey-Bass, Inc., Publishers, 1983, p. 11.
3 Eble. p. 11.
4 James Kjellan, "Where Have All the Teachers Gone? Bringing the Ecrosystem into Balance," *American String Teacher*, Spring, 1996. p.25.
5 Kjellan, p.27.
6 Emily Davis. "How Important Is Continued Performance?" Research study. Texas Christian University, 1999.
7 Frank Abrahams. "National Standards for Music Education and College Pre-service Music Teacher Education: A New Balance." *Arts Education Policy Review*, Spring 2000. p. 27.
8 Hope, Samuel. "Teacher Preparation and the Voluntary K–12 Music Standards." *The Quarterly Journal of Music Teaching and Learning*, 1995, pp. 14–21.
9 Michele L. Henry. "An Analysis of Certification Practices for Music Education in the Fifty States." *A Study*. Baylor University, 2001.
10 Froseth, James O. "The Standard: Surveys of Undergraduate and Graduate Values." *Aiming for Excellence: The Impact of the Standards Movement in Music Education*. Reston, VA: Music Educators National Conference, p. 45.
11 Eble. p. 11.

Chapter 13

Avoiding Burnout

Be- gone! Dull care!
I prithee be-gone from me;
Be-gone! Dull care,
You and I shall never agree.

Long time thou hast been tarrying here
And fain thou would'st me kill.
But I've faith dull care
Thou never shall have thy will.

Too much care will make a young man turn gray
And too much care will turn an old man to clay.
My wife shall dance and I will sing,
So merrily pass the day.

For I hold it one of the wisest things,
To drive dull care away.

—Old English Song

I enter the process of writing this chapter daunted by the task as well as the subject. I have turned the subject over and over in my mind, hoping to achieve some bright insight into the cause and prevention of music teacher burnout.

We need every good teacher we have, and certainly so with the music teacher shortage we face in this country. Having never experienced this thing called "burnout," I feel reluctant to console those who are experiencing it. Yet no epiphany has come, just random thoughts on why I have never burned out after forty-five years of music teaching and administration. Eventually, it occurred to me that the reason I should include this chapter in the book is just that! Should I be able to articulate to others the reasons why I remain as passionate about my art and my profession as I was forty-five years ago, just possibly my thoughts will be of value to others. So here goes, and may my message have some meaning. Consider the following:

1. LIVE WITH PASSION.

Enter any faculty lounge and what you see are people who are tired. Fatigued. Worn out. Burned out. They seem to have just given up and become bitter. They are tired and have no idea why they are tired, and so physicians name it *chronic fatigue syndrome*. But even if it is not diagnosed, in my estimation many are suffering from a kind of chronic energy shortage. How many people respond to your "How are you?" by saying "Superb! Fantastic!" How many people do you know who are alive with anything that resembles a deep kind of energy? Sometimes we get the feeling "Why bother?," but somehow the elasticity of the human spirit snaps us back, and on we go. Each year, the elastic gets older, and you know what worn-out elastic is like. Well, you are just going to have to get new underwear! You must keep that passion for your life, your art, and your work alive! I believe we behave according to how we feel and not according to what we know. Do not merely count your days, but make your days count. Light the fire, catch the flame, and enjoy the glow.

When a person lives heedlessly,
his craving grows like a creeping vine.
He runs now here
and now there,
as if looking for fruit:
a monkey in the forest.

If this sticky, uncouth craving
overcomes you in the world,
your sorrows grow like wild grass
after rain.

If, in the world you overcome
this uncouth craving, hard to escape,
sorrows roll off you,
like water beads off
a lotus.

—Dhammapada, 24,
translated by Tharissaro Bhikki

2. EXPECT LITTLE FREE TIME.

If you expect little free time, you will cherish the free time you do have. My fast pace and work ethic has been disrupted due to retirement. Now I find myself prone to irritability because I expected so much free time and it simply is not there. Who knows…possibly I will experience burnout in retirement because I am so busy. I do not even seem to have the time to do the things I did when I was working. When I was professionally under contract, I did not anticipate much free time; thus, the lack of it did not bother me. Trust me, this is all good! People who work forty hours or less a week usually work for someone who works sixty hours a week or more.

Many who say that someone is rich
mean only one thing:
He never had to work another day in his life.
So enter the sweepstakes
and try the lottery
and never work another day in your life.

Money comes and goes,
and so does the meaning of rich,
but most will retire before they learn
that nothing pays off
like having work to do.

—Author Unknown

3. UNDERSTAND THAT CHANGE IS A CERTAINTY.

What a great word "uh-oh" is. In fact, Robert Fulghum wrote an entire book on the word. "Uh-oh" embraces "Here we go again" and "Now what?" and "You can never tell what's going to happen next" and "So much for Plan A" and "Hang on, we're coming to a tunnel" and "No sweat" and "Tomorrow's another day" and "Let's try this again."

No matter how difficult it appears to be, attempt to celebrate change. Change can bring new opportunities, new life, and new stimulation. For many reasons, the music education profession has become less and less mobile. Many times, a job change is not economically feasible because salary schedules are similar everywhere; however, changes in our professional life seem to come when we least expect them. My personal life of change encompassed four basic segments: ten years as a public school music teacher, ten years as college professor, fifteen years as the director of music education in a large public school district, and twelve years as a university music administrator. Each change was stimulating to me professionally. It kept the adrenaline flowing, the creative juices alive along with many "uh-ohs." I learned to welcome the mysterious and the unknown, for change makes us discover about ourselves things that we never knew existed. When one is reluctant to change, the excitement of life is diminished. Make certain your life is filled with "uh-ohs."

4. ENJOY TODAY.

Do not allow your mind to be where you are not. Do not spend your time brooding over the mistakes you have made or the sorrows that have befallen upon you. What is done is done and cannot be changed, but you have your entire future life in which to make good. To be concerned about the past creates guilt and anxiety. Too much concern over the future produces worry. As time flies, you must be the navigator. Live for today!

> It is the best of times, it is the worst of times...it is the season of light, it is the season of darkness, it is the spring of hope, it is the winter of despair....
>
> —Charles Dickens (paraphrased)

5. THINK POSITIVE THOUGHTS AND CONNECT WITH POSITIVE PEOPLE.

Is the cup half full or half empty? Avoid blaming others for your problem or mistakes. Be a doer rather than a critic, for it is useless to be anything else. Positive thoughts come and go, but negative thoughts accumulate. How many times do you miss the opportunity to see the good in a situation? Years may wrinkle the skin, but the lack of positive thought could wrinkle the soul.

> All that we are is the result of our thoughts; it is founded on our thoughts and made up of our thoughts. With our thoughts we make the world. If you speak or act with a

harmful thought, trouble will follow you as the wheel follows the ox that draws the cart.

All that we are is the result of our thoughts; it is founded on our thoughts and made up of our thoughts. With our thoughts we make the world. If you speak or act with a harmonious thought, happiness will follow you as your own shadow, never leaving you.

—Dhammapada

6. Distance Yourself from Persons You Find Difficult.

Do this as much as possible. When a person earns your rejection, reject them in only the most discrete manner possible. Do not allow this person to access you. Do not let criticisms worry you. Be careful not to take other people too seriously. It is impossible to please all people all the time. The difficulties of life need to make us better, not bitter.

To avoid criticism, do nothing, say nothing, be nothing.

—Elbert Hubbard

7. Recognize that an Angry Exchange of Words Changes Few Minds.

Neither side is listening well enough for any thought of change. Remember that we frequently judge others by their actions but ourselves by our intentions. Certainly, if there were not two sides to a disagreement, there would be no disagreement. Happiness is not the absence of conflict but the ability to cope with it.

8. UNDERSTAND THAT NO ONE CAN MAKE YOU ANGRY.

Only you can allow yourself to become angry. I would suggest that it is most important for you to remain in control of your emotions, even if you must take an occasional "timeout" to regain control. You only injure yourself by relinquishing that control to others. Don't cherish enmities and grudges. Don't keep up old quarrels. Don't remember all the mean things someone has done to you. Forget them. Hate is a dreadful chemical that we distill in our own hearts that poisons our own souls. It takes all the joy out of life and hurts us far more than it does anyone else. There is nothing so depressing as having a grudge against someone, for it makes you unhappy and uncomfortable to be stirred up in wrath against the person.

> Anyone can become angry—that is easy. But to be angry with the right person, to the right degree, at the right time, for the right purpose, and in the right way—that is not easy.
>
> —Aristotle

9. BECOME ANALYTICAL ABOUT THE BEHAVIOR OF OTHERS.

Ask yourself what the other person's justification might be for the action he/she exhibits. Kenneth E. Eble, in his book *The Art of Administration*, speaks of his concern about those individuals who are running below expectations, commonly called *deadwood*. He states, "I once suggested a deadwood conference, to which only certified deadwood would be invited without, of course, their being told that this was the basis for their being chosen. Who might better discuss what causes deadwood and how it might be brought back to life? The very fact of being invited someplace and asked about something might spark some new life. Alas, no one had the courage to fund the conference." At least he attempted to analyze the behavior of "deadwood."

We all live under the same sky, but we do not necessarily have the same horizon. Be kind.

10. ATTEMPT TO ALWAYS RESPOND TO PEOPLE RATHER THAN REACT TO PEOPLE.

Only when you drink from the river of silence,
shall you indeed sing.
And when you have reached the mountain top,
then shall you begin to climb.
And when the earth shall claim your limbs,
then shall you truly dance.

The Prophet—Kahil Gibran

It is far more impressive when others discover your good qualities by themselves. Think with your brain, not with your emotions. To change this attitude could well change your life.

11. RECOGNIZE THAT THE LONGER YOU REMAIN CALM, THE MORE LIKELY YOU ARE TO GET YOUR POINT ACROSS.

Anger gets in the way of rational thinking and prevents you from seeing opportunities and possibilities. Don't borrow anger. You have to pay compound interest on that, and it will bankrupt you in the end. Again, be kind.

12. Know that Success Breeds Success, and the More Success you Attain, the More Critics you will Attract.

To succeed, do the best you can where you are and with what you have. Understand that the world is divided into people who get things done and people who get the credit. We cannot all be shining examples, but at least we can twinkle a bit.

13. Never Apologize for Excellence— or the Quest for It.

When we take time to draw on the leadership center of our lives, what excellence is all about, it spreads like an umbrella over everything else. It renews us, it refreshes us, particularly if we recommit it. The goals I set for myself are not to be what I am not, but rather to be the best that I can be.

14. Know that You can Fail Effectively.

More things are learned in failure than in success. It is difficult when one fails, but it is worse if you have never attempted to succeed. Every entrepreneur knows the risks of failure. Remember that failure is a normal part of life, it is not disastrous. Besides, we live in a world that does not always pat us on the back. Develop the entrepreneurial spirit! The greatest mistake you can make is to be constantly fearful that you will make one.

15. Attempt to Love Yourself at All Times, and Know that Not Everyone will Share that Love.

Make the best of your lot. Of course, you are not everything you would like to be; nobody is that lucky. There isn't a single human being who hasn't plenty to cry over, but make certain the laughs outweigh the tears. I read an article in the Washington Post entitled

"Dreamers, Start Your Engines," by Iris Kransow. It deals with allowing your fantasies to outmuscle pragmatism and take you where you belong. It is reprinted in entirety in Appendix N. With "focused imagining, and perseverance, we can be any self we want to be."

You yourself should reprove yourself,
should examine yourself.
As a self-guarded monk
with guarded self.
Mindful, you dwell at ease.
Your own self is
your own mainstay.
Your own self is
your own guide.
Therefore you should
watch over yourself—
As a trader, a fine steed.

—Dhammapada, 25
Translated by Thanissaro Bhikkhu

16. KEEP A SENSE OF HUMOR.

Laugh at yourself; enjoy yourself in spite of the stock markets coming and goings. Don't take yourself too seriously. We are never happy until we find humor in our life, so don't wait for a crisis to discover what is really important.

17. PARTY!

Party every time you have the chance. When you party and have fun, you do not need the first twelve considerations ascribed here. Keep in circulation. Go around and meet people. Belong to organizations or clubs. Travel as much as you can. Have as many interests and friends as possible. This is the formula for happiness and thinking that this is the best of all possible worlds. But above all, PARTY! This is the true way to discover the enjoyment life can offer.

Well, these were/are the rules of my professional life, and I attempt as much as possible to apply them to my private life. Please understand that I am not presenting myself as a model of mental and physical health. As with you, I have won some and I have lost some, but the most important part of that process is how I have emerged from the loss or win. I have had times of frustration, times of disappointment, and times of exhilarating exhaustion. A good night's sleep (I never have difficulty sleeping) always seemed to well prepare me to charge on. If bitterness creeps into the heart in the friction of a busy day's unguarded moments, it is important for it to steal away with the setting sun. If I accept the sunshine and the warmth, then I must also accept the thunder and the lightening. The happiest people do not necessarily have the best of everything, but they do make the best of everything. May you be happy, may you be at peace, and may you live all the days of your life and have many happy returns.

Chapter 14

The Future

In his book *Waiting for Foucault*, Marshal Sahlins notes that "two things are certain in the long run. One is that we will all be dead. The other is that we will all be wrong." This thought will caution anyone to look too far into the crystal ball; however, the temptation is there, and how else would one end a book entitled *Aspiring to Excel?* There must be some hope, some reason to go on, and some reason to celebrate those wonderful musical moments we all cherish.

I come to this concluding chapter with some level of nostalgia, as it represents a nearing of the end of my professional career as a music educator. While I will have a few more years in which I can share my enthusiasm and experience with music educators in my summer seminars, state and national music conferences, and occasional consulting jobs in school districts and higher education, this chapter represents the culmination of my celebration of the past and the present in my own career. Even more, I look to the future with great anticipation and hope for music educators everywhere.

I undertook each position that I held over the past forty-five years with great enthusiasm. None were easy. All held significant challenges. Each had a unique history of development that I needed to learn to *aspire to excel* in that position. Our ability as a profession to meet the challenges of the future requires a combination of knowledge of the past and a vision of what the future can be. Both define the present. As I look to the future, it is my hope that the skills and understandings, along with the history and philosophy of my career, will enable others to *aspire to excel*. If I have done that much, then I shall be quite happy.

I can remember a much slower world of my youth, both as a student and as a young teacher in K–12 and college. We were certain music education—growing exponentially at the time—would be a profession that continued to grow and earn the respect and commitment of communities and the nation. We were gently pushed by technology as we coped with the electric guitar, the cassette, and pop radio stations that supported the rise of a vibrant popular culture. Our students came from pretty stable homes with high levels of parental involvement. We were comfortable with a repertoire based on Western European traditions and students who shared a common set of mostly Western European cultural values. Student enrollments were high, few students worked, and sports participation was fairly limited (compared to today), because there were fewer teams and so few women allowed to participate in athletics. I can remember times when I was impatient and bored over moments and time, a much more leisurely time, when I longed for ACTION. I certainly don't mean to imply that things were easy. Building any kind of music program in any period of history is hard work. But it did seem less complicated and more predictable in the 1950s and early 1960s.

Of course, I got what I asked for. I think the last time I was bored was about 1963. Think of what change I have experienced since the 1960s! The very essence of the profession to which I committed my personal and professional life changed—its relationship to K–12 education, its place in our schools, its perceived value to society. Technology has become a rampant, unrelenting force, creating vast new opportunities while at the same time challenging the relationships between performer and creator, consumer and producer. We work with students from many different cultures, 65 percent who will live in a single-family situation by the time they are eighteen, who do not necessarily value Western European musical traditions. School reform has changed the structure of schools, teacher and student achievement, testing, and accountability. Our students are pulled six ways from Sunday, both boys and girls, by a host of options and choices from the full range of varsity, junior varsity, freshman, middle school, and pee-wee athletics to jobs, theater, debate, after-school programs, church, special camps, the Web, computer games and computers, and the list goes on and on.

Now that the *action* has overtaken all else, I wonder whether all of you, as I, live a life of anticipation, forever looking beyond the present, eyes scanning the horizon seeking tomorrow, thinking about how we must lead music education programs into unknown times and uncharted water.

Yet even as we anticipate the future, there are constants that have not changed and will not change. Schools. Students. Music. The power of music. People who share and love music. Teachers. The never-ending need for good teachers. Leadership. Courage. Strength. Love.

I know we all have a tomorrow inside of us, the part of our being that measures out our lives in semesters, by assignments we need to complete, papers we need to grade, rehearsals we need to plan, performances we have to give, or by the promise of a spring or summer break. Life just seems to wait for us somewhere out in the future, just beyond today, and the days go on and the months flow by and the years sweep onward. All of a sudden you ask, "Whoa! What happened? How can I stop this treadmill?" Well, obviously, you cannot stop it, but you need to be able to say in retrospect that your years were meaningful and productive. You need to be certain you are able to look back with joy.

As we contemplate a future of what will always be times of change, the one constant predictor of program success in music education that will remain in the future is the need for leadership, a passion for quality, and a never-ending quest to *aspire to excel*. If we do not work to constantly improve our situation, to constantly improve the quality of teaching and learning for our students, to renew the commitment to quality music and experience, and to be committed to seeking innovation and improvement, then our noble profession will atrophy. Certainly if concerned constituents of public education, those who value the art of music in their lives and culture, do not see a formal connection between "educational" music and the deeper experience of the arts, music education will remain a peripheral subject.

Hopeful Signs

Over the past few years, there have been some beacons on the horizon that may portend some important new directions. In some ways, we are lacking a real blueprint for the future, resources developed nationally that can be adapted to local conditions. In Lewis Carroll's *Alice in Wonderland*, Alice asks the Cheshire Cat which road she should take. He answers that it depends on where she wants to go. When she replies that she doesn't really care where she goes, he points out that it doesn't really matter which road she takes. Well, it *does* matter which road you take, but there are many potential directions. I am encouraged by some important resources and directions now available to the profession.

The MENC publication *Vision 2020* attempts to both emulate and update the powerful Tanglewood Symposium Report from 1967, a truly seminal document that is as valid today as it was more than thirty-five years ago. *Vision 2020* is based on the premise that music educators must determine where they want to go before they can figure out how to get there.[1] As a document, it asks a series of questions that are important for the year 2000, and the answers, taken from panels of "experts" who assisted in framing the texts, provide a philosophical grounding that clearly places MENC initiatives of the last thirty years, from national standards to advocacy, as the foundation point for the future of music education. Whether these initiatives will stand the test of time and answer all the issues in the future remains to be seen, but it does help us see where we are at present. Only you as a music educator *aspiring to excel* can determine if those questions will be the right questions in 2020.

Once you know where you want to go, the enactment of the Goals 2000: Educate America Act (and the National Standards in Music Education) have helped provide a curricular direction that has potential to shape program direction, instructional effectiveness, and the comprehensiveness of our music programs. The National Music Education Standards may provide a leverage point in the debate about our place in the American school curriculum, a vital step if American music education is to finally gain control of its own destiny. This will require tremendous effort from teachers, the teachers of teachers, and university music schools, for standards alone cannot ensure program integrity, viability, or instructional excellence. But it can be done, and certainly will be aided by those who think broadly and comprehensively about their role as a music educator—that is, those who *aspire to excel.*

Linked to a quality curriculum is the crucial necessity to recruit and retain good music teachers. Without quality instruction, a curriculum is literally worthless. Here the laundry list of needs is long: better working conditions and salaries, and a different way of rewarding excellence than seniority. The issue of retention of teachers will not be significantly improved, I believe, until we abandon our insistence on paying our weakest teachers as much as we pay our best teachers with equal experience. That practice is so at odds with common sense that it undermines the public's confidence (especially that of the business community) in the ability of schools to allocate their salary budgets wisely. It is a crucial step in rewarding hard work, entrepreneurial behaviors, creative solutions, and student and school improvement. Yes, there are threats with a system of reward based on merit, because we are suspicious of who will be providing the evaluation. But if we are smart enough to find cures for disease, scientific advancements, and social problems (well, some), surely we can figure out a better system of teacher evaluation *and* compensation. Of course, my concern is that merit will be assigned by "value"—that is, that math might be valued more than music. If we go to a merit-based compensation system (which I hope we do someday), my hope is that merit across all teaching becomes something that further dignifies the profession and helps us retain the next generation of quality music teachers.

Finally, I come to the issue of advocacy and our place in American education. There does remain a general skepticism on the part of many educators as to whether or not the arts do play a significant role in making education comprehensive in the United States. We must remember that we are but one part of the whole of our educational programs. Our teaching colleagues are those we have trained; they grew up under our system of music education. Now we must deal with the way they view us as apart and indifferent from the entire educational process. We have been so busy being a star that it becomes important not to forget that we are also a member of a team. We must work together to support the movement that all children should have an education in music, not just the brightest and the best. We must acknowledge that the eventual assessment of arts education will reveal that musical knowledge and performance ability in music are distributed thinly among American students.

Perhaps we must look at ourselves when considering who is to blame for the thinness of our music programs. On one hand, music education programs are valued when they are perceived as vehicles of high-profile entertainment, social interaction, and competitive pride. On the other hand, lower-profile programs that emphasize a solid, sequential, and comprehensive program of music learning, programs that eschewed expensive travel, commercial-style concerts, and competitive performances, may be perceived by the public as lower-quality programs and their leaders and teachers, persons not committed enough to spend their time fund-raising and tour promoting. In the words of Shakespeare's *Julius Caesar*, "Men at some times are masters of their fate. The fault, dear Brutus, may lie among ourselves." Perhaps music educators themselves have sometimes promoted the perception that the only goal of education through music is to entertain and/or win a competition. We must be ready for that kind of self-scrutiny. But I do believe that with some new resources and a willingness to think boldly, we can be prepared for what lies ahead.

Areas We Must Consider in the Future

After all of these years of teaching and leadership, I do believe there are some critical areas that, were I to continue to lead and teach in music programs, would play a key role in shaping the music education agenda in the coming decades. I wish I could be there with you to continue this fascinating career, but I won't. However, in thinking about these areas, it is clear that there are already events, trends, and history that tell us that the future will not be like the past. I feel strongly about these trends and issues because I am convinced that our actions in the past have sewn the seeds that those who *aspire to excel* in the future will have to deal with. I really have written this book to help future leaders develop the leadership skills that will help them conquer these challenges. As I think about the future, I have turned to my longtime friend and futurist Jeff Kimpton, a leader in K–12 music education and higher education, who has spent much of his career looking at the implications for change on our profession. With his input and advice, I've formulated some thoughts to close this book. I hope they will guide you in the initial decades of the twenty-first century.

1. TECHNOLOGY AND MEDIA:

I can remember when technology was a mimeograph machine and a manual typewriter. I remember the first time I began using a computer for word processing. I have watched the progression from 16mm film and filmstrip to videocassette to DVD, the first electronic keyboards to the introduction of MIDI and sophisticated synthesizers, CDs to CD-ROM and MP3. I am still grappling with how to program my VCR.

There is not one of us for whom technology has not permeated our culture. The increasing rate of technological change is staggering and will continue. For many of us, technology is a threat to the musical traditions that have supported our careers. We expect things instantly, faster, and grow impatient when our computers are slow or we can't get a cell to make a call. That impatience is part of the lives of our students, who have a level of instant access to a level of information (including musical information and, yes, entertainment) greater than all past generations combined. This level of immediacy is influencing how students want to receive information in structured learning situations. Today's students are restless, distracted, and possess very short attention spans, influences that will increasingly play a role in whether or not they want to patiently learn to hold an instrument, form an embouchure, learn fingerings, and wait for the accumulation of knowledge and physical capacity that is part of music learning. This is changing relationships between technology, teachers, and students.

Technology has steadily accentuated generational differences between those who use technology and those who won't, those who have access to it and those who don't. Music technology has changed the perceptions of students; some view acoustic instruments and the sounds they produce as old technology, and therefore difficult, while the music produced with/by music technology, or combinations of electronic and acoustic instruments, is viewed as new and, therefore, considered easy and acceptable. Finally, we are increasingly interacting with technology rather than organizations or institutions to make music. Too many of us aren't experiencing music through a jazz club or a symphony concert. We are experiencing music through our home stereo system and Walkman CD. This is what is scaring us the most as a profession.

I sometimes worry that music educators are not very aware of the vast media and informational influence that is "downloaded" to or by our students every day, cognizant of what these students see and hear outside the music class, and understand that part of our success will be to relate to the way in which we present music *in* the music class. We must understand that our students are constantly processing music, and how we learn to bridge and integrate these influences will be important to our success.

Part of the challenge that technology presents to music educators is that the profession has built almost its entire hierarchy on the reproduction of music that others have composed, rather than on the creative opportunities inherent in technology. It seems strange that the performance of music has been so important to music educators, but the creation of music has not. So few school music programs, in my experience, have ever looked seriously at the issue of creativity. Yet the cumbersome nature of music composition in the past—a composer hunched over a piano with ink pen and 26-line score—has been simplified greatly by technology to the point where many students today, both those who participate in music and those who don't, are venturing into adding composition and scoring software on their home music technology centers. Of course, the creation of music that is interesting and engaging requires an extensive knowledge of music—styles, history, compositional techniques, theory, and form. It is music education that will transmit that information, and no software package can replace what *we* can teach. For our future, we must determine how to present the musical content that will be of value to future society in the largest number of *contexts*. This is what will require programmatic, curricular, and instructional innovation.

As we look at the future of the arts, we know that art is shaped by the technology with which it is created, but technology is also shaped by the process of producing the art. The tension between that dichotomy is what is pushing the creative relationships with the arts—film, video, and interactive media—and will seed an interactive and creative setting for musical expression that could be a tremendous opportunity for school music programs. For instance, I notice an increasing use of classical music on television advertising. Certainly this music has a timeless staying power that is an excellent contrast to media messages of many kinds. A discussion about the role of classical music in this light would be excellent, whether in a performance ensemble or classroom. How do students understand the juxtaposition between classical music and contemporary marketing images? Would a band director think of having this discussion? This is precisely the way we make connections between music and student life. I have one caution, however. We must be very careful that the musical life at "High Tech High" and "Media University" will not be dominated by a male majority among the participants who tend to be overwhelmingly involved with technology. This will require careful monitoring to avoid a new round of sexual stereotyping beginning in American society (girls play flutes, boys use the computers!).

We must touch, feel, and hear in as many ways as we can.

2. ADVOCACY AND THE MEDIA:

I must confess that the entire range of media—newspapers, radio, television, and even music merchants—is a tough nut to crack. I have worked on this personally for my entire career and finally found that if I used a gimmick of some sort, I could attract the media's attention. Consequently, I make no predictions here other than to stress the great effect it has on public thought and opinion. Music educators have not even begun to explore the unique and powerful potential that the media could make to our profession and our industry. But we must be equally careful that the media does not distort our profession or that music educators, in desperate attempts to advocate for the profession, do not distort or cheapen the essence of the message we are trying to send. The wrong message—the gimmick—that is sent about music can do irreparable damage.

I am very fearful of staged events and the use of thin research to push the advantages of music. Our publics are extremely skeptical of messaging, and so we must make sure the message we send—loudly and clearly—through our students and their achievements supports the advocacy for the role of music that we feel is important. If we are just another message, then will that really change public opinion? I think not. I am not sure rock musicians who were not a part of school music programs can really send the right message about the value of music education. Ultimately, I fear that our use of this kind of advocacy will serve to hurt our cause, not help it. With media, especially media that can tell the stories of the value of music in the lives of people, we have a chance. While there may be public indifference, there are no widespread negative perceptions regarding music education. In fact, music educators are often highly respected for their commitment to their subject, their art, and their students. Let us take this positive base and build upon it. We represent one of the few disciplines remaining in the school curriculum that stimulates the senses, feelings, and emotions. We must not allow this opportunity to escape—this opportunity to show to our colleagues in other academic disciplines, our administrators, our school board members, and our communities the curricular worth of music education and our interest in sharing our art with all students so they may better understand the potential of music to produce a better quality of life. This must be our blueprint for the future.

The family of organizations that serve the profession, such as MENC, NASM, NCATE, ABDA, CBDNA, ACDA, MTNA, NAJE, ASTA, NSOA, NAMM, TIME, the state organizations, the Orff Association, the Kodaly Association, the Suzuki Organization, and many more, must finally begin to work together in support of their parent—*music education!* I am pleased to note that we are slowly beginning to move in this direction, but more must be done. As we learned in kindergarten, "When you go into the world, watch out for traffic, hold hands, and stick together." (I must confess that I borrowed this from Robert Fulghum in his book, *All I Really Need to Know I Learned in Kindergarten.*)

3. STUDENTS, OPTIONS, AND CHOICES:

The students of the twenty-first century have more musical alternatives and more choices of participation in and with *music* than at any other time in our history. Now I want to be sure that I have clarified this. I didn't say school music—I said participation with and in *music*. Music remains a powerful, almost addictive attraction to today's students. The connections that we make with students in school music can no longer turn out re-creative practitioners— first-class fingerers, if you will—without paying at least equal attention to the creative aspects of music and the aesthetic understanding necessary to give needed, added credibility to our profession. This is a given, and it will require us to prepare new music teachers differently to cope with that change.

The choice that students have today is between individual options and choices versus a system of music education largely built on group performance. Contrast this with the choices facing the musical society, choices between participating with music live or via recordings and technology, school music or personal experience through technology or the Web. Those who *aspire to excel* must understand the world of choices students confront every day. Actually, *both* kinds of choices must be offered within the context of a music education.

Music educators have long had a tendency to limit student choices because, when given *too many* choices, students would often not choose the performing group that continues to be the foundation for school music today. I am afraid those days are about to end. However, I do not feel this will have a negative effect on quality performing groups, particularly with a quality director. I continue to believe that music has a power that, with the right kind of teacher and experience, can be a powerful force in the lives of all people and the education of our youth.

We are also going to have to become much more sensitive to the families our students come from, the need for communication between and among families, and the cultural diversities that our students bring to school. Without the ability to bring music to meet the need of increasingly diverse communities, we risk further isolation. I've seen a huge shift in family structures in my lifetime in education, and we must understand that families are giving students options and choices and allowing them to negotiate and make decisions much earlier than in the past. This presents even more difficulty in our present system of music education. This will require us to become much more understanding of the vast world of music that lies beyond Western European traditions.

4. Music in Types, Styles, Lifestyles, and Cultures:

The art of music is a gestalt that consists of a variety of styles and kinds of music throughout the world that the American music establishment and the public are finally beginning to recognize and appreciate. Art (classical) music is beginning to extend beyond the domain of the privileged through summer concerts, pop concerts, and summer festivals where audiences come to enjoy music of a variety of styles, perhaps with a glass of wine in hand and a freedom to respond in ways that suit each individual. As recently as June 13, 2002, the *New York Times* reported, in an article titled "Loaf of Bread, Jug of Wine and Puccini in Central Park," that an "estimated 45,000 to 50,000 people gathered in Central Park for a performance of Puccini's 'La Boheme' at the opening of the Met in the Park series." I predict that this trend of offering music of all types to all people in new and exciting venues will continue. We shouldn't view this kind of experience that is outside the plush concert hall as a threat; we should view the fact that 50,000 people want *some* kind of connection to music as an incredible opportunity. As a society, we are addicted to music, and we are no longer willing to separate music from life and approach its performance as a cultural ritual isolated from our daily rituals in austere concert halls. Music has become a glorification of life and leisure. If we aren't a part of that, and we don't help music educators understand how to contribute to that, then we are endangered as a species.

Our very limited and largely Western European-based approach to music teaching, learning, and consumption will continue to digress from the long-perpetuated myth that great music was composed at some high pulpit by White, European males between 1700 and 1900. Grout will no longer be the only "Bible" for music scholars. The increase in new music venues—ethnic, jazz, blues, gospel, country, folk, chamber, choral, hip-hop, reggae, electronic,

classical, opera—is ample proof that as a society we are heavily connected with *music* and involved with *music* of all types and genres.
We embrace it all. My question to you is, "Do you, too, embrace *all*
music?" As the line between pop culture and "high" culture becomes
increasingly blurred, will you fight this or understand it, for by the
end of your lifetime, the lines of demarcation will be gone.

It has also been my concern that professional educators, parents,
and communities who pay taxes and influence education have a
limited interest in, or appreciation of, participatory music
experiences that have a lasting cultural value. It seems there is also
the perception that if individuals are convinced they have no talent,
there is then no reason to learn about or understand the power of
music, even when they do not actively participate as performers.
In the context of a society that for the past decade has sought
satisfaction in the pursuit of material wealth rather than humanitar-
ian service, such visions of the arts are unlikely to result in the
perception of music as a cultural component of the curriculum. This
profession must aggressively address this issue in future years.

5. CURRICULUM:

With the publication and gradual implementation of the
National Standards for Arts Education, a focus is being placed on a
sequential and conceptually based curriculum of music teaching and
learning that for many teachers is a very new world. That we have a
baseline of conceptual learning and understanding that is broadly
accepted across the country is remarkable for this profession, but not
so remarkable for math, English, or science. The difference here is
real: music has been taught and perceived as an activity, while math
and English have been *subjects* and *courses*.

Like John Kennedy and Martin Luther King, Jr., music educators
who have developed these standards "have a dream," and they
are confident they can bring music to every child and produce a

musically educated public unique in the history of the world by adhering to standards. Yet standards by themselves are not a curriculum; standards are baselines of conceptual and content understanding around which a curriculum of experiences is developed and framed. To bring it down to basic understanding, the standards are to education what par is to golf. A curriculum cannot fulfill any hopes of music literacy and real student achievement without teachers prepared and capable of teaching that curriculum and meeting the standards. That will require teachers who *aspire to excel*. Even more, the standards movement will begin to reshape teacher preparation, which is a huge challenge for American colleges and universities to change their program of music teacher education.

I also think that curriculum will have to become far more eclectic in design, multi-cultural, and less dependent on particular pedagogies or singular philosophies. While many pedagogies have contributed to the overall history of American music education, they were also pedagogies shaped around a particular music, period of time, and societal imprint that may not be valid today. The quality of curriculum will not be determined by the adherence to one particular pedagogy or philosophy, but by how well the curriculum—which may contain concepts and strategies from many pedagogies—teaches music to diverse learners.

6. SCHOOL ORGANIZATION:

One of the difficulties of prediction in this area is that we are constantly tinkering with the *organization* of learning and schools in hopes that it will raise student achievement. School reorganization may provide a new framework for better curricular management and instructional program organization, but by and large, school reorganization is akin to moving the deck chairs on the Titanic. Issues such as block scheduling, site-based management, lengthened school days, and reconfigurations of age groupings (middle schools, freshman centers, etc.) may have changed the time requirements and organization of education, but the jury is out as to whether they have significantly changed curriculum, teacher competence, and student achievement.

We should expect more changes in school organization; this is how *systems* attempt to overcome *instructional and curricular shortfalls*. The only prediction I can make here is that we will continue to tinker with school and district organizations, and that kind of change will be a constant. My hope is that the National Standards in music education will establish a base framework for music instruction that might weather re-organizational restructuring. That would allow music to become a basic component of education in the United States—at least, that is my hope.

7. MUSIC TEACHER PREPARATION AND IN-SERVICE:

As I travel and teach around the country, I find so many music teachers who are quite paranoid that the story line of the movie Mr. *Holland's Opus* will be played out in their own schools. I am not sure this paranoia is in the best interest of our profession and, certainly, in presenting the model of teaching that is essential to recruiting future teachers to this profession. After all, the movie tells us that Mr. Holland was a *very good teacher*.

Today, however, in many states we are faced with a severe lack of qualified music teachers who are willing to teach. Even the most supportive superintendents and school boards have concerns over the supply and quality of teachers. There are critical shortages in rural and urban areas, where districts are often left with the option of either eliminating non-state-mandated areas of the music program or hiring non-certified teachers. The American Association for Employment in Education (AAEE) has recently reported that the music teacher supply and demand showed shifts toward shortages nationally during the last three years. Unfortunately, only about 60 percent of those earning degrees in education actually take teaching jobs. Of those who do choose to teach, 30 to 50 percent will remain in teaching for less than five years.[2] The very students we want to attract into the music teaching profession—our best and brightest with the most music potential—spend twelve long years watching you, their music teacher, engage in your profession. They see everything about you, and yes, I am afraid they also make their career decisions based on watching you. This is leadership placed upon you, whether or not you want it. Rise to the occasion!

The strong mentor and apprentice model that we think we have in teacher education may not be as strong as it once was. The old adage, "We teach as we were taught," bears witness to the fact that our personal music teachers are usually the strongest models we take into the profession. I am wondering if the *circularity* of music teacher preparation as we know it today will give us the kinds and numbers of teachers we need in the future. That circularity is a time-honored tradition, and it goes something like this. Public and private school teachers shape the music horizons, skills, and attitudes of music students entering collegiate institutions. Collegiate institutions prepare music teachers to go out with various levels of skill and competency, but the range of classes is very limited and almost topical in its coverage of major issues of pedagogy and instructional management. Student teaching, still on average only ten weeks in this country, serves as a "fly up" ceremony but a weak clinical model. After those experiences, the students are on their own. Mentor and apprentice programs are virtually non-existent, and professional development is often left to the state convention or occasional workshops. If the current model isn't supplying us with either the quality or quantity of teachers we need, then the circularity of teacher preparation really becomes a "cycle of limitations" that I feel can only be broken at the collegiate level.

Critics of the competence of public school music teachers must recognize that most of their deficiencies are directly traceable to the collegiate institutions that prepared them. In the future, music teacher education must undergo a major transformation. Jeff Kimpton feels that the system may actually have to be completely rebuilt from the ground up, with every part of the time-honored traditions examined, some parts kept and others tossed away, even if this means violating certain standards and parameters if they are, indeed, preventing music teacher education from succeeding. He feels that bold new partnerships and alliances must be forged between K–12, college, professional, and non-profit institutions, and that it is the isolation and territoriality of these various levels from each other that is weakening music teacher education and the supply of music teachers.

Along the way, we must develop new systems to enculturate teachers–new as well as career teachers—into the contemporary classroom, where current professionals in the K–12 teaching ranks will become an important part of the mentoring and professional development of future teachers, helping them challenge their own skills, values, and understandings about the profession. It is unlikely that we can make these changes without radically thinking outside the box, but the alternative to *not* thinking outside the box is to lose the next generation of music teachers altogether. We cannot let that happen. We must be certain that budding entrepreneurs in our profession are not plucked from the vine and trampled, that generational differences do not become more acute, and that the nation does not view us as apart and different rather than integral.

8. Music, School, and Curricular Accountability:

Professional accountability will become even more critical in the schools of the twenty-first century. In one sense, accountability is the price we are paying for a highly decentralized national and state process of educational control. Testing and school accountability measures, unwieldy, flawed, punitive, and biased, are the price we pay for not having policed our own profession enough and getting caught with a product that was not as good as it should have been.

Testing and assessment are not going to go away. We have a penchant in this country for wanting to know what is best, what works, and who scores highest. It's just a part of who we are as an American culture. I do see a future when testing is finally brought into perspective—and where this obsession with standardized examinations finally reaches a point where we aren't willing to expend more resources, especially if increasing accountability really does not solve the problem of student achievement as it relates to race, ethnicity, and class. My hope is that eventually our profession will be judged by the impact it makes on society, not by a test score. Only through conscious assessment of and reflections on our practices will we gain assurances that what we do reflects the principles in which we believe.[3]

School, program, and professional assessment are not bad things. We need to know whether the human and financial investments we are making in public education are, indeed, working. There is nothing wrong with demonstrating that our school meets certain criteria, or that teachers are competent to teach in the primary subject area. My concern with testing is that it has become mindless, punitive, unfocused, and without a real purpose. Testing has become a ritual, and "teaching to the test" is how teachers are coping in order to be viewed as successful. I am not sure we all can see the value of testing and assessment in its present form. When we test, we have winners and losers, and when we have winners and losers, a test score greatly influences the self-esteem of the students upon hearing the results, even though they may not be reaching their full potential, or they take tests poorly, or possibly they simply do not care. I have yet to have worked with a student whose test scores changed his/her motivation for learning in the truest sense.

Students win or lose, schools win or lose, and school districts win or lose based on test scores, and consequently, communities win or lose. The affective dimension of a student who desires to do well or possesses the desire to excel is not exhibited on a standardized test. *Aspiring to excel* must become a basic drive for students as well as teachers. This drive, along with those leaders who inspire it, is an essential element in the cultivation of students into successful adults and future leaders. My hope is that the art of music will become available to all—regardless of race or class, culture, disadvantaged or elite. By the same token, along with the requirement that music education will exist in schools comes the requirement that teaching effectiveness be assessed. New and improved methods of assessment must and will be found, and my hope is that we can eventually demonstrate through a rational kind of assessment the value of music learning. I have often suggested that a test might be designed to measure the "goose bumps" a student derives as a result of an aesthetic experience. Alas, no one has come forth with such a test, but if such a test could measure joy, creativity, or the relationships that build between performance or musical enjoyment and life success, wouldn't it be wonderful?

9. THE ROLE OF NEW DEVELOPMENTS IN BRAIN RESEARCH:

Even though I believe strongly that feelings, communication, self-esteem, and aesthetic reactions are a central issue of music education, we must acknowledge that we have a long way to go in making music become a subject in its own right. This lofty goal remains difficult for many to comprehend—and we have waited so long—but there is a price to pay here. Whether we like it or not, it is increasingly unlikely that we will be able to justify the place, and price, of music programs based only on the traditional performance-based programs and the limited enrollment they provide. We will not be able to continue to talk about the intrinsic values that are immeasurable, or use lofty descriptions about beauty, self-worth, and involvement even though they are true benefits, when only a few students participate in music programs. We will need to demonstrate what students know about music, not the experience they have had with it.

I am convinced that recent developments in brain research about music, nascent as they are, hold tremendous import for music education in the future. As our educational system continues on its cognitively oriented path, and many school districts have special programs for the gifted and talented that deal virtually or entirely with the academically gifted, we must ask why? And the answer is because these things can be measured. However, talent, creativity, expressiveness, emotional and aesthetic reactions are very difficult—if not currently impossible—to measure.

The emerging work in brain research about the role of music is gradually expanding. Earlier in this book, I mentioned the education research of Harvard psychologist Howard Gardner and his concept of the seven basic intelligences, as described in his book *Frames of Mind: The Theory of Multiple Intelligences*. As brain researchers and psychologists work together to explore the intersections of the brain, learning, and music, we may be developing a new dimension of understanding about the complexity of music, its role in learning, and its involvement as a basic form of education.

Other psychologists provide equally compelling arguments for arts education through the theory of hemispheric dominance. This concept, simply stated, describes the psychological functions of the cerebral cortex. The left hemisphere is involved in analytical and logical thinking (verbal and mathematical skills), while the right hemisphere is more holistic (spatial orientation, artistic ability, body image, and recognition). Education, as currently practiced, is almost exclusively aimed at developing the left hemisphere, a serious omission if we are to realize the full potential of human intelligence.

As this work progresses in future decades, I believe it will further underscore the role that music plays in learning. But notice once again that I have not said *music education*. It doesn't say involvement with band or jazz ensemble; those are only vehicles in which music is conveyed. As I look back on my career, and look forward to the future, I am convinced that our greatest challenge will be unpacking the group mentality which implies that you must belong to the group in order to have the privilege of learning music. Musical intelligence opens those doors only if it is exercised; thus, to be denied the opportunity to develop these various intelligences becomes a form of deprivation of the mind.

By allowing *music* to become a dynamic force in all of education, a vibrant connector in learning and life, we have a chance of surviving as a profession. Those who *aspire to excel* must look carefully at the transitions that current music education must undergo to get to this higher state of music learning and enjoyment. It is what my career has been about in the past—and what it would be about in the future.

Conclusion

The *Arts Education Policy Review*, Volume 102, Number 2, November/December 2000, dedicated an entire issue to "Arts Education in the 21st Century" (2099 to be precise). It included futuristic views of prominent and daring thinkers in this profession. I have included excerpts from this issue in Appendix O.

When we look at music education as one part of the perspective of the real world beyond the lens, we see that we are more than the moment and more than the hype. Philosophically, we must tell the world that the pulse of the culture of this country does not reside in its politics, it lives in its arts...and in its music. Music education will either be permitted into the club of comprehensive education or left to muddle along on the sidelines. This manner of viewing music education places it squarely within the academic, cognitive priority of schooling in the United States. But the philosophical view must be translated into practice. If music does enlighten, then it must be taught in an enlightened way. If music is to become an important part of the serious business we call education, then it must be taught as a discipline that develops both skill and knowledge.

As music educators, we must not abdicate our responsibility for accountability and for the cultivation of an appropriate sequential curricular document. Beyond a doubt, achieving the desired status for music education in all of education today suggests a Herculean effort. Those who *aspire to excel* are the ones who can make this happen.

The terrorist tragedy of September 11, 2001, as well as the terrorist activities around the world, has provided a dichotomy between the ongoing secularization and dehumanization of our society, and the terrorist activities in the name of religion. How one can kill in the name of any God or any religion seems unimaginable, and somehow the secularization of our country seems more humane than the wars around the world in the name of religion. Of course, the hindsight is only useful when it improves our foresight. I noted, with approval, that in the aftermath of September 11, educational institutions at all levels—local, state, and national governments as well as people around the world—became humanized and called upon music to relieve the sorrow and shock of this tragedy. For that period of mourning, music became basic and necessary, as it does in any troubling time. It will always be that way.

Music is a language of the whole range of human experience and emotion and is, consequently, important for students from the very beginning. If the adult individual of tomorrow is to live to enjoy a creative, human, and sensitive life, education must create a condition wherein free time is not a personal source of dread. The world cannot tolerate another generation that knows so much about preserving and destroying life but so little about enhancing it.

Bottom line...the first aim of education must be to prepare young people to develop respect for life. Music can do this! To this end, let us proceed.

A Fermata!

Go Andante,
and make each day Tenuto.

May there be few Marcatos,
and many Legatos

If there be Dissonance,
resolve and form a Cadence.

If there be Consonance,
Rallantando and enjoy!

---

1 See Paul Lehman, "How Can the Skills and Knowledge Called for in the National Standards Best Be Taught?" Clifford K Madsen, ed. *Vision 2020*. Reston, VA: MENC, 2000, pp. 89–107.
2 May, William V. "Our Future Threatened: The Teacher Shortage." *Southwestern Musician*, October 2001, pp. 18–22.
3 Bennett, Peggy D., and Douglas R. Bartholomew. *Song Works I*. Belmont, CA: Wadsworth Publishing Company, 1997, p. 40.

Appendices

Appendix A
Dropout Letter

Dear _____,

I am sorry to learn that _____ has discontinued participation in lessons in instrumental music in school. I hope that it might be possible to help solve the problems that have caused the student to withdraw from the program, and perhaps make it possible for lessons to resume more successfully. If continuing lessons is not an option, possible or desired, perhaps some information from you might help us to improve our program of instruction and help to reduce the number of dropouts.

I would appreciate your returning this questionnaire with any information you can give me regarding the reasons why your son/daughter dropped out of the program. The music teacher will be asked to file a report on the child's withdrawal.

For most questions, one or more checkmarks will be enough to indicate your answer. If you feel you would like to write more, please do so, or feel free to telephone me at _____.

Thank you for your interest and help in this important matter.

Sincerely,

_____

Chair
Department of Music Education

[Note to Reader: This letter may be altered to come from the band or orchestra director instead of the Chair.]

Appendix B
Instrumental Music Survey for Parents

Who was your child's teacher? _____

Student's Name:_____

School: _____

1. How would you describe the student's interest and willingness to work at the instrument?

    ❏ good at one time, but became less interested as time went on
    ❏ moderately interested from the beginning
    ❏ never very enthusiastic from the beginning

2. How much practice did the student normally do at home?

    ❏ 30 minutes or more daily   ❏ some time
    ❏ 10–25 minutes daily   ❏ every other day
    ❏ 0–15 minutes daily   ❏ once or twice a week
                                     ❏ none

3. How regularly were the lessons scheduled and met by the teacher and/or student?

    ❏ seldom missed   ❏ sometimes missed   ❏ often missed

4. If lessons were missed, was there any one reason that was common?

    ❏ student "forgot"
    ❏ music teacher absent or cancelled lessons
    ❏ classroom teacher discouraged student from going to lessons

5. Does the student feel that the teacher made the lessons interesting?

    ❏ Yes   ❏ No

6. Did the student get along well with the teacher?

   ❑ Yes   ❑ No

7. Did the teacher seem to be able to help the student solve his/her problems?

   ❑ Yes   ❑ No

8. Did you regularly check and sign the practice sheet?

   ❑ Yes   ❑ No

9. Did you assume the responsibility to see that your child practiced regularly at home, or was this responsibility solely that of the child?

   ❑ I insisted that the child practice
   ❑ Practice times were solely that of the child
   ❑ we both worked on practice time

10. Are you aware of any specific causes for your child's loss of interest?

    _____

    _____

11. Did the teacher ever call home to discuss the student's progress?

    ❑ Yes   ❑ No

12. Did you attempt to contact the teacher before the student dropped from the program?

    ❑ Yes   ❑ No

    _____   _____
    Parent's Signature   Date

[Note to Reader: This form must be used to only establish the parents' perception of the process. It is not intended to in any way bring discredit upon the music teacher.]

Appendix C
Performing Group Participation Guidelines

_____ School District Address

The music program of the _____ School District takes great pride in the successes of its musical ensembles. The members of the organizations have based these successes on an attitude of pride, discipline, and hard work. They have provided a rich heritage for the department. It is these same qualities that must be ongoing, for they provide not only musical success but also success in the multifaceted pursuit of life, whether the endeavors are musical or personal. Thus, it is in this spirit that the following guidelines are established to aid the successful guidance of students through the music program of the _____ School District.

Participation Guidelines
Performing Music
Band(s), Orchestra (s), Choir(s)

This course has the same objectives as any other elective course, with the added dimension of the performance of music. The course is designed for interested and talented students and may be elected by students in band, orchestra, and choir. Permission of the instructor(s) through audition is required for admission into the course. Students will follow the same procedures as any other elective course when dropping, adding, or electing the courses.

1. Each director will notify students of all special rehearsals and all performances scheduled at least two weeks in advance (except in rare emergency situations). Students will be expected to notify their parents.
2. Attendance at these special rehearsals and performances is required.
3. In the event of an emergency, the director must be contacted and legal absence must be established. Conflicts with regard to

the definition of the term "legal absence" will be resolved in consultation with both the high school principal and the Director of Music Education.

4. Should a student not be diligent in music preparation, the director is at liberty to remove the privilege of performance in any given concert.

5. A student's failure to meet these obligations will have an unfavorable effect upon his/her grade.

Note: Students will receive this document at the beginning of the course so they are aware of what is expected of them.

GRADING POLICY

(State here the grading policy of your school district.)

Choir

The members of all choral groups are expected to comply with the *Participation Guidelines* presented to each student at the beginning of the course.

Grades for students are established by the following criteria:

60% Preparation of Music (judged by individual and small group performance)

10% Written work

30% Attitude (diligence to task, commitment to excellence, self-discipline, effort, and initiative)

Note: Failure to meet the *Participation Guidelines* will affect the grade of the student unfavorably. The degree to which a given situation will affect a grade will be determined by the teacher with regard to the individual situation.

Band and Orchestra

The Band and Orchestra members are expected to comply with the *Participation Guidelines* that are presented to each student at the beginning of the course.

Grades for students are established by the following criteria:

35%   Supplemental Study Material (lessons)

35%   Preparation of Ensemble Music (judged by individual and small group performance)

30%   Attitude (diligence to task, commitment to excellence, self-discipline, effort, and initiative)

Lessons – Each student is provided with one small group instrumental lesson per week on a rotating basis. The prime purpose of these lessons is to provide instruction on the respective instrument in basic and advanced fundamentals and technique. Lesson books as well as ensemble music and curriculum materials will be used to advance this purpose. Each group will contain students of similar playing levels and abilities. All lessons are required with the following exceptions:

1. *Examination* in the class to be missed for the lesson. The student should report to the scheduled lesson immediately after the test should the test not encompass an entire period.
2. *Illness* and excused absence from school.
3. *Participation in school district-sanctioned events* that excuse a student from all classes during a given time period (e.g., athletics, publications, seminars, etc.).
4. At the discretion of the instructors (music and subject area) involved, a student may be excused for a *major review* prior to a *major test*.
5. A student has the right to request exception from the entire lesson process upon presenting proof that he/she is studying privately with a competent and qualified teacher on his/her instrument at regular intervals. Periodic evaluations of progress will occur by the band or orchestra instructor consulting with the private instructor.

A minimum of 80 percent of scheduled lessons must be attended in any given nine-week period in order for the student to receive full credit in that portion of the grading period. Students may request a make-up lesson at a time mutually acceptable to both student and teacher. Any student not possessing grades for a minimum number of scheduled lessons will receive a grade of 60 for each unexcused lesson to be averaged against other lesson grades. Long-term illness will be handled on a case-by-case basis. Two weeks before the end of the grading period, the instructor (thus giving the student an opportunity to make up lessons missed unless the problem is too extensive) will notify students who are deficient in this area.

All students are required to maintain an up-to-date practice record that is signed by a parent on a weekly basis. Ten points will be deducted from the lesson grade if this requirement is not met.

ATTENDANCE POLICIES

The following policies are strictly enforced:

Performances:

1. All performances are required except in emergency situations. In the event of an emergency, the director must be contacted and legal absence must be established. Conflicts with regard to the definition of the term "legal absence" will be resolved in consultation with both the high school principal and the Director of Music Education (or department head). Unexcused absence from a public performance may result in the expulsion of the student from the program at the end of the respective school year as well as the loss of any awards for that current year.

2. Where possible, the student is expected to notify the director at least two weeks in advance of a request for an excused absence.

3. In the event the student belongs to a non_____ high school performing organization that may be appearing or rehearsing the same evening, the _____ high school group will take preference. Most community groups respect and indeed encourage this policy.

4. Illness is, of course, excused if the student is absent from school that day or has a doctor's excuse. Any other emergency

situation must be discussed with the director of the group involved.

5. Part-time employment – Case-by-case arrangements are made between the student, the director, and the employer to ensure the performing organization, the student, and the employer are treated fairly.

6. Unexcused absences for rehearsals. A first offense for an unexcused absence may result in the loss of student eligibility for all awards that year. A second offense may result in dropping a student from the program at the end of the respective school year.

GENERAL REGULATIONS FOR BAND, CHOIR, AND ORCHESTRA

Concert Attire:

a. Band
   1. Full uniform (provided)
   2. Red shirt and white bow tie
   3. Black socks and black shoes

b. Choirs
   1. Females: solid black dress or skirt and blouse (these may be purchased, made, or frequently procured from graduated choir members), black shoes (ballet slippers or China flats acceptable, comfortable, moderately heeled shoes suggested).
   2. Males: black dress shoes, black socks, black dress trousers, white shirt (preferably long-sleeved), black tie (long), and red choir blazer (provided).

c. Orchestra
   1. Females: long red dress (provided by the Orchestra Parents Association) and black shoes.
   2. Males: tuxedo-style uniform (provided), button-on ruffles (provided), white shirt, black socks, black shoes, and black bow tie.

Music:

Each student is issued a folder and copies of all music. Each student is responsible for his/her MUSIC AND FOLDER. This music is required at all rehearsals. Should the music or folder be lost or damaged, the student will reimburse the department at the current market value needed to replace the parts. Music that is carefully marked during rehearsals expedites the learning of notes, rhythms, pronunciations, etc., and allows for the making of music. Pencils (not pens) are, therefore, required at all rehearsals.

State/Regional/All State/National Music Festivals:

Each year, the Music Department participates in district, regional, and all-state music events. Any student in tenth, eleventh, or twelfth grade is eligible to audition for the music faculty (also ninth grade, in the case of orchestra). These auditions generally occur in early or mid-October. All registration fees for acceptance and expenses are paid by the _____ School District.

Auditions:

During the course of the school year, there are several times when students have the option to audition for events, solos, groups, etc. It is the intent of the music faculty that a commitment of completion be understood. In each case, rehearsal times, music to be learned, performance dates, etc., will be explained. Should a student audition for any such event, he/she is expected to complete that commitment. In the event a student does not complete a commitment where monies paid by the _____ School District are involved, the student will reimburse the school district.

Image:

The reputation of any musical organization is created by its performance, its visual appearance, and its professional demeanor. The following regulations will ensure the proper standards of professional demeanor for the _____ School District Music Department.

- Smoking in designated attire (uniforms) is prohibited at all times.

- When performing, complete concert attire will be worn to, during, and from the event (unless otherwise instructed).
- WARNING: THE USE OF ALCOHOL OR DRUGS IS STRICTLY PROHIBITED AT ALL MUSIC DEPARTMENT FUNCTIONS. Violation of this may result in immediate expulsion of the student from the music program and the loss of any awards for that current year. The high school principal will be notified and apply any further disciplinary action required.

STUDENT RESPONSE

I have read the attached rules and regulations with regard to participation in the Band, Choir, and Orchestra of the _____School District. I have also shared the contents with my parent or guardian. I understand what is expected of me and will keep a copy of these regulations available for future reference. My signature and that of my parent(s) signifies my agreement to comply with the Participation Guidelines contained herein.

Signed _____
        Student

Signed _____
        Parent(s)

Appendix D
Student Population Distribution Survey

School District
Instrumental Music Program
Date _____
Total number of students in program: 1,646

Grade	Violin	Viola	Cello	String Bass	Strings total by grade	Flute	Clarinet	Saxophone	Oboe	Bassoon	Coronet/Trumpet	Horn	Trombone	Baritone	Tuba	Percussion	Band totals by grade	Combined totals by grade
12	30	7	3	2	42	10	9	8	1	1	13	3	7	4	4	8	68	110
11	34	8	4	3	49	9	11	6	2	1	12	6	5	3	6	9	70	119
10	33	10	6	2	51	14	13	9	1	1	10	2	8	6	3	7	74	125
9	37	9	5	3	54	12	15	14	1	2	15	5	6	2	8	9	89	143
8	36	13	8	3	60	13	17	11	2	1	14	3	7	3	4	12	87	147
7	42	10	12	4	68	12	16	10	3	2	16	4	9	4	5	11	92	160
6	47	12	6	5	70	17	18	14	0	1	18	6	11	6	4	10	105	175
5	46	15	9	3	73	14	20	11	1	0	25	6	10	9	1	11	108	181
4	50	18	18	4	90	16	21	17	8	0	32	5	13	4	3	12	131	221
3	73	24	22	6	125	20	24	20	6	0	27	6	18	5	1	13	140	265
Total	428	126	93	35	682	137	164	120	25	9	182	46	94	46	39	102	964	1,646

Appendix E
Instrumental Curriculum

_____School District
Instrumental Music Program

Woodwinds and Brass

_____   _____
(Instrument)   (Month/year of first lesson)

Level 1 Instructional Objectives for:

_____
(Name of Student)

Date Completed

1. The student will consistently exhibit posture and
   hand/arm position while playing the instrument.   _____

2. The student will consistently play with a
   properly formed embouchure.   _____

3. The student will consistently play with adequate
   breathsupport while using proper techniques to
   inhale and exhale.   _____

4. The student will demonstrate the ability to attack
   and release tones using the tongue and breath
   support correctly.   _____

5. The student will be able to play a sustained tone or
   slurred phrase lasting a minimum of four seconds
   before takinga second breath.   _____

Date Completed

6. The student will march the tempo beat while
   singing the words to a simple song.   _____

7. The student will demonstrate knowledge of fingerings
   (positions) by a prompt oral and/or visual response
   to the teacher's call of letter names or tones within
   a five-note range.   _____

8. Within a five-note range, the student will be able
   to play, using half-note values, any scalewise progression
   of four tones requested by the teacher.   _____

9. The student will name and identify the various
   parts of his/her instrument.   _____

10. The student will demonstrate musical independence
    by playing a short tune or exercise alone with
    proper regard for pitch and rhythm.   _____

    Etc.

The student is now ready to begin Level Two of the curriculum.

Signed_____
   (Teacher)

Instrumental Curriculum

_____School District
Instrumental Music Program

Percussion

_____   _____
(Instrument)   (Month/year of first lesson)

Level 1 Instructional Objectives for:

_____
(Name of Student)

Date Completed

1. The student will consistently exhibit posture and hand/
   arm/finger position while playing the instrument.   _____

2. The student will consistently play with the sticks
   (mallets),striking the instrument at the proper angle
   and on the proper location on the instrument.   _____

3. The action of the student's wrists and arms during
   the stroke will be consistently correct.   _____

4. The student will consistently achieve a resonant
   sound that is relatively equal with either hand.   _____

5. The student will march the tempo beat while
   singing the words to a simple song.   _____

6. The student will march the tempo beat while
   clapping the melodic rhythm to a simple song.   _____

Date Completed

7. The student will demonstrate knowledge of the location of pitches of the C major scale on the mallet instrument without reference to letter names printed on the bars. (Use a keyboard without letter names or with the letter names covered.) _____

8. The student will be able to recognize when two other players are playing the same pitch or different pitches. _____

9. The student will be able to recognize when he/she is playing the same pitch or a different pitch when playing with others. _____

10. The student will identify the various major parts of his/her instrument. _____

Etc.

The student is now ready to begin Level Two of the curriculum.

Signed_____
(Teacher)

Instrumental Curriculum

_____School District
Instrumental Music Program

Strings

_____	_____
(Instrument)	(Month/year of first lesson)

Level 1 Instructional Objectives for:

_____
(Name of Student)

Date Completed

1. The student will consistently exhibit correct posture
   withhis/her instrument both sitting (violin, viola, cello)
   and standing (violin, viola, bass)   _____

2. The student will consistently exhibit proper left-hand
   position while playing his/her instrument.
   a. Curved fingers   _____
   b. Proper placement of thumb   _____
   c. Proper placement of elbow   _____
   d. Proper placement of wrist   _____
   e. Relaxed hand while playing   _____

3. The student will consistently exhibit proper right-hand
   position on the bow.
   a. Curved thumb   _____
   b. Proper placement of thumb   _____
   c. Proper placement of first finger   _____
   d. Proper placement of two middle fingers   _____
   e. Proper placement of little finger   _____
   f. Proper placement of wrist   _____

Date Completed

g. Proper placement of elbow   _____

h. Proper tilt of the bow   _____

4. The student will consistently exhibit proper right-hand
   position when playing pizzicato:
   a. Without holding the bow   _____
   b. While holding the bow   _____

5. Using the lower half of the bow and keeping it perpendicular
   to the strings at all times, the student will play four quarter
   notes on each of the four open strings producing a steady,
   controlled tone (legato).   _____

6. The student will play the D major scale (bass using the D
   and A strings), ascending and descending, producing a
   steady, controlled tone (legato).   _____

7. The student will march the tempo beat while
   singing the words to a familiar song (e.g., Twinkle,
   Twinkle Little Star).   _____

8. The student will march the tempo beat while
   clapping themelodic rhythm to a familiar song
   (e.g., Twinkle, Twinkle Little Star).   _____

9. The student will demonstrate correct procedure
   in taking the instrument and bow out of the case.   _____

10. The student will demonstrate correct carrying
    position for instrument and bow.   _____

Etc.

The student is now ready to begin Level Two of the curriculum.

Signed_____

    (Teacher)

Appendix F
Woodwinds and Brass

										Student Names	Level One	Class Brass and Woodwinds	Individual Student Progress Chart / Instrumental Music Curriculum / _____ School District
10	9	8	7	6	5	4	3	2	1				
													1. Posture and Position
													2. Embouchure
													3. Breath Support
													4. Attack and Release
													5. Sustained Tone
													6. March While Singing
													7. Fingerings / Letter Names
													8. Scalewise Progression
													9. Name Parts of Instruments
													10. Musical Independence

etc.

Appendix F
Percussion

Student Names	1	2	3	4	5	6	7	8	9	10													

_____ School District
Instrumental Music Curriculum
Individual Student Progress Chart
Percussion
Level One
Class _____

Student Names	1	2	3	4	5	6	7	8	9	10
1. Posture and Position										
2. Stick Angle										
3. Wrists and Arms										
4. Equal Hands										
5. March While Singing										
6. March While Clapping										
7. Location of Pitches										
8. Same/Different Pitches										
9. Play Scales										
10. Parts of Instruments										

etc.

Appendix F
Strings

_____ School District

Instrumental Music
Curriculum

Individual Student Progress
Chart

Class Strings
Level One
Student Names

Student Names	1	2	3	4	5	6	7	8	9	10	Criteria
											1. Posture
											2. Left Hand Position
											3. Right Hand Position
											4. Pizzicato – Right Hand
											5. Bowing –Lower Half
											6. D Major Scale
											7. March While Singing
											8. March While Clapping
											9. Taking Instrument In and Out of Case
											10. Carrying Position

etc.

Appendix G
On the Selection of Music
for the Marching Band

—by Kenneth R. Raessler

Alas! The marching band season is over for another year. Now the time has come for the citizens of this great democracy to judge the music selected this past year and give advice on the selection of music for future seasons.

As one might suspect, no one speaks to the band director concerning his or her opinions. They share with each other so as to not hurt his/her feelings, and of course, the musical palate of each person must be satisfied. This is the time when one might like to provide a menu of choice to all, since each person is certain that his/her taste is ultimate. Before providing all factions with this opportunity, the wise band director will solicit and then assess the various requests that have been expressed as well as considering the various political ramifications. One year I compiled a list of the opinions of the band fans that were certain that music of their choice would guarantee the marching band a winning season. Some of these choices follow:

1. SUPERINTENDENT OF SCHOOLS – The taste of this person is usually quite eclectic, but he/she likes to hear the music he/she knows. Consequently, his/her opinions are unpredictable. One thing is certain: these opinions need to be carefully considered.

2. ASSOCIATE SUPERINTENDENT OF SCHOOLS – The taste of this person lies midway between Country Western and the Romantic Era. The key here is "schmaltz."

3. THE DIRECTOR OF ELEMENTARY EDUCATION – This person would like to hear what could be done with some of the all-time gospel favorites—"The Holy City," "Jesus Loves the Little Children," "Jesus Loves Me," etc. Since no words would be rendered, there would be no problem with separation of

church and state. (Do not be too sure of this!)

4. THE HIGH SCHOOL PRINCIPAL has no opinion—he/she avoids hearing the band as much as possible. The principal can be seen leaving the press box at halftime of every football game.

5. THE SCHOOL BOARD PRESIDENT – Absolutely anything that pleases the football ticket holders in rows AA to MM in the reserved seat section of the stadium. They are critical to his re-election. (Music popular in the 1950s would work best here.)

6. THE DIRECTOR OF PUBLIC RELATIONS has been looking forward to an all-circus theme with all the well-known circus music, balloons, clowns, horses—high GE (general effect) but "tacky." Possibly worth considering. Out with the education of the students (or the fans either) at all cost! The purpose of marching band is ENTERTAINMENT.

7. SCHOOL BOARD MEMBERS – Each has a vested interest request just for them—"You'll Never Walk Alone," "Pennsylvania 65000," "Star Dust," and "We Are the World." These folks admit that they know little about music, but they do know what they like.

8. FOOTBALL COACHING STAFF – They are open to any music since they never hear it anyway, as long as the band gets off the field in the allotted time to avoid the team being penalized. Also, do not play during the game—the team cannot hear the signals.

9. THE BAND SHOULD PLAY MORE AT FOOTBALL GAMES GROUP – In the interest of school spirit, keep the band playing pep songs during the football game.

10. FOOTBALL TEAM – They do not concern themselves with band or band music, but they do attempt to contribute to the overall morale of the band by labeling them in endearing ways such as "Band Buddies," and other unmentionable names. Put to a test, however, these gentleman will be happy to pay due tribute to the band in front of family and press.

11. FOOTBALL MOTHERS – All music should inspire team spirit because the raison d'etre for a band is to support athletics. Also, the band should cheer more and provide a pep band for the basketball team.

12. THE BOOSTER CLUB – This group concerns itself only with athletic matters; however, they do feel that the school district shows partiality to the band parents by allowing them to run the concession stand at football games for paying bus transportation to away games.

13. CHEERLEADERS – The cheerleaders will always cheer for the band at football games regardless of the music selected. They will not attend competitions since it is not in their contract.

14. THE STUDENT BODY – This large group has a strong preference for rock, so they listen to their Walkman during halftime.

15. BAND PARENTS – The majority of this group never really get to hear the band because they are selling hot dogs during halftime of the football games to people who would rather support the band financially than listen to it.

16. CHAIRMAN OF THE MUSIC DEPARTMENT – This person just hopes everyone likes the music. He has long since lost his/her musical taste.

17. THE MUSIC TEACHERS WHO DO NOT DIRECT BAND (and would not be caught dead doing it!) – This group strongly prefers that the marching not even exist, unless they have a child in the band. They seem to spend the entire season decrying the band's existence.

18. JAZZ BUFFS – They are pleased that a few of the jazz "all-time greats" are being explored by the marching band, but the director needs to be more discriminating with regard to the quality of most of the jazz chosen. Also, the band director needs to "swing" more.

19. CLASSICAL MUSIC BUFFS – These folks are pleased that the caliber of music performance on the field has grown from "merely marches" to music of genuine quality, but they never really hear the band unless they have a child or grandchild in

the band or on the football team.

20. SYMPHONY ORCHESTRA MEMBERS – This elite group is of the firm opinion that music of the higher order should never be prostituted by being performed on a football field.

21. "CITIZENS FOR THE PRESERVATION OF PATRIOTISM AND ALMA MATERS" – These folks like shows with small American flags, medium-sized American flags, large American flags, many American flags, the Statue of Liberty, the school flag, the alma mater...and marches!!

22. THE "THEY DID NOT PLAY ONE SONG I KNEW" CLUB – Every halftime or competition lost by the band brings this group to the fore. They are presently compiling a list of the songs they know to assure the band of a winning season.

23. THE GENERAL CITIZENRY – They really don't know or care what music the band plays because they attend neither football games nor competitions; however, they relay opinions received from friends who do have opinions.

24. RADIO OR TV COMMENTATORS – They really don't care what bands play, just as long as it lasts long enough to cover five commercials.

25. BAND DIRECTOR – The band director's taste is not an issue. He or she is hired to please others!

26. BAND MEMBERS – Obviously with twenty-five other opinion groups who have the power and/or potential to influence decisions, no one really considers what the performers themselves prefer. Their lot is simply to entertain—WAIT A MINUTE!—what about education? Obviously, most people view the marching band endeavor as strictly show business and the students are there to entertain. But some of us view this as education. I would suppose this is why music ensembles are looked upon as extracurricular frills.

I would rather view music as education for the fans/audience as well as for the performers. No one ever said that education was an easy process, and neither is playing Holst, Beethoven, Wagner, Moussorgsky, Bernstein,

Gershwin, etc., on the marching (football) field. On the other hand, how else will we ever prove to the public that music is curricular and that our task with regard to taste is to elevate, not fall prostrate—to educate as well as entertain?

Reprinted from *Southwestern Musician*
October 1998

Appendix H
The TCU (Marching) Horned Frogs vs.
The SMU (Marching) Mustangs

—by Kenneth R. Raessler

Would it not be interesting if the halftime ceremonies of this week's TCU/SMU encounter were interrupted by four quarters of football? Let us imagine that....

During the warm-up pregame time, it was marvelous to see all those band members in their colorful uniforms out there warming up for this great contest. No sooner was I thinking about how my "blood flowed purple" for TCU, these muscular men came running on the field to the theme of "Ceremony of Texas Politics." It was really difficult to tell the Democrats from the Republicans, especially when they kept hitting each other. At any rate, it fortunately was short, and we could quickly get to the band game.

As the bands returned to the field, the fans were on their feet cheering as the TCU Marching Band, in their gorgeous purple and white uniforms, strutted across the field in fantastic style. They played well despite serious lip injuries to two of their lead trombone players. The SMU Mustangs appeared in their usual red blazers. In a pregame interview, the director of the SMU Marching Mustangs was asked what he thought of today's game. "Well", he said, "there is no question that the loss of TCU's two lead trumpet players for academic reasons will hurt them; however, they were able to draft two capable substitutes from Fort Worth's Paschal High School, and despite the fact that they have only six tubas, they are good— and fast—especially on their left obliques. There is no question that they will give us a tough battle. They are really up for the game!"

The avid band fan will quickly observe the Director of the Texas A&M Band in the press box scouting both bands. Later in the season, A&M will come up against both of these musical groups. After speaking with this fine director (a TCU grad), his only comments were, "We'll be ready for them! Our brasses will kick their brasses, and if our rifles can come through, we will definitely be a strong contender in both battles. Neither TCU nor SMU have rifles, and both of their color guards are inexperienced. I do have concern, however, for the strength of the TCU showgirls."

As the half-time gun sounded and the bands left the field, the announcer stated, "For your entertainment at halftime, we present the TCU Horned Frogs battling the SMU Mustangs in a game of football. Let's give these men a rousing welcome."

However, the teams recognize the fact that few will be aware of their hard work all week long. You see, many people leave for refreshments, tailgating, and a restroom break during halftime. Many also listen to the statistics of the two bands on their transistor radios, along with the progress of other band games around the country. Others speculate on the condition of the TCU piccolo player who fell on her instrument while executing a "to the rear march" near the end of the show. Alas, the trials of marching bands are acute these days.

One of the highlights of the TCU/SMU contest was a very impressive post-game salute to the band parents of both schools. It was indeed a thrilling sight to see all those mothers and fathers out there on the field— for they have given so much in time and money for the thrill of affording their children the opportunity to perform in these two outstanding organizations.

Obviously, football fans, there must be a moral to this story, so here it is. Both the TCU and the SMU marching bands spend endless hours to make halftime a treat for the fans. Why not begin now by giving them the attention and the support they both earn and deserve during the halftime and pre-game. Performers love and work hard for applause, and these marching bands are no exception. Let's hear it at the next home game!

Reprinted from The TCU Daily Skiff
September 12, 1990

Appendix I
Choir Rules and Regulations

1. If the choir has an engagement and you cannot be present, don't say anything about it. Keep it a secret!

2. Don't wear your gown unless you desire it; your citizen's dress will make the audience think you are a soloist.

3. Remember a little decoration improves the gown, such as a flower stuck on you. People notice you that way.

4. Always wait until the choir is about to sing and then ask: "what are we singing?" and no matter what it is don't fail to remark: "What, that miserable thing?"

5. Always sing as loudly as you can, to show people you are the whole show.

6. When anyone asks you where you learned to sing so well, just say: "Oh, I picked it up." Never give your director or teacher any credit.

7. Always chew gum when singing. It acts as a lubricant.

8. Always slouch in your seat when singing. In this way you can show your opposition to physical fitness.

9. Develop the artistic temperament. Criticize the director and buck all tempos. You have studied and you KNOW!

10. Don't attend rehearsal if you can find anything else to do; the other fellows are the only ones who need to rehearse. If you do attend, be sure to come late.

11. If you are not asked to sing a solo, pack up and go home; let your slogan be "solo or nothing."

12. Never look at the director when singing – he is only up there to provide decoration anyway.

13. Always talk during rehearsals – this provides the director with security – he knows he is not alone in the room.

Appendix J
Landmark Decisions:
Religion and Religious Music
in Public Schools

1962 – ENGEL V. VITALE

A prayer written by the New York Board of Regents for every public school child in the state of New York to say every morning in school was deemed an unconstitutional establishment of religion.

It is important to know that the First Amendment to the Constitution does not forbid all mention of religion in the public schools. It states:

"Congress shall make no law respecting an establishment of religion, or prohibiting the free exercise thereof...."

The courts continue to struggle to find a neutral course between the two religious clauses.

1963 – ABINGTON (PA) SCHOOL DISTRICT V. SCHEMPP
MADALINE MURRAY O'HARE V. CURLETT (374 U.S. 203)

Bible devotional reading and prayer were prohibited in the schools of the United States.

Chief Justice Thomas Clark Campbell stated:

"It certainly may be said that the Bible is worthy of study for its literary and historic qualities. Nothing we have said here indicates that such study of the Bible or of religion, when presented objectively as part of a secular program of education, may not be affected consistently with the First Amendment to the Constitution.[1]

Justice Brennon mentioned that "the scope and quality of holiday concerts has historically been left up to local school systems, a situation that has created much uncertainty and diversity of opinion as to what is proper for school music study and performance.[2]

1971 – LEMON V. KURTZMAN (403 U.S. 602)

To ensure that any music class or program is conforming to the constitutional standards of religious neutrality necessary in public schools, the following questions raised by Chief Justice Warren E. Burger should be asked of each school-sanctioned observance, program, or institutional activity involving religious content, ceremony, or celebration:

1. What is the purpose of the activity? (Is the purpose secular in nature—that is, studying music of a particular composer's style or history?)
2. What is the primary effect of the activity? (Does the activity either promote or inhibit religion?)
3. Does the activity involve an excessive entanglement with a religion or a religious group, or between the schools and religious organization?[3]

If the music educator's use of religious music can withstand the test of these questions, it is probably not a violation of the First Amendment and can withstand a constitutional attack. This became known as the "Lemon Test."

1973 – GOETZ V. ANSELL

Teachers must grant students the right to not participate in musical activities that oppose their religion or religious beliefs. This ruling opened the door to many situations, right or wrong, that made music educators skeptical of accepting or giving lead solos or lead parts to non-Christians, or even those Christians not belonging to the mainstay denominations.

1980 – FLOREY V. SIOUX FALLS (SOUTH DAKOTA) SCHOOL DISTRICT (619 F 2D 1.311 [8TH CIR. 1980] [CERT: DENIED 449 US 987 [1980])

Florey, an avowed atheist, objected to the use of the hymn "Silent Night" in the school Christmas program. This created a statewide furor in South Dakota. The court applied the "Lemon Test" and ruled in favor of the school district, allowing religious songs for educational purposes.

1984 – LYNCH V. DONNELLY (104 S.CT. 1355)

Filed against the city of Pawtucket, Rhode Island, charging that the city endorsed Christianity by displaying a nativity scene in the city park. The "Lemon Test" again was applied, and the court ruled against the city. However, the court later reversed its decision by a 5–4 vote, stating that the nativity scene depicted the history of Christmas, which is a national holiday.

1988 – JANE DOE V. DUNCANVILLE (TEXAS) SCHOOL DISTRICT

The issues revolved around basketball and choir. In basketball practice, group prayer was held at each practice, in the locker room before games, after games in the center of the basketball court in front of the spectators, and also on the bus traveling to and from games.

Jane Doe no longer participated, and her friends and fellow students began to question her on whether she was a Christian. Her history teacher referred to her as "our little atheist." In choir, she was required to sing the choir's theme song "Go Ye Now In Peace," which had a Christian text, and their traditional song, "The Lord Bless You and Keep You."

The school district also distributed Gideon bibles to fifth grade students.

The Federal District Court ruled against the school district. The school district appealed to the Fifth Circuit Court, but they upheld the injunction against the school district.

In 1995, the Fifth Circuit Court reversed part of its ruling by a

2-to-1 vote and gave permission for the religious theme songs because "60 to 75 percent of serious choral music is religious."

FEBRUARY 7, 2000 – CAMP HILL HIGH SCHOOL, HARRISBURG, PA
School district officials ruled that they would allow no religious music to be performed by the high school choirs. The choral director was required to submit the music he planned to use for his five choral groups to the administration for approval. Choir members wore black armbands to school to protest the action. No court case occurred; however, the situation did attract a great deal of media attention, especially newspaper, radio, and television, throughout the state.

---

1 Greer, R. "Sacred Music in the Schools: An Update." *Music Educators Journal*, November 1968, p. 43.
2 Whitmoyer, Robert N. "Sacred Music in the Public Schools." A research paper on Educational Administration. Pennsylvania State University, December 1989, p. 2.
3 "Religious Music in the Schools." *Music Educators Journal*, April 1984), p. 32.

Appendix K
Mr. Wolfgang Mozart Applies
for a University Teaching Position

Dear Dean:

This is in response to your suggestion that we appoint Mr. Wolfgang Mozart to our music faculty. The music department appreciates your interest, but the faculty is sensitive about its prerogatives in the selection of new colleagues. While the list of works and performances the candidate has submitted is very full, it reflects too much activity outside academia.

Mr. Mozart does not have an earned doctorate and has very little formal and teaching experience. There is also significant evidence of personal instability in his resumé. Would he really settle down in a large state university like ours? Would he really be a team player? I must voice a concern over the incidents with his former superior, the Archbishop of Salzburg. They hardly confirm his abilities to be a good team man and show a disturbing lack of respect for authority. Franz Haydn's letter of recommendation is noted, but Mr. Haydn is writing from a very special situation. Here we are concerned about everybody, not just the most gifted. Furthermore, we suspect cronyism on the part of Mr. Haydn. After Mr. Mozart's interview with the musicology faculty, they found him lacking in any real knowledge of music before Bach and Handel. If he were to teach only composition, this might not be a serious impediment. But would he be an effective teacher of music history? The applied faculty was impressed with his pianism, although they thought it was somewhat old-fashioned. That he also performed on violin and viola seemed to us to be stretching versatility dangerously thin. We suspect a large degree of dilettantism on his part.

The composition faculty was skeptical about his vast output. They correctly warn us from their own experience that to receive many commissions and performances is no guarantee of quality. The senior professor pointed out that Mr. Mozart promotes many of these performances himself. He has never won the support of a major foundation. One of our faculty members was present a year ago at the premiere of, I believe, a violin sonata. He discovered afterward that Mr. Mozart had not written out all the parts for the piano before he played it. This may be very well in that world, but it sets a poor example for our students. We expect deadlines to be met on time, and this includes all necessary paperwork.

It must be admitted that Mr. Mozart is an entertaining man at dinner. He spoke enthusiastically about his travels. It was perhaps significant, though, that he and the music faculty seem to have few acquaintances in common. One of the female faculty members was deeply offended by his bluntness. She even had to leave the room after one of his endless parade of anecdotes. The propensity of his to excite the enormity of some is hardly conducive to the establishment of community to which we aspire to maintain on our faculty, let alone the image that we wish to project to the academic community at large.

We are glad, as a faculty, to have had the chance to meet this visitor, but we cannot recommend his appointment. Even if he were appointed, there would be almost no hope for his being granted tenure. The man simply showed no interest in going to school to collect his doctorate. This is egotism at its zenith.

Please give our regards to Mr. Mozart when you write him. We wish him our best for a successful career. All are agreed, though, that he cannot fulfill the needs of this department. We wish to recommend the appointment of Antonio Salierni, a musician of the highest ideals and probity that accurately reflect the aims and values that we espouse. We would be eager to welcome such a musician and person to our faculty.

Sincerely Yours,
The Chair and Faculty of the Department of Music

P.S. – Some good news. Our senior professor of composition tells me there is now a very good chance that a movement of his concerto will have its premiere within two years. You will remember that his work was commissioned by a foundation and won first prize nine years ago.

—Author Unknown

Appendix L
Parody: When Guidelines are Unclear

I offer this parody as an example of the difficulties that sometimes can occur when one is involved in leadership. True, in this instance, I was a music administrator, but similar occurrences can happen to those leaders not in an administrative role.

Memo to: Dean

From: Dr. Kenneth Raessler, Director of the School of Music

Re: Guidelines for the Director of the School of Music
with regard to the Band Director and Associate Band Director
Position

A very difficult situation is in existence. It is that of the relationship between the School of Music as a whole, on one hand, and the band program on the other. My perception here is that the lack of guidelines in the relationship of the School of Music and the band program creates frequent situations that end in conflict. A child whose parents are not consistent or clear in their expectations of that child generally becomes a troubled child. Likewise, a director of a school of music who gets mixed messages as to his role in the development and execution of the band program ends up very frustrated because he is not quite sure what is expected. Initially, it must be understood that this is not a cry for power on my part, but rather a cry for role clarification. I have an extensive background in the development of band programs at both the public school and the university level; however, I do not wish to go beyond your expectations, or that of the Provost or the Chancellor. Since assuming the Directorship, I have received many mixed messages on this subject, so I will attempt to articulate them in order to help establish my own role.

1. The band director welcomed me with open arms, saying that it "will be so great to have a director who knows and understands bands. We have never had this before." (Message: Become involved.)

2. When involvement began, there was suddenly a change of mood—a defensive posture takes over with the band director. Some "behind the back" manipulation begins. (Message: Whoops, you went too far. You are only to be the ceremonial "Director of the School of Music" who considers the band program great and tells everyone so. Above all, keep your opinions to yourself if they do not coincide with those of the band director.)

3. Band budget, scholarships, and graduate assistantship time comes around. It becomes apparent that the band program receives $30,000 per year more than the rest of the School of Music combined. I would not have known of this had the band director not shared the amount of his budget in a weak moment. The band budget is separate from the other budgets in the music unit. The band director is the budget manager for his budget, and the director of the music school is the budget manager for all other areas. No one except these two individuals is given access to the budget amounts.

   At any rate, the band director, in another weak moment, shared the amount of his budget with a few colleagues. The word got around, and other faculty and performing directors complained all the way to the Dean, Provost, and Chancellor. As a result, the Provost sent out a memo that from now on the Director of the School of Music is responsible for assigning budgetary and salary amounts, along with assistantship and scholarship monies. (Message: Wow! This is certainly a no-win situation for the director of the music unit. Am I to be involved or am I not to be involved? Any cuts in the band budget would now be blamed on me by the Band Department, and if the overall budget remains inequitable, that too will be my fault.)

4. A new graduate assistant comments to the music unit director (innocently) that the band director had "gone to the Dean and the Dean gave him the money for the new percussion

equipment that I had denied for budgetary reasons." (Message: Great! They got the new percussion equipment. Possibly more happens when I stay out of it than when I am involved.)

5. The Summer Music Institute begins, and Tim Lautzenheiser is hired to do a band director workshop. The band director was asked to go and greet the many high school band directors visiting campus. The band director agrees to do this; however, he never shows up—thus, no communication between the university band director and the many high school directors present—something the director of the music unit deemed politically valuable. (Message: The band director only supports those programs that he himself initiates and in addition to that, he has tenure.)

6. The band director was appointed to the search committee for the new orchestra director. He states to the director of the music unit that he knows who should get the position (along with reasons why), has notified the person, and the person has applied. The Director of the School of Music suggests that all candidates must be equally considered—the band director resigns from the committee stating that he cannot approach the issue with an open mind. He also reminds me again that I did not know the workings of the state, and he did. (Message: The "good old boy" syndrome is alive and well. Exploring all options is not an option.)

7. A search for a new Associate Director of Bands begins. It became apparent from the beginning that the individual had already been decided upon before the search began. (Message: Just let this one go because it is only a one-year position. Choose your battles wisely. The band director already feels insecure, so why ruffle any feathers?)

8. A significant number of football fans, alumni, and professors have said, "I hope you are able to upgrade the (marching) band program." (Message: These people are holding me ultimately responsible for the band program.)

9. Monthly Student Forum – Students discussed the morale problems in the band program, so we did some problem-solving, using care not to do or say anything unprofessional. (Message: This group also views the Director of the School of Music as ultimately responsible for the quality and workings of the band program.)

10. Student Evaluation – The director of bands is presently receiving the lowest student evaluations in the School of Music (Message: The Provost has recently told the Dean to tell me to keep "hands off" the band director; thus, don't get involved in this problem until someone else suggests that you work with him on his communication problems.)

11. The band director receives the highest salary in the School of Music, some $10,000 a year more than even the director of the school. (Message: This is the most important position in the School of Music.)

12. The summer stipend for the Director of the School of Music is $800, and the summer stipend for the band director is $18,000 plus an Associate Director of Bands and a full-time administrative assistant. (Message: This is the most important position in the School of Music.)

13. The band director offers to share his full-time administrative assistant with the orchestra director, the choral director, and the Director of Music Education when she has time. They have no administrative help. (Message: This is the most important position in the School of Music.)

Implied or indirect messages one receives are sometimes more accurate and poignant than the direct ones, even though they may be less palatable.

Appendix M
Dentistry and Standardized Testing

My dentist is great! He sends me reminders so I don't forget check-ups. He uses the latest technique based on research. He never hurts me and I've got all my teeth, so when I ran into him the other day, I was eager to see if he'd heard of the new state program. I know he'd think it was great.

"Did you hear about the new state program to measure the effectiveness of dentists with their young patients?" I said.

"No," he said. He didn't seem too thrilled. "How will they do that?"

"It's quite simple," I said. "They will just count the number of cavities each patient has at age 10, 14, and 18, and average that to determine a dentist's rating. Dentists will be rated as Excellent, Good, Average, Below Average, and Unsatisfactory. That way parents will know which are the best dentists. It will also encourage the less-effective dentists to get better," I said. "Poor dentists who don't improve could lose their license to practice."

"That's terrible," he said.

"What? That's not a good attitude," I said. "Don't you think we should attempt to improve children's dental health in this state?"

"Sure I do," he said, "but that is not a fair way to determine who is practicing good dentistry."

"Why not?" I said. "It makes perfect sense to me."

"Well, it's so obvious," he said. "Don't you see that dentists don't all work with the same clientele; so much depends on things we can't control? For example," he said, "I work in a rural area with a high percentage of patients from deprived homes, while some of my colleagues work in upper middle-class neighborhoods. Many of the parents I work with don't bring their children to see me until there is some kind of problem, and I don't get to do much preventive work. Also," he said, "many of the parents I serve let their kids eat way too much candy from an early age, unlike more educated parents who understand the relationship between sugar and decay. To top it all off," he added "so many of my clients have well water, which is untreated and has no fluoride in it. Do you have any idea how much difference early use of fluoride can make?"

"It sounds like you're making excuses," I said. I couldn't believe my dentist would be so defensive. He does a great job.

"I am not!" he said. "My best patients are as good as anyone's, my work is as good as anyone's, but my average candy count is going to be higher than a lot of other dentists because I choose to work where I am needed most."

"Don't get touchy," I said.

"Touchy?" He said. His face had turned red from the way he was clenching and unclenching his jaws, I was afraid he was going to damage his teeth. "Try furious! In a system like this, I will end up being rated average, below average, or worse. My more-educated patients who see these ratings may believe this so-called rating actually as a measure of my ability and proficiency as a dentist. They may leave me, and I'll be left with only the most needy patients. And my cavity average score will get even worse. On top of that, how will I attract good dental hygienists and other excellent dentists to my practice if it is labeled below average?"

"I think you are overreacting," I said. "Complaining, excuse making, and stonewalling won't improve dental health...I am quoting from a leading member of DOC," I noted.

"What's the DOC?" he asked.

"It's the Dental Oversight Committee," I said, "a group made up of mostly lay persons to make certain dentistry in this state gets improved."

"Spare me," he said. "I can't believe this. Reasonable people won't buy it," he said hopefully.

The program sounded reasonable to me, so I asked, "How else would you measure good dentistry?"

"Come watch me work," he said. "Observe my processes."

"That's too complicated and time consuming," I said. "Cavities are the bottom line, and you can't argue with the bottom line. It's an absolute measure."

"That's what I am afraid my parents and prospective patients will think. This can't be happening," he said despairingly.

"Now, now," I said, "don't despair. The state will help you some."

"How?" he said.

"If you're rated poorly, they'll send a dentist who is rated excellent to help straighten you out," I said brightly.

"You mean," he said, "they'll send a dentist with a wealthy clientele to show me how to work on severe juvenile dental problems with which I have probably had much more experience? Big help."

"There you go again," I said. "You aren't acting professionally at all."

"You don't get it," he said. "Doing this would be like grading schools and teachers on an average score on a test of children's progress without regard to influences outside the school, the home, the community served, and things like that. Why would they do something so unfair to dentists? No one would ever think of doing that to schools!"

I just shook my head sadly, but he had brightened. "I am going to write my representatives and senator," he said. "I'll use the school analogy— surely they will see the point."

He walked off with that look of hope, mixed with fear and suppressed anger that I see in the mirror so often lately.

John S. Taylor
Superintendent of Schools
Lancaster County School District
Lancaster, Pennsylvania

Appendix N
Dreamers Start Your Engines

—By Iris Krasnow

(Reprint from the *Washington Post*, January 2002)

I am dropping off my fourth-grader, Isaac at school when his teacher raises her arms in a jubilant V. "I'm 64 today!" exclaims Katherine Haas. The sunlight shimmers through her pixie-cut gray hair, and I'm seeing a wide-eyed girl, not a soon-to-be grandmother. As she embarks on the third third of her life, Haas credits her age-defying exuberance to loving what she does – teaching third and fourth grade.

"I love, love, love it," says Haas, twirling a red rubber pen with a gaping shark on its top. " I think my family always saw me as the black sheep because my sister has a PhD. My brother is a doctor. And I teach 9-10-year-olds. But I have always felt I was doing something wonderful. There is always fun in my days.

"I may be 64, but I still climb trees. I can't wait to come to school each day and see these little, loving people who have so many questions and keep me thinking. How could anyone spend 10 hours a day doing something they don't like to do?"

We have all suddenly been forced to reflect on overarching questions about personal happiness, jolted by the slap of a black September and uncertainty over a war without a foreseeable end. At parties and on playgrounds, conversations no longer linger in superficial places. Dialogues now include urgent probes that penetrate right to the marrow of the meaning of existence: Who am I? Who do I want to be? Is it time to quit a so-so job and start living my dreams?

Are you living your dreams? Does going to work fill you with exhilaration or dread? How can you shift from the grind of the ordinary into the extraordinary? Follow your gut into the passion of your soul, say those who have boldly chased their dreams. Some 15 years ago, New Yorker Dick Caples, 52, left the law firm of Shearman & Sterling, where he made lots of money as an international banking specialist, to become executive director of the Lar Lubovitch Dance Company. In his new post as director of the nonprofit modern dance troupe, he shifted from a shiny skyscraper and starchy suits to blue jeans, half the salary and a loft in Chelsea. What Caples told me back then about why he turned his life upside down are words that continue to goad and to guide:

> "Essentially the practice of law was lacking emotional and psychic satisfaction. Only in the arts have I been able to feel that my life has greater purpose than merely helping a client make more money. I wanted to be in a job that was touching people in their deepest selves."

Before a profound metamorphosis can occur, we must first be awakened to our own deepest selves. Then comes the courage to create a life that feels authentic to the bone and spiritually right. I have known since the first grade in Oak Park, IL, under the withering stare of stout Mrs. Steger, that figuring out words and composing sentences was that I most enjoyed. Becoming an author and journalism professor is not out of luck, but due to an unwavering commitment to stick with my gut passion and not be lured off track by jobs offering larger wages and less soulful rewards, I am in luck.

Yet, plugging into your passions doesn't have to mean leaving huge earnings behind. The most successful people I know got that way because their fire within and deep-seated self-knowledge gave them an edge and tenacity to do their jobs better than anyone else. Abbey Butler is a Wall Street legend who grew up in middle-class Brooklyn, where his father managed a variety store. In his second year of college, he started reading the Wall Street Journal every day. "I just knew that was where I belonged." Says Butler, 64.

In his first job on Wall Street, running errands at a big investment firm, Butler made $47.50 a week. But what he calls his "real passion and knack" for analyzing stocks and bonds and companies quickly turned into some real money. By the time he was 27, Butler was a millionaire – this from "devouring more financial news in a week than most people read in a lifetime." The Butler Pavilion and the Norman and Charlotte Butler Learning Institute (named after his parents) at American University are his gifts back to the institution where he studied business, worked to pay his tuition and graduated from in 1958.

"Even when I wasn't making a lot of money, my work has always given me an emotional high," adds Butler, who heads an investment firm called C.B. Equities Capital Corp. "I have always loved waking up in the morning. I am excited every day. That's what people should strive for. You never want to wake up and say, 'Damn, I have to get up and go to work today.'" Some of the more interesting twists along Butler's road to fulfillment and fortune has been to do investment work for various rock groups, such as the Beatles and the Kinks. Butler recalls walking down the streets of London in the mid-'60's, Ringo Starr and John Lennon a few steps ahead of him, and exclaiming, "Wow, what a great life I am having" – a great life he continues to have by adhering to basic life principles, which include "You are what you think" and "Always take action."

"After Sept. 11, a lot of people are telling me they are going after their dreams as quickly as they can," Butler says. "It is never too late to start over."

Many of those dreamers smitten by the notion of fresh forays into more meaningful lives are in their forties, fifties and beyond, no longer shackled by the limits of youth and inexperience. This is precisely the market that is driving AARP's latest magazine, My Generation, launched last spring and targeted to the front edge of the 76 million baby boomers in America.

With sexy covers of aging boomers such as Sissy Spacek and Ed Harris, My Generation's thrust is that anything is possible after age 50, in fitness, work, romance and adventures not yet pursued.

"The old conception is gone that after a certain age, it all goes downhill," says Hugh Delehanty, 52, the magazine's editorial director and a man whose own career has had several renditions. "With huge advances in medical research, we have not only added 20 years to the average lifespan, but there is a whole new change in the consciousness of what it means to be alive. People have really opened up to ways they can reinvent themselves at every step.

"When you enter your forties and fifties and get that first glimmer of mortality, many people get released from some of the things that have been holding them back." In past lives, Delehantly was an editor at Sports Illustrated and People. Along the way he started practicing Zen Buddhism "fairly radically", a journey that led him into a different practice of journalism. In

1995 he co-authored the bestseller "Sacred Hoops" with then-Chicago Bulls Coach Phil Jackson and the following year became the editor of the *Utne Reader*, a magazine that reprints articles from the alternative press.

"I made a decision in my life that I was going to search out work that would integrate where I was evolving as a person," says Delehanty. Joining *Utne* meant moving away from journalism that "celebrated materialism in our culture" to journalism that celebrates basic human values. Under Delehently's hand, writing for the soul also is a key part of the editorial push at *My Generation*.

"We give people inspiration to think in alternative ways and do work that is true to who they really are," he adds. "Too many people are prisoners to conceptions of what they are supposed to be. Real liberation comes from understanding, and following, what is happening in your heart."

I got a call last week from a college friend in California who said that a mutual friend, in her early forties, had advanced cancer. The stricken woman, a mother of three young children, had loved hard and lived hard and always done work she loves. Looking back on her life, she was feeling no major "I should haves" about terrain unexplored. Are there any "should haves"currently churning in your gut? Becoming the self of your dreams is for right here and right now, not to be posted on some future to-do list that may never pan out.

Our 8-year-old son, Jack, recently came bounding into the kitchen, whooping and beaming. He said that he had just discovered that when he was sad he could become happy by just imagining himself smiling. "Mommy, I am the president of my imagination so I can tell myself to be any way I want to be." With focused imagination, and perseverance, we can all be any self we want to be.

I am in midtown Manhattan having lunch with a man who is one of the biggest names and talents in the publishing world. I ask him who he would want to be if he wasn't who he was. Green eyes flashing, face flushed, this editor in his early forties tells me: "Inside of me is a jazz pianist. And that will happen. You will see."

What will you do for an encore? This is the year to let your fantasies outmuscle pragmatism, and take you where you belong.

Appendix O
What Others Are Saying
About the Future

The *Arts Education Policy Review*, Volume 102, Number 2, November/December 2000, dedicated an entire issue to "Arts Education in the 21st Century" (2099 to be precise). It included the futuristic views of prominent and daring thinkers in this profession. Here are excerpts of what some said:

BENNETT REIMER, NORTHWESTERN UNIVERSITY

"...we do expect every kid to be able to enjoy and treasure the arts they choose for their lives as intelligent consumers, and those who take that path get as much attention and respect as the ones who get into art-making professionally or as devoted amateurs. There's still that holdover from the twentieth century illusion that every child will choose to be an art maker, and only those kids who do so are worthy of our concern. We've made good progress toward including all the others, which is why we are now a well established, secure, basic, know - do domain in American schools, but the public still needs to be assured that we care about the arts health of *all* kids."[1]

SAMUEL HOPE, EXECUTIVE DIRECTOR OF THE NATIONAL ASSOCIATION OF MUSIC SCHOOLS (NASM)

"It is 2099. The term "arts education" is used more than ever. Applied to so many types of learning and experience, arts education has become a general good to the point that it carries no particular reference to the study of anything, much less the various arts disciplines...."

"One can only hope that the field of arts education will develop a policy analysis capability to address the growing complexity that the twenty-first century is likely to bring."[2]

J. CARTER BROWN, DIRECTOR EMERITUS
OF THE NATIONAL GALLERY OF ART

"The fundamental problem [is] the increasing divergence over the course of the century between the rich and poor, and the dominance, in a highly decentralized system of local school boards, of economic priorities, driving curricula to an exclusive focus on training the young for immediate economic return. By 2099 the schools have become basically vocational training centers but are still unable to stem the tide of dropouts and school violence."

"Within the field of [music education] the teachers of [applied music], the teachers of the understanding and history of [music], the teachers of [music methodology and practicum, and the performing group directors] could not get along. [In addition], as teachers status continued to decline over the century, by virtue of egregiously low pay and the lack of appreciation by the society as a whole, the kind of self-fulfillment prophecy brought the quality of teaching to a new low." (Granted, I took some editorial liberty with this paragraph, but I did not destroy the message or intent of the author)[3]

PAUL R. LEHMAN, PROFESSOR EMERITUS
OF THE SCHOOL OF MUSIC AT THE UNIVERSITY OF MICHIGAN

"Schools themselves will recognize that preparing students to live rich, satisfying and rewarding lives should take precedence over preparing them narrowly for the world of work...music will become technology based...[and] by 2099 every student from early childhood throughout the years of education, will have access to comprehensive, balanced and sequential instruction in all four arts."[4]

JOHN J. MAHLMANN, EXECUTIVE DIRECTOR OF MENC,
THE NATIONAL ASSOCIATION OF MUSIC EDUCATION

"What impact will the next half century have on music education? Here the story line is not as likely to cause jaws to drop because the tale may well be a familiar one. Without a sustained breakthrough in the way taxpayers and educational policy makers think about music and the other arts, they are likely to languish in the backwaters of the curriculum; in other words, more of the same."[5]

SCOTT C. SCHULER, ARTS EDUCATION CONSULTANT
OF THE CONNECTICUT STATE DEPARTMENT OF EDUCATION

"Under pressure from alternative centers of learning, the universities finally began to 'get with it,' but too late to preserve their traditional monopoly on teacher preparation...Increasingly, sophisticated teacher assessment systems enable states to abandon their traditional certification approach, which permitted an increasing proportion of alternative candidates to enter the profession. University teacher preparation programs that were of lesser quality or more bureaucratic collapsed under the weight of heightened expectations, as their graduates poor test scores were publicized in the media"[6]

(Authors Note: This has already begun...the practice of printing the composite average of students' test scores on the teacher's examination in newspapers.)

JAMES UNDERCOFLER, DIRECTOR AND DEAN
OF THE EASTMAN SCHOOL OF MUSIC

"The instruction at the pre-K and elementary levels will engage students actively in music making and creating. However, as students move into middle and high schools, active music making during the traditional school day will become increasingly rare. It will be accommodated in the community. Time allocated at the secondary level to the arts will focus increasingly on learning about the arts, as now found in history, 'appreciation,' and criticism."[7]

RICHARD COLWELL, VISITING PROFESSOR
OF MUSIC AT THE UNIVERSITY OF MICHIGAN

"Given the context of the early years of the twenty-first century, music educators faced with a plethora of outcomes trumpeted by advocates were forced to define the knowledge and skill base of the discipline or lose control of music as a curricular subject. Intelligent curriculum research was not possible without guidelines for in-school and out-of-school experiences. Thus, the first move was a needs assessment, which given the lack of interest in assessment by music educators, involved a great deal of trial and error."[8]

SUSAN MCGREEVY-NICHOLS, FOUNDER AND DIRECTOR
OF THE ROGER WILLIAMS MIDDLE SCHOOL DANCE PROGRAM
IN PROVIDENCE, RHODE ISLAND

"Students no longer go into a specific grade. Instead, each child has an Individualized Educational Plan (IEP) and is required to complete a well-rounded course of study based on standards and proceed at his or her own pace. All students have a mentor teacher who guides them through their entire educational experience and oversees their IEP. The child's plan is submitted to the governing board in their state for approval. As students progress toward their established educational goal and the completion of the standards, they are monitored by a computer chip that is implanted in every child at birth. These chips track grades, participation and cumulative scoring and maintain an inventory of what standards have been met and which still have to be mastered. The chip deactivates at age twenty-one, and student records are stored in federal data banks.

As students reach specific benchmarks, they are eligible for a variety of incentives, scholarships, apprentice opportunities, and eventually employment. These implanted chips also decreased school violence and gang activity because of the ability to monitor students."[9]

GRETTA BERGHAMMER, PROFESSOR OF DRAMA EDUCATION
AT THE UNIVERSITY OF NORTHERN IOWA

"I believe that one hundred years from now, the arts will provide the only soul in an educational environment that is based largely on information manipulation. I believe that the arts in education will exist in the twenty-first century, but what we perceive as art will most likely have changed. It may be less aesthetic and more politically or socially driven. It may be more didactic and less artistic. But it will exist and it will have meaning for those who make it."[10]

1 Reimer, Bennett. "The Way It Will Be." *Arts Education Policy Review*, Volume 102, Number 2, November/December 2000, p. 8.

2 Hope, Samuel. "Arts Education in Wonderland." *Arts Education Policy Review*, op. cit. p. 11.

3 Brown, J. Carter. "A Modest Projection." *Arts Education Policy Review*, p. 10.

4 Lehman, Paul R. "A Vision for the Future." *Arts Education Policy Review*. op. cit., p. 15.

5 Mahlmann, John J. "Music Education Half a Century Hence," *Arts Education Policy Review*, op. cit., p. 24.

6 Schuler, Scott C. "The Shape of Things to Come." *Arts Education Policy Review*, op. cit., p. 26.

7 Undercofler, James. "Trends and 'Megatrends." *Arts Education Policy Review*, op. cit., p. 28.

8 Colwell, Richard. "Music Education in 2050." *Arts Education Policy Review*, op. cit., p. 29.

9 McGreevy-Nichols, Susan. "Dance Education 2099: An Odyssey." *Arts Education Policy Review*, op. cit., p. 35.

10 Berghammer, Gretta. "Danger! Will Robinson!" *Arts Education Policy Review*, op. cit., p. 40.

About the Author

Dr. Kenneth R. Raessler has recently retired as Director of the School of Music at Texas Christian University (TCU). He was formerly Director of Music in the Williamsport Area School District, Williamsport, Pennsylvania. The Williamsport Music Education Program achieved national prominence during his tenure, not only for excellence in performance but also for excellence and innovation in classroom music. The program was awarded the MENC "Exemplary Program Award" in 1985.

Dr. Raessler holds a bachelor's degree from West Chester University, Pennsylvania, where he was named a *Distiguished Alumni* in 2003, a Master of Music Education from Temple University, and a Ph.D. from Michigan State University. He has taught in the public schools of East Stroudsburg and Hatboro-Horsham, Pennsylvania, as well as Belvidere, New Jersey. He also served for ten years as the Director of Music Education and Chairman of the Department of Music at Gettysburg College.

A frequent guest speaker, lecturer, consultant, and clinician, Dr. Raessler has served as state president of the Texas Association of Music Schools (TAMS) and College Chair and Vice President of the Texas Music Educators Association from 1998–2000. He presented invited papers at conferences of the National Association of Schools of Music (NASM), along with Keynote Speeches for the Florida Music Educators Association Conference (FMEA) and the New York State School Music Association (NYSSMA). He served as Consulting Editor of the Yamaha Corporation publication *NEW WAYS* and has presented week-long seminars on music administration at such schools as the Eastman School of Music, the Hartt School of Music, Duquesne University, Villanova University, and TCU. Dr. Raessler was interviewed in the March 1997 *Instrumentalist* magazine, and he serves on the Board of Trustees of the Phi Mu Alpha Foundation. He has appeared in numerous "Who's Who" publications, including the 2003 edition of "Who's Who in America," and has received Hall of Fame designations.

The author of over seventy articles, using his experiences as the catalyst, Dr. Raessler offers this book on leadership in the music education field as a definitive work on the state and future of music education in the United States. *Aspiring to Excel* **will** challenge all music educators in the United States to assess their priorities, their goals, and the sequence of instruction in their school district or their university. It will inspire leadership in the music educator through the investigation of many processes, and when these processes fall in place, students will then experience excellence through music, and music through excellence.

Index